HUMAN ACTION SIGNS IN CULTURAL CONTEXT
The Visible and the Invisible in Movement and Dance

edited by
Brenda Farnell

The Scarecrow Press, Inc.
Metuchen, N.J., & London
1995

British Library Cataloguing-in-Publication data available

Library of Congress Cataloging-in-Publication Data

Human action signs in cultural context : the visible and the
   invisible in movement and dance / edited by Brenda Farnell.
        p.   cm.
      Includes bibliographical references.
      ISBN 0-8108-2867-7 (alk. paper)
        1. Man—Attitude and movement.   2. Human locomo-
   tion.   3. Nonverbal communication (Psychology).   4. Dance—
   Social aspects.   5. Body, Human—Social aspects.   6. Body,
   Human—Symbolic aspects.
   I. Farnell, Brenda M. (Brenda Margaret)
   GN231.H85   1995
   306.4—dc20   94-5537

CONTENTS

iii

FOREWORD

The origins and context of a book like this sometimes throws light on its content. As the author points out in her elegant and exhaustive Introduction, all of the chapters in the volume, except two—Chapters 7 and 9—were given as papers at a panel entitled, *The Visible and the Invisible: Meaning in Systems of Human Movement,* (Session 4–019), of an American Anthropology Association annual conference in Phoenix, Arizona, in November 1988.

The meeting where the papers were presented was well-attended. I remember waiting to begin and a somewhat noisy scramble as audience members filched chairs from adjoining conference rooms. In spite of these efforts, many people stood leaning against walls, or sat cross-legged in the aisles. But no one left.

That says something about the intensity of interest generated by the subject. New theoretical developments and current working papers were long overdue.

I remember, too, the presence of two Sign Language interpreters. In fact, I became so fascinated with their rapidly moving, articulate hands and faces, I nearly forgot what I had to say. Someday, we may be able to have movement-writing texts of such signed performances, adding yet another dimension to the indexicalities of lived situations that would undoubtedly extend our notions of translation beyond its present verbal boundaries.

Sitting high above the night lights of Phoenix in a slowly revolving restaurant whose windows revealed one majestic landscape after another made it easy to scale slippery, (often rocky) cliffs of criticism, gain new perspectives on pioneering educational tasks, and discuss intricate intellectual issues with the same dedication and care as mountaineers assaulting a snow-covered peak.

Where the author sees that, without new alternatives, we are "left swinging on a pendulum between objectivist and subjectivist perspectives," I see us swinging over an abyss supported by nothing but our climbing gear (consisting of *moving* bodies, action sign systems, reflexivity, the idea of a personal anthropology, the literacy of human movement and semantic primitives), while we call to our friends in the valleys below hoping they might share the clarity, the heady atmosphere of higher altitudes achieved by divesting ourselves of cumbersome weights; in sum, the entire Cartesian legacy.

To pursue the metaphor: I stood on the rim of the Grand Canyon after the conference ended, pondering over an epistemological gap of equal proportions that will always divide dualists and behaviorists from those of us who refuse to accept alienation-cum-disembodiment as the *sine qua non* of human movement study. As Varela so aptly puts it, we have learned to talk *from* the body, in contrast to talking *about* the body or *of* the body.

Given that we are all inheritors of the philosophical and scientific mind-sets that produced the Cartesian legacy, learning to talk *from* the body isn't easy. Kaeppler says, "In order to understand movement as a cultural artifact with an internal structure and as part of socially given categories, the performer and the observer must have "competence" in an evolved Chomskian sense." In other words, spectators or observers who don't know the rules aren't going to be able to make sense of the game and players who (with mind-boggling arrogance) think they create the rules, not recognizing the essential *social* nature of culturally learned body language games are likely to fall into an abyss of their own making.

As David Pocock once put it, "we do not 'float free' of our historical selves," but we *can* get rid of the suffocating cloaks of outmoded cultural, methodological and theoretical assumptions we wear, and that, to me, is the outstanding feature of this book.

The author has managed to ring the changes that the study of human movement has made during the last fifteen years with penetrating accuracy and laudable brevity. She has backed her claims not only with a variety of recent ethnographic studies, including her own, but two closing chapters that are both anthropologically and theoretically sound. The whole book contains unique and excellent examples of a new kind of ethnography that seeks, first, to *understand* what human actions amount to, then to write from that understanding. It is an important contribution to the social sciences, especially sociocultural anthropology, and to linguistics, ethnomusicology, philosophy and folklore as well.

Drid Williams
May 3, 1994
Columbia Heights, Minnesota

INTRODUCTION

In recent years the study of human movement within sociocultural anthropology has been undergoing profound changes. Although many anthropologists are familiar with approaches known as proxemics and kinesics[1] there is as yet little awareness of developments in both theory and method that have either built upon or departed radically from these earlier approaches.[2] Adrienne Kaeppler's ethnoscientific structuralism, Adam Kendon's approach to gesture and sign language studies and Drid Williams' semasiology represent three such developments.[3]

Essays by each of these three leaders in the field, together with the work of seven other authors, are offered in this volume as a sample of current work. Set in a wide variety of ethnographic contexts, the essays in Part I present a view of human movement as an expressive medium used by persons for the construction of meaning. Throughout these essays the concept of person entails specifically human powers and capacities for the exercise of agency. Body movement is a medium that in all cultures generates an enormous variety of forms of embodied knowledge, systematized in various ways and to varying degrees, involving convention as well as creative performativity. The authors whose work is represented herein share the realization that understanding human movement requires close attention to the varied and complex cultural resources that are used to organize human actions and cannot be understood from observation alone. It is an interest in the centrality of these culture-specific resources to an understanding of perceivable action which has provided common ground. The ethnographic essays are followed in Part II by detailed theoretical commentaries.

THE VISIBLE AND THE INVISIBLE: BEYOND OBSERVATION

There is no one "school" of thought represented herein, but two major theoretical developments can be identified that distinguish this work from earlier approaches. First, there has been a theoretical shift from an empiricist and observationist view of human movement to an agent-centered perspective.[4] The observationist stance has been typical of many studies in nonverbal communication and is frequently accompanied by experimental methods that remove cultural context. Even though such studies are primarily psychological rather than anthropological, they have had their effects, as, for example, in Birdwhistell's functional-anatomical explanations of movement as a "kinesic stream." Such studies created ever more detailed microanalysis of visible movement but prove barren, because from an anthropological perspective it is the "invisible"—features of social organization, cultural values, and human beliefs and intentions—that determine the meanings of the visible. It is social taxonomies of the body and the semantics attached to space and time as they emerge in specific cultural contexts and historical moments that create and are created by the signifying person.

This change in perspective has coincided with theoretical shifts in sociocultural anthropology generally during the 1970s and 80s; toward new notions of objectivity, for example, and toward a model of humankind as "meaning-maker."[5] Related to this are developments that shifted language to center stage in anthropological theory and practice,[6] and deeply affected conceptions of the kinds of relationships that could be said to exist between movements of the body and spoken languages. Herein lies the second theoretical shift.

Current interest in connections between language and human movement does not reside in the simple application of spoken language models, and there has been some misunderstanding on this point (cf. Royce 1977, Jackson 1983a) because of a failure to note the difference between the application of a model and the use of linguistic analogies in theory-building. We have every reason to believe that liberation from a frame of reference dominated by spoken language will be theoretically productive. It would be a mistake, however, to interpret this to mean that theories of the body and human action should be removed from the realm of spoken language meaning, because as these papers clearly demonstrate there would appear to be important connections between these two kinds of semiotic systems at several levels.[7] Such a separation, whether made in the interests of behaviorism or anti-intellectualist subjectivism, only perpetuates a Cartesian attitude toward persons as mind/body, when much of current philosophy and social theory has overcome such dualistic thinking.[8] Even if that were not the case, failure to recognize that such a brand of mind/body dualism is a Western ontological position and not a philosophy adhered to by many non-Western peoples threatens severe clouding of theoretical spectacles.

All the authors whose essays are represented here illustrate a sensitivity to spoken language and a commitment to exploring in various ways the possible relationships between action and speech and between "body languages" and spoken languages.[9] In fieldwork practices this demands that an investigator make central the learning of actions as well as speech patterns. It includes focusing upon what people do and what they say about what they do. Important too, are actions that people perform but never put into words because the knowledge is a "knowing how"—to use Ryle's (1949) term—rather than a "knowing that." How people classify the body itself and classify their actions, how they organize and assign value to the space(s) in which they act, and what such "doing" means to these individuals and groups in specific cultural and historic moments are of central concern. In sum, neither observation alone (objectivism) nor its subjectivist opposite in the form of an appeal to some kind of shared prelinguistic but "lived" somatic experience is any longer viewed as sufficient as the basis for an understanding of human movement.

The title of the book addresses this fact. What is at issue here is that the "visible"—the observable movement—is only a starting point for investigation. Although necessary, it can never be sufficient as an explanation of that movement. A common thread that runs throughout the papers suggests that unless such observation is informed in important ways by knowledge of various semiotic practices, including uses of spoken language, cultural conceptions of the body, persons, space, time, action, and much more, it is empty of everything that makes it part of a social world of human be-ing.

THE VISIBLE AND THE INVISIBLE: BODY MOVEMENT AND SOCIAL THEORY

This book also aims to make more visible to our colleagues that which has been a virtually invisible arena of inquiry within the discipline, for there is no doubt that the human body—in particular the moving body—has remained virtually invisible to the vast majority of sociocultural anthropologists until recently. This is largely due to a long-standing bias against the body in the western philosophical tradition, which in turn has led to few social theorists taking the embodiment of persons seriously. Harré suggested this when he noted that in philosophy, the body has "been left on the butcher's slab more or less since Descartes credited it only with extension."[10] This absence of the body in social theory has meant that most sociocultural anthropologists (although they are by no means alone in this) literally do not *see* movement empirically. When they do, it is most often viewed as "behavior" and not as "action." Many find it hard to imagine how movement might "mean" at all, far less contribute anything to our understanding of social and cultural practices.

Jackson (1983a) offers a revealing glimpse into the possible depth of this problem in a confessional account of his own alienation from "bodily praxis." He recalls his discovery of a close kinship between economy of effort and grace of movement through an everyday task such as lighting a fire. This allowed him to "break the habit of using a linear communicational model for understanding bodily praxis." He notes that "to participate bodily in everyday practical tasks was a creative technique which often helped me grasp the sense of an activity by using my body as others did" (p.340). One can only wonder what counted as participation in Jackson's notion of participant-observation prior to this event, if indeed he previously chose "to stand aside from the action, take up a point of view and ask endless questions." He has discovered what Langer (1942) has called "presentational [non-discursive] meaning," and Polanyi (1958) "tacit knowledge." In semasiological terms we can say that Jackson has discovered signifying acts done with movement in addition to signifying acts done with words. One is led to suspect that Jackson's prior alienation may be quite a common experience for investigators socialized into the mores of Western academia.

Unfortunately, this discovery leads Jackson to the romantic assumption that "recognition of the embodiedness of our being-in-the-world is to discover a common ground where self and other are one" (p.340). He thereby catapults himself into the Cartesianism he is attempting to overcome by privileging body over mind, but maintaining the separation between the two. Jackson wrongly assumes that actions require no translation from one culture to another; that what looks the same will mean the same and provide the same experiences (how does he know?); and that the sheer fact of embodiment allows one to inhabit the world of the other. Jackson's position continues the tradition of positing a reality sans language, sans culture, sans history that has been criticized by Rorty (1979). In this case the reality is that of a bifurcated person: the experience of the body apart from the mind, and therefore—in a position that strikes one as extraordinary for an anthropologist—apart from cultural context, beliefs and intentions.[11]

There can be little doubt that the legacies of Plato and Descartes have left assumptions about body and mind, thinking and feeling, knowledge and experience, subjective and objective, largely unexamined and unchallenged. Or, alternatively, these oppositions remain intact and we are left swinging on a pendulum between objectivist and subjectivist perspectives.[12] Yet such basic philosophical presuppositions are crucially important, since it is they that ultimately determine the theories and the very perception of the problems at issue. That such basic presuppositions are involved seems self-evident. Their import for anthropological theorizing, however, has been insufficiently recognized. Indeed, the problem of the disembodied actor in social theory may prove to be a fruitful arena for anthropology and philosophy to meet, as Varela's chapter in this volume clearly illustrates.[13]

There is of course significant anthropological and historical research waiting to be done on the complex reasons for such an absence of discussion about the body and human movement in social theory. In addition to the Platonic legacy, surely it is, in part, a reflection of the Western Christian tradition wherein the body as flesh is the location of sinful desire, corrupting appetites, and irrational passions (Turner 1984). Such theoretical neglect of the body has occurred despite the obvious fact that we are embodied; and that we *have* and *are* bodies, these English verbs marking both notions of ownership and our sense of being-in-the-world. Ironically perhaps, such theoretical neglect remains intact despite a virtual cult of the body in contemporary Western cultures, with fetishes ranging from fitness (body as machine kept in shape by other machines) to fat control (liposuction and implants) and from the politically correct body (Pollitt 1982) to the use of fashion and non-vocal rhetoric by political dissidents (O'Neill 1972). In response, perhaps, we now find a virtual explosion of writing on "the body" in post-modern literature.

As Bryan Turner (1984) has suggested, perhaps for many sociologists and anthropologists, reference to the corporeal nature of human existence raises the specter of social Darwinism, biological reductionism, or sociobiology.[14] But these are no longer the only theoretical options, as the papers in this collection and other contributions to the anthropology of the body clearly demonstrate.[15]

The problem has been a complex ontological dualism between matter and spirit, which inevitably created an insoluble problem, because in rejecting a dualism of the body/mind variety, one does not want to end up with an ontological monism that reduces subjectivity to physiology or genetics. Previous attempts to transcend reductionist thinking of this biological kind, however, seem to have led us to a somewhat ethereal conceptualization of our being-in-the-world, in that recent developments in social theory and the philosophy of action that concentrate on conceptualizations of the person and the notion of self, on the whole, define people in terms of their social location, beliefs and values, and speech acts and discourse, and people remain strangely disembodied.

Current anthropological discourse, however, appears to be on the brink of a groundswell of interest in the physical body as cultural construct, much of it stimulated by the work of Foucault. Foucault, Armstrong, Brain, Freund, Hudson, Martin, Turner, and others, have focused attention on such topics as the sexual body, the medical body, the civilized body, and the decorated body.[16] These developments should be extremely fruitful, because at the very least, they draw attention to the ethnocentricity that has permeated our spoken-language-centered approaches to systems of meaning until recently.[17] However, in these developments, in addition to agent-centered philosophical contributions,[18] there remains one major lacuna: the human body as a *moving* agent in a spatially organized world of meanings.

It is precisely here that the essays in this volume offer a potential contribution to developments in sociocultural anthropology generally. If social theory is to embrace fully the notion of "person," it would seem necessary not only to treat the actor as embodied but also recognize that this embodied person moves. In other words theories of social action without the action can no longer be deemed adequate.

Despite seminal contributions from Durkheim's students Robert Hertz and Marcel Mauss[19], until Bourdieu reintroduced the notion of habitus in 1977 (see also 1984, ch. 3) there had been only peripheral interest in a moving body.[20] The habitus, while certainly a sensitizing concept, in fact offers a somewhat blurred conception of the body and human agency and offers no systematic strategies for the inclusion of embodied action in cultural practices.[21] The essays in this volume presume Bourdieu's identification of the importance of ways of moving (e.g. stance, gait, posture), ways of making things, and practical taxonomies rooted in sensory experience. A general anthropology of human movement, however, aims to be all inclusive rather than limited by arbitrary divisions between practical or instrumental uses of body actions—that may be out of focal awareness through habit but not therefore "unconscious"—and "symbolic" actions such as those found in dances, theatrical events, ceremonies and rituals of all kinds.

Unfortunately, and as a result of the same Cartesian legacy mentioned above, when attention has been paid to a moving body, it often appears to have lost its mind. That is, some earlier approaches to human movement that entered the anthropological arena also acquired the appellation "nonverbal communication" and were for the most part behavioristic and scientistic.[22] The label "nonverbal" is itself problematic because apart from being a logocentric maneuver,[23] as a negative appellation—the designation of something in terms of what it is not—it tends to direct attention away from the many ways in which complex symbol systems as diverse as sign languages, dance idioms, martial arts, religious ritual, and fighting are deeply interconnected with spoken language concepts and depend equally on the human capacities for meaning-making. These attributes are considered essential to an agent-centered notion of person in what Harré (1971) has usefully called an "anthropomorphic model of man." In addition, to reduce such systems to "communication" is to ignore the many other functions of semiotic systems.

In contrast to these former approaches, most of the essays herein are best understood in light of the new realist philosophy of science with its specific conception of agency and causal powers that transcends the Cartesian material/immaterial dichotomy and so dissolves the problem of agency set up by Descartes.[24] This is discussed in detail in Varela's analysis in chapter 8. The ethnographic essays are direct examples of ways in which such inquiry might proceed within a post-Cartesian framework. As Varela puts it, we are at last able to talk, not only *about* the body and *of* the body but also *from* the body in action.

This collection also marks a potential shift in the definition of the field, from two separate areas called the anthropology of dance and nonverbal communication to a more inclusive anthropology of human movement. Pioneered separately by both Kaeppler and Williams, the inclusion of any and all manifestations of human movement in cultural contexts has brought together interested parties previously separated by arbitrary anthropological distinctions between art and nonart, between whole-body action and the use of parts of the body (such as the arms and hands) in specific contexts.[25]

Along the way it has been necessary to leave behind encumbrances of an ethological nature to which even Hall's proxemics was prone, as well as some problematic assumptions from psychologistic and naive universalist perspectives. Ethological approaches, though they usually recognize species-specific cognitive abilities, implicitly allow the faculty for language use to "stop at the neck" as it were—as if such faculties somehow don't apply to our actions or our conceptions of those actions.[26] Such an omission implies that the same mind that uses spoken language somehow switches off when the body starts to move. Psychologistic approaches under whose rubric fall many of the early nonverbal communication studies, usually insist upon the aforementioned observationist perspective and on the whole assume that whereas we speak what we mean, we don't move what we mean, assuming that gestures are primarily a kind of emotional incontinence.[27]

Naive universalism or that of a Darwinian kind[28] is problematic in its assumption that because we share the same basic physical makeup with all other human beings, therefore somehow the actions produced mean the same things across cultures because they look the same. While the romantic nature of this escape from relativism is seductive to some—and especially so when it comes to aesthetics and "art"—the fact remains that this attitude is equivalent to and just as problematic as insisting that all spoken languages are alike and mutually understandable because they use the same parts of the mouth and throat and select from the same set of possible vocal sounds. The essays in this book present a plethora of examples that oppose these kinds of reductionism, and one dares to hope such hoary old dragons will have finally breathed their last.

Williams insisted as long ago as 1975 that if we view human movement not as simply body movement or behavior but as action, the very heart of our terminology shifts to an agentive perspective. This means that human bodily movement is performed by meaning-making agents that possess a hierarchy of powers and capacities that are specifically human. Kaeppler's structured movement systems, Kendon's gesticulation and codified gesture systems, and Williams' action sign systems are all conventional structured systems of human movement that are best understood as they exist in the sociolinguistic sphere of human life. They are not behaviors or raw physical data of some kind, nor are they the result of biologically triggered impulses that can be separated from the capacity of humans to create multiple and complex levels of meaning. They are not so much theories of movement as theories of culturally and semantically laden actions couched in indigenous conceptual models of organization and meaning as they apply to "various idioms of dancing, signing, liturgy, greeting systems, the martial arts" (Williams 1982); presenting ritual food, mixing ritual *kava*, and the performance of sung speeches with choreographed movements (Kaeppler 1985); and mediating kinship by way of body signs and choosing speech or sign language in daily interaction (Kendon 1989).

SYNOPSIS OF CHAPTERS

Part I presents seven papers set in a wide variety of ethnographic contexts. These include Hawaiian dance and poetry, the Roman Catholic post-Tridentine Mass, the Chinese exercise technique tai chi chuan, classical ballet, Plains Indian and Australian Aboriginal sign languages; Waridjuri (Australian) fighting; Philadelphia's black youth street theater/dance forms, Bharata Natyam (Indian classical dance), and Martha Graham's American modern dance. Part II consists of anthropological and philosophical commentaries on the ethnographic papers in Part I.

In chapter 1, Adrienne L. Kaeppler examines the intricate connection between poetry and the Hawaiian hula, in which "movements may allude to the surface meaning of the poetry, thereby making the text visible, or they may allude to the hidden meaning of the poetry, thereby enhancing the meaning of the invisible." She connects this to a central concept in Hawaiian life, that of *kaona*, meaning "veiled or layered meaning," which brings an aesthetic or evaluative way of thinking to many cultural forms. Like the more widely known concept of mana, *kaona* is a creative power of understanding the invisible through the visible, thereby gaining a more profound understanding of both what is seen and what is unseen. The intricate and complex ways in which poetry and dance combine to illuminate Hawaiian history, social structure, and cultural practices presuppose that such performances are not for the uninformed. The dancer's skill and the audience's knowledge come together here, for one has to know the spoken poetic and movement metaphor being employed, the social and cultural context of the specific performance event, and the general social and cultural background, in order that both visible and invisible emerge in all dimensions.

In this context Kaeppler is careful to stress another dimension of the notion of invisible: the structure of the dance system itself. One has to know how meanings are attached to movement conventions, and how these are formed into patterned sets within the dance form in order to decode the messages. She likens this kind of shared cultural knowledge to the Chomskian notion of competence and the Saussurian idea of langue. It is only such competence that enables a viewer to understand a movement sequence never seen before and to recognize that grammatical requirements of the system have been fulfilled.

In chapter 2, Drid Williams moves us to a comparative perspective and presents an additional theoretical level of invisibles. She suggests that although specific dance or sign systems, rituals or ceremonies may be very different from each other, the kinds of cultural concepts necessary to understand any particular action sign system in perfor-mance can in turn be understood with reference to a universal theoretical framework. This makes sense of diverse particular facts, and makes useful comparison possible. Citing examples from three widely disparate systems—tai chi chuan, classical ballet, and the Roman Catholic post-Tridentine Mass—she clears a careful path for the reader to follow by demonstrating the analytical power of a semasiological approach. Distinctive spatial characteristics and semantics are elucidated for each sys-tem/event and shown to be the invisible resources inform-ing the visible actions that take place.

Following Williams' semasiological theoretical frame-work, in chapter 3, Brenda Farnell challenges the implicit Cartesianism at work in current definitions of language, wherein words are privileged but gestures are not. Farnell argues that Western theories of meaning are not relevant to the Assiniboine Indians of Montana. "Mind" in their culture is not a thing, but a disposition toward others and so is fundamentally a social state. Illustrating with data from Plains Indian sign language (abbreviated to Plains Sign Talk or PST) as it is used today, she explains how it is that everyday action and interaction as well as storytelling performances—all of which use both speech and signs—are permeated and structured by two particularly salient spatial symbolic forms. An Assiniboine speaker is likely to incorporate elements of PST into speech to the degree that a PST-Assiniboine continuum may be suggested, depending on context and skill. The systems are not monolithically distinct. In particular the same deictic features appear in both speech and sign at both the syntactic and semantic levels. It is argued that the "here and now" and "there and then" for the mover no less than for the speaker represent articulated conceptions of space and time, and deixis is connected to an embodied sense of direction. This provides a clear illustration of the kind of links Williams refers to when she says there are "semantic primitives" common to both spoken languages and action sign systems. In addition, and like Williams and Kaeppler (1990), this chapter illustrates the methodological importance of the movement writing system Labanotation for the detailed recording and analysis of data. Writing with symbols that record the movement itself enables investigations to be freed from real time and from dependence on difficult if not impossible translations into spoken language terms.[29]

In chapter 4, Adam Kendon also deals with a sign language. Drawing upon his extensive research on sign languages of Aboriginal Australia (Kendon 1989) he focuses here upon interactive contexts. Kendon hypothesizes that signing is widely used in Australian Aboriginal society because of its special properties as a mode of communication: its silence, its visual nature, and its lexicon, which appears less elaborate than spoken language units but in fact carries an increased semantic load in interaction contexts. These features suit signing to certain deliberately indirect, semiexplicit communicative tasks Aborigines face daily. Signing is not restricted to the ritual contexts in which spoken language is prohibited, such as during men's initiation rites and women's mourning practices. In the complexity and delicacy that characterize Aboriginal interaction, signs often prove to be more useful than speech for many kinds of communication. As with the Assiniboine, the choice of speech and/or signs would appear to depend on personal skill, knowledge, and subtleties of the interaction context itself.[30]

A similar theme in the utilization of movement rather than of explicit speech to keep things hidden arises in a very different context in Gaynor M. Macdonald's work in chapter 5 on Wiradjuri fighting. The failure of well-meaning interferences by non-Aboriginals to get people to talk things over rather than fight highlights some of our own deeply-rooted assumptions about the respective roles of spoken language and what we perceive as physical violence. It was only through her gradual understanding of fights, Macdonald tells us, that she came to comprehend many of the dynamics of Wiradjuri life. Thus our notion that "sticks and stones may break my bones" is reversed, words being viewed as effective and explosive weapons that reveal far too much and therefore are far more harmful than physical encounter. Fights act as an implicit form of censorship by which the society prevents invisible contradictions from becoming visible and damaging. A fight weaves the protagonists back into society and facilitates reestablishment of the orderly form of daily relations. Rather than being divisive, fights actually lead to social involvement, and they reestablish or maintain communication rather than impede it; they are assertions of sociality, not the reverse.

In contrast, in chapter 6, LeeEllen Friedland's research on children and youths in Philadelphia's African-American community reveals how movement becomes a medium that encodes very explicit social commentary. The politics of representation are especially at issue here: what is visible is what the collector has allowed to be visible. Previously ignored by historians of popular dance whose attention was taken up with adult virtuoso performers of tap dancing in the entertainment industry, the actual pinnacle of skill and artistic expression resides rather in adolescent culture, and is perfectly visible in the everyday life of African-American communities. Scholars confined by their definitions of what dance was supposed to look like hadn't learned to see the fast-changing and more flowing genres within communities, which, like the Hawaiian dances analyzed by Kaeppler, contain rich social commentary encoded into movement and aimed at different sections of the adolescent and adult worlds. Because these dancers are at a disadvantaged place in the class structure, their knowing audience may not even count as audiences, and the performers are no longer dancers but just a bunch of poor kids. This is in some ways comparable to the situation of the Waridjuri Aborigines, in which non-Aboriginal outsiders see fights and assume "just a bunch of drunk Aborigines!"[31]

The final chapter (chapter 7) in the ethnographic section discusses improvisation and composition in two radically different dance idioms. Rajika Puri is a performer in the south Indian classical dance idiom *Bharata Natyam*, and Diana Hart-Johnson is a former soloist with Martha Graham's modern dance company. Their chapter is a response to Sheets-Johnstone's "Thinking in Movement" (1981) and illustrates serious problems with Sheets-Johnstone's phenomenological approach. The authors also expose the ways an audience's preconceptions can totally misconstrue the meaning of the visible if the audience lacks knowledge of the structure and practices within a specific dance idiom. The content is not discussed in Urciuoli's commentary because it was not written for the AAA panel that gave rise to the other chapters. It is included here because of its relevance to the general theme, and because it provides ethnographic grounding for the critique of Sheets-Johnstone's work found in Varela's commentary.

The first discussion in Part II is a detailed commentary by Bonnie Urciuoli on the previous essays. Urciuoli, as both anthropologist and linguist, views the work from a double vantage point. She perceives the central importance of indexicality in those essays and shifts the focus of attention away from grammatical-semantic organization, which makes spoken language structurally distinct, and centers instead on its indexical nature, as Silverstein (1976) suggested. Theoretical space emerges wherein speech as action (speech act) and movement as action both become centered in indexicality itself; "the indexical creation of the social person (and the terms of action) is the performative nature of action," and "indexicality is at every moment symbolically mediated." Urciuoli suggests that we embrace a broader concept of the signifying act, making a speech act a signifying act done with spoken language in contrast to signifying acts done with dance, martial arts and the like. She notes the power of Williams' phrase "action sign system" to capture this, and its reminiscence to Saussure's vision of a "science of signs" of which spoken language would be only one kind.

Urciuoli's discussion brings to the fore theoretical points not always explicit in the essays themselves, and, in addition, she articulates theoretical connections at several levels. She discusses emergent performativity and the enactment of self, the embodiment of social and historical moments, formal and informal performativity, and aspects of the politics of visibility and invisibility.

Whereas chapter 8 provides anthropological and linguistic commentary, chapter 9 combines philosophical discussion with a historical perspective. Charles Varela's analysis articulates several conceptual errors found in recent attempts to return to the work of Merleau-Ponty in order to find ways to transcend the exclusion of the body from social theory. Philosophers and anthropologists who emphasize Merleau-Ponty's existential phenomenology and ignore his later emphasis on the philosophy of history, in which he himself saw the need to connect bodily gesture with language, in fact bring his approach to a dead end. Indeed it is argued that in order to accept Merleau-Ponty's invitation to discover that connection between language and gesture one must go to theoretical and philosophical resources beyond Merleau-Ponty's work itself. Those resources are identified in Varela's chapter as the new realist philosophy of science articulated by Rom Harré and the ethogenic standpoint that Harré has developed from it for the purposes of sociocultural investigations. These developments transcend Cartesian dualism without renouncing the significance of Merleau-Ponty's suggestions.

Resorting to the body as lived, experienced, or intentional does not transcend Cartesianism because agency remains a ghost; it has simply been relocated from being in the mind to being in the body. The new realist philosophy of science argues for a definition of agency that properly connects it to a conception of substance that is compatible with causation (as causal power, not the Humean variety). Without causation there can be no agency, and for causation to be possible there must be substance for its grounding. A new conception of substance has been developed, which is neither the materialist nor the phenomenalist version, but a dynamical one: an immaterialist model of substance as a structure of powers and capacities in which the natural powers grounded in the human organism make possible the realization of personal powers that are grounded in, and thus afforded by, social life. Powers thus belong to the person, not the organism, and the Cartesian material/immaterial dichotomy underlying the body/mind duality is no longer viable. The key is the primacy of the person, gesture (including vocal gestures) and social action, not the primacy of the body, experience, and individual perception. Since powers are grounded in social life and therefore belong to the person, the organism is thus transformed into the body viewed as a bio-cultural entity. Embodiment, the cultural fact of the body, is therefore the result of the social construction and empowerment of the person. Varela thus makes explicit certain metatheoretical themes essential to understanding why the actor in Western social theory has remained disembodied for so long. His contribution from recent work in the philosophy of science allows us to transcend this problem and thereby illuminates how fruitful these ethnographic studies are—not only for an anthropology of human movement but for sociocultural anthropology in general.

Brenda Farnell

I would like to thank Raymond J. DeMallie, Adrienne Kaeppler, Adam Kendon and Drid Williams for their helpful comments on an earlier draft of this introduction.

NOTES

1. See, for example, Hall 1966a, 1966b and Birdwhistell 1970.
2. It is not my purpose in this introduction to present a comprehensive review of the field but rather to identify certain general theoretical themes and to situate the concerns of the contributing authors. The interested reader can consult Kaeppler 1978 and Williams 1986 and 1991 (especially chapter 9) for discussion of theories and developments.
3. See Kaeppler 1967, 1972, 1986; Williams 1975, 1979, 1982, 1991; Kendon 1989 provides an extensive bibliography of his work.
4. See Harré and Secord 1972 for discussion of agency in the social sciences.
5. Polanyi 1958, Gadamer 1960, and Kuhn 1962 developed new notions of objectivity, arguing against the objectivism prevalent in the positivist conception of science. The underlying theme in all three works is encapsulated perhaps in Gadamer's comment that the objectivist position is based on a self-contradiction; that is, it is a prejudice against prejudice. This involves two mistakes: the illusion that any act of thought can be bias free and that bias is necessarily negative. Value judgment being built into the process of thought is positive; it promotes thought and does not distort it. Bias can of course become negative, but that is a secondary matter and not a primary one. Objectivity depends then, not upon denying such bias, or pretending that it doesn't exist, but making these necessary biases explicit such that critical judgment can be brought to bear systematically. David Pocock's notion of a "personal anthropology" applies this new view of objectivity directly to anthropological concerns (Pocock 1973) and was an early expression of a reflexive approach to social science. For a working out of this problem in sociology, see Gouldner 1970 and Friedrichs 1970. For a discussion of the emergence of objectivity without objectivism, that is, a conception of mind without the idea of neutrality, in both sociology and anthropology, see Varela 1984. Crick 1976 discusses the shift to a definition of human beings as "meaning-makers" in semantic anthropology.
6. Structural linguistics had major effects on anthropological theory during the 1960s and 1970s. In America, Kenneth

Pike's "emic" analysis was a concept in linguistics which anthropologists applied to broader anthropological thought in what came to be called the "new ethnography." Conklin, Frake, Gladwin, Goodenough, Sturtevant and others realized the potential of applying contrastive analysis and componential analysis to other cultural domains such as kinship systems, color categories, religion, and botany (Hymes 1964 and Tyler 1969). The new ethnography had its roots in ethnoscientific analysis that employed linguistic models and analogies. Kaeppler's analysis of dance is based in this tradition (Kaeppler 1986).

In England, the influence of Saussurian linguistics in the 1970s was profound in an anthropological tradition that had largely ignored language (apart from Firth). Unlike the American tradition, the history of linguistics and anthropology in England is largely one of separate development (Henson 1974). For the impact of Saussurian linguistics on semantic anthropology see Crick 1976. Williams' semasiology is centered on this development. Both Kaeppler and Williams utilize linguistic analogies to help build theories about structured movement systems but this should not be confused with the application of linguistic models that characterized the "new ethnography."

7. See also McNeill 1985, 1992; Kendon 1983, 1989 and Farnell 1990.
8. In philosophy, Heidegger, Ryle, Dewey, and Wittgenstein have all abandoned the Cartesian distinction as invalid.

In the sociological tradition, Durkheim, Weber, Simmel, and Cooley, as well as Mead in social psychology and Vygotsky in psychology, were all working toward overcoming Cartesian dualism. G. H. Mead, in particular, was perhaps the first to achieve the breakthrough explicitly in a series of papers during 1909-1913 (Joas 1980). Dualistic thinking created problems that centered on subject (inner world) versus object (outer world), distinctions that denied the social nature of mind and the individual. The discovery of the social nature of the individual began the demise of Cartesianism. If the nature of human being is social—in mind, body and action—there cannot be a primordial split between mind and body, between inside and outside. To think that way, as many people in Western cultures still do, of course, is a secondary cultural achievement particular to Western modernity, but not a primary given.

In the first half of the twentieth century both philosophy and social theory converged on this abandonment of Cartesian dualism. Paradoxically, while this led to a social view of mind, it did not lead to an inclusion of the body. Our particular interest in the Cartesian mind/body split as it affects studies of human movement is therefore a subset of a much larger concern. If mind is the locus of the subject in an inner world of meaning, then the body is relegated to sensating matter outside that world. See Varela, this volume, for further discussion.

9. The term "body language" was taken up originally in Williams' semasiology as the best available alternative for "non-verbal communication" (Williams 1991:207). Unfortunately, the term was popularized in a superficial and misleading book of the same title by Fast 1970, which has made many scholars, including Williams, uncomfortable with the label.

10. Harré 1986a. Farnell 1994, Turner 1984 and Varela (this volume) discuss the absence of the body in social theory.

11. This problem is not one confined to a male perspective, nor does being a dancer guarantee that one will know better. For a similar error by a female philosopher and former dancer see Sheets-Johnstone 1981. For a critique of this error see Varela 1983 and this volume.

12. See Best 1978 and 1992 for cogent discussions of "subjectivism" and "objectivism" and the fallacies and misconceptions involved.

13. See also Johnson 1987 and Lakoff 1987 for interesting developments of their earlier concerns with metaphor and categories into examinations of the role of body, movement, and space in the development of mind, imagination, and reason.

14. The specter of socio-biology has been legitimately exorcised by Stephen Jay Gould's essays "Cardboard Darwinism" and "Genes on the Brain" in Gould 1987, and by Sahlins 1976.

15. Scheper-Hughes and Lock 1987 provide a representative bibliography of recent work on the anthropology of the body, particularly as used in medical anthropology.

16. Armstrong 1983, Brain 1979, Freund 1982, Hudson 1982, Martin 1987, Turner 1984.

17. Exceptions are the multi-sensory approaches advocated by Stoller 1989, Feld 1982 and Tedlock 1983.

18. Cf. Hampshire 1965 and Harré 1984.
19. Hertz 1909 and Mauss 1935.
20. I am referring here to the lack of general interest and to the marginalization of such interests to a specialist subfield within the discipline. Apart from Hall's proxemics and Birdwhistell's kinesics, there has been ongoing work by specialists in the anthropology of dance and human movement (see Williams 1986 and 1991 for bibliography and discussion). Douglas 1970 continued the tradition of examining the body via a Durkheimian model of society; Benthall and Polhemus 1975 and Blacking 1977 provide a mixed bag of examples from approaches to the body in anthropology, sociology and nonverbal communication extant in the 1970s. My point is that such work has remained peripheral, making little or no impact on social theory generally or on anthropological methods.
21. Varela's chapter in this volume builds on the work of Harré to clarify such blurred conceptions of agency.
22. Cf. Argyle 1970, Hewes 1955, Lomax 1971.
23. This was noted by Polhemus in Benthall and Polhemus 1975. "Logocentric" is a term used by Derrida and writers of the French *Tel Quel* circle, such as Kristeva. Although I sympathize with the criticisms implied by the term, I do not hold to the view that the answer to logocentricity lies in the championing of the body as an (often romantic and primitive) opposition to spoken language meaning. A notion of subjectivity or attention to physical being that involves a rejection of spoken language meaning only perpetuates the problem, as if nonvocal semiotic systems exist in a realm apart. Rather, it would seem more fruitful to investigate overlapping semiotic processes; the ways in which people use all kinds of semiotic systems for different purposes.
24. See Harré 1986b, Warner 1990.
25. See Kaeppler 1971, 1985 and Williams 1975, 1982.
26. Examples of ethological approaches can be found in Eibl-Eibesfeldt 1989, Hewes 1955, Morris 1979 and Peng 1978.
27. See Harper et al. 1978; Scherer and Ekman 1981; Siegman and Feldstein 1987.
28. See Hinde 1972.
29. Birdwhistell 1970 recognized the importance of this problem and attempted to devise an adequate notation system for kinesic investigations. Unfortunately, his system fails to fulfill some of the criteria necessary to be considered a

script rather than a mnemonic device — problems such as the finite differentiation of space for example (Goodman 1969). Farnell 1989 summarizes the historical development of scripts of writing movement and briefly compares three extant scripts: Benesh, Eshkol-Wachman, and Labanotation. Page 1990 provides an in-depth comparison of Benesh and Labanotation. Williams and Farnell 1990 and Farnell 1994a advocate the Laban script for social scientists and discuss the value of literacy in relation to movement. Kendon has also recognized the need for a script; in his recent work he adapted William Stokoe's notation, which was designed to write American Sign Language.

30. See also Kendon 1989:4–6.
31. I am indebted to Bonnie Urciuoli for these observations, made in her preliminary notes on the essays.

REFERENCES

Argyle, M. 1970. The communication of inferior and superior attitudes by verbal and non-verbal signals. *British Journal of Social and Clinical Psychology* 9:222–231.

Armstrong, O. 1983. *The Political Anatomy of the Body: Medical Knowledge in Britain in the 20th Century.* Cambridge, U.K: Cambridge University Press.

Benthall, J., and T. Polhemus, eds. 1975. *The Body as a Medium of Expression.* London: Institute of Contemporary Arts.

Best, D. 1978. *Philosophy and Human Movement.* London: Allen and Unwin.

———. 1992. *The Rationality of Feeling.* London and Washington: Falmer.

Birdwhistell, R. 1970. *Kinesics and Context: Essays on Body Motion Communication.* Philadelphia: University of Pennsylvania Press.

Blacking, J., ed. 1977. *The Anthropology of the Body* (ASA 15). London: Academic Press.

Bourdieu, P. 1977. *Outline of a Theory of Practice.* Cambridge, U.K.: Cambridge University Press.

———. 1984. *Distinction: A Social Critique of the Judgement of Taste.* Cambridge, Mass.: Harvard University Press.

Brain, R. 1979. *The Decorated Body.* New York: Harper & Row.

Crick, M. 1976. *Explorations in Language and Meaning: Towards a Semantic Anthropology.* London: Malaby.

Douglas, M. 1970. *Natural Symbols.* New York: Vintage.

Eibl-Eibesfeldt, I. 1989. *Human Ethology.* Hawthorne, N.Y: Aldine De Gruyter.

Farnell, B. 1989. Body movement notation. In D. Barnouw, ed., *International Encyclopedia of Communication.* Philadelphia: Oxford University Press and University of Pennsylvania Press.

———. 1990. Plains Indian sign talk: Action and discourse among the Nakota (Assiniboine) of Montana. Ph.D. dissertation, Indiana University, Bloomington, Indiana.

———. 1994. *Do You See What I Mean?: Plains Indian Sign Talk and the Embodiment of Action.* Austin: University of Texas Press.

———. 1994a Ethno-graphics and the moving body. *MAN*, December.

Fast, J. 1970. *Body Language.* New York: Evans.

Feld, S. 1982. *Sound and Sentiment: Birds, Weeping, Poetics and Song in Kaluli Expression.* Philadelphia: University of Pennsylvania Press.

Foucault, M. 1973. *Madness and Civilization: A History of Insanity in the Age of Reason.* New York: Vintage.

————. 1975. *The Birth of the Clinic: An Archaeology of Medical Perception.* A. M. Sheridan Smith, trans. New York: Vintage/Random House.

————. 1979. *Discipline and Punish: The Birth of the Prison.* New York: Vintage.

————. 1980. *The History of Sexuality. Vol. 1, An Introduction.* R. Huxley, trans. New York: Vintage/Random House.

Freund, P. E. S. 1982. *The Civilised Body: Social Domination Control and Health.* Philadelphia: Temple University Press.

Friedrichs, R. W. 1970. *A Sociology for Sociology.* Toronto: Collier Macmillan Canada.

Gadamer, H. 1975 [1960]. *Truth and Method.* New York: Continuum.

Goodman, N. 1969. *Languages of Art: An Approach to a Theory of Symbols.* London: Oxford University Press.

Gould, S. J. 1987. *An Urchin in the Storm: Essays about Books and Ideas.* New York: W. W. Norton.

Gouldner, A. 1970. *The Coming Crisis of Western Sociology.* New York: Basic Books.

Hall, E. T. 1966a. *The Silent Language.* Garden City, N.Y.: Doubleday.

————. 1966b. *The Hidden Dimension.* Garden City, N.Y.: Doubleday.

Hampshire, S. 1965 [1959]. *Thought and Action.* London: Chatto & Windus.

Harper, R. G., A. N. Wiens, and J. D. Matarazzo, eds. 1978. *Nonverbal Communication: The State of the Art.* New York: John Wiley and Sons.

Harré, R. 1971. An anthropomorphic model of man. *Journal of the Anthropological Society of Oxford* 2(1):33–37.

————. 1984. *Personal Being.* Cambridge, Mass.: Harvard University Press.

————. 1986a. Persons and powers. In S. G. Shankar, ed., *Philosophy in Britain Today.* Albany, N.Y.: State University of New York Press.

————. 1986b. *Varieties of Realism: A Rationale for the Natural Sciences.* Oxford: Basil Blackwell.

Harré, R., and H. Secord. 1972. *The Explanation of Social Behaviour.* Totowa, N.J.: Littlefield Adams.

Henson, H. 1974. *British Social Anthropologists and Language*: Oxford, U.K.: Clarendon.

Hertz, R. 1960 [1909]. *Death and the Right Hand*. Aberdeen, U.K.: Cohen & West.

Hewes, G. 1955. World distribution of certain postural habits. *American Anthropologist* 57:231–244.

Hinde, R., ed. 1972 *Non-verbal Communication*. Cambridge, U.K.: Cambridge University Press.

Hudson, L. 1982. *Bodies of Knowledge: The Psychological Significance of the Nude in Art*. London: Weidenfeld & Nicolson.

Hymes, D. 1964. *Language in Culture and Society*. New York: Harper & Row.

Jackson. M. 1983a. Knowledge of the body. *Man* 18:327–345.

———. 1983b. Thinking through the body: An essay on understanding metaphor. *Social Analysis* 14:127–149.

Joas, H. 1980. *G. H. Mead: A Contemporary Re-examination of His Thought*. Cambridge, U.K.: Polity.

Johnson, M. 1987. *The Body in the Mind. The Bodily Basis of Meaning Imagination and Reason*. Chicago: University of Chicago Press.

Kaeppler, A. L. 1967. The structure of Tongan dance. Ph.D. dissertation, University of Hawaii, Honolulu, Hawaii.

———. 1971. Aesthetics of Tongan dance. *Journal of Ethnomusicology* (May) 15(1).

———. 1972. Method and theory in analyzing dance structure with an analysis of Tongan dance. *Ethnomusicology* 16(2):173–217.

———. 1978. The dance in anthropological perspective. *Annual Review of Anthropology* 7:31–39.

———. 1985. Structured movement systems in Tonga. In P. Spencer, ed., *Society and the Dance: The Social Anthropology of Performance and Process*. London: Cambridge University Press, 92–118.

———. 1986. Cultural analysis, linguistic analogies, and the study of dance in anthropological perspective. In C. J. Frisbie, ed., *Explorations in Ethnomusicology: Essays in Honor of David P. McAllester*. Detroit Monographs in Musicology No. 9. Detroit: Information Coordinators.

———. 1990. The use of archival film in an ethnohistoric study of persistence and change in Hawaiian hula. In *Proceedings of Colloquium*. Archives of the International Council for Traditional Music, Canberra, Australia 1988.

Kendon, A. 1983. Gesture and speech: How they interact. In J. Weimann and R. Harrison eds., *Non-verbal Interaction.* Sage Reviews of Communications. Vol. 11:13–46. Beverly Hills, Calif.: Sage.

———. 1986. Current issues in the study of gesture. In J. L. Nespoulous, P. Perron, and A. R. Lecours, eds., *The Biological Foundations of Gesture.* Hillsdale, N.J.: Lawrence Erlbaum, 23–47. Reprinted in *Journal for the Anthropological Study of Human Movement* 1989, Vol. 5(3):101–133.

———. 1989. *Sign Languages of Aboriginal Australia.* Cambridge, U.K.: Cambridge University Press.

Kuhn, T. 1962. *The Structure of Scientific Revolutions.* International Encyclopedia of Unified Science 2(2). Chicago: University of Chicago Press.

Lakoff, G. 1987. *Women, Fire and Dangerous Things: What Categories Reveal about the Mind.* Chicago: University of Chicago Press.

Langer, S. 1942. *Philosophy in a New Key: A Study in the Symbolism of Reason, Rite and Art.* Cambridge, Mass.: Harvard University Press.

Lomax, A. 1971. Choreometrics and Ethnographic Filmmaking. *Filmmakers Newsletter* 4(4):22–30.

Martin, E. 1987. *The Woman in the Body: A Cultural Analysis of Reproduction.* Boston: Beacon.

Mauss, M. 1979 [1935]. Techniques of the body. In *Sociology and Anthropology.* London: Routledge & Kegan Paul.

McNeill, D. 1985. So you think gestures are non-verbal? *Psychological Review* 92(3):350–371.

———. 1992. *Hand and Mind: What Gestures Reveal About Thought.* Chicago: University of Chicago Press.

McNeill, D., and E. Levy. 1982. Conceptual representations in language activity and gesture. In R. J. Jarvella and W. Klein, eds., *Speech, Place and Action.* Chichester U.K. and New York: John Wiley.

Morris, D. 1979. *Man-Watching: A Field-guide to Human Behaviour.* London: Abrams.

O'Neill, J. 1972. *Sociology as a Skin-trade: Essays towards a Reflexive Sociology.* New York: Harper & Row.

Page, J. 1990. A comparative study of two movement writing systems: Laban and Benesh notations. M.A. thesis, University of Sydney, Sydney, Australia.

Peng, F. C. C. ed., 1978. *Sign Language and Language Acquisi-*

tion in Man and Ape: New Dimensions in Comparative Pedo-linguistics. Boulder, Colo.: AAAS with Westview.

Pocock, D. 1973. The idea of a personal anthropology. Paper presented at the Decennial Conference of the Association of Social Anthropologists, Oxford, July.

Polanyi, M. 1958. Personal Knowledge: Towards a Post-Critical Philosophy. Chicago: University of Chicago Press.

Pollitt, K. 1982. The politically correct body. Mother Jones (May):66–67.

Rorty, R. 1979. Philosophy and the Mirror of Nature. Princeton, N.J.: University of Princeton Press.

Royce A. 1977. The Anthropology of Dance. Bloomington, Ind.: Indiana University Press.

Ryle, G. 1949. The Concept of Mind. London: Hutchinson.

Sahlins, M. 1976. The Use and Abuse of Biology: An Anthropological Critique of Socio-biology. Ann Arbor, Mich.: University of Michigan Press.

Scheper-Hughes, N. and M. M. Lock. 1987. The mindful body: A prolegomenon to future work in medical anthropology. Medical Anthropology Quarterly 1:6–41.

Scherer, K., and P. Ekman. 1981. Handbook of Methods in Nonverbal Behaviour. Cambridge, U.K.: Cambridge University Press.

Sheets-Johnstone, M. 1981. Thinking in movement. Journal of Aesthetics and Arts Criticism xxxix 4:399–407.

Siegman, A. W., and S. F. Feldstein, eds., 1987. Non-Verbal Behaviour and Communication. 2nd ed. Hillsdale, N.J.: L. Erlbaum.

Silverstein, M. 1976. Shifters, linguistic categories and cultural description. In K. Basso and H.A. Selby, eds., Meaning in Anthropology. Albuquerque: University of New Mexico Press.

Stoller, P. 1989. The Taste of Ethnographic Things. Philadelphia: University of Pennsylvania Press.

Tedlock, D. 1983. The Spoken Word and the Work of Interpretation. Philadelphia: University of Pennsylvania Press

Turner, B. 1984. The Body and Society. Oxford: Blackwells.

Tyler, S. 1969. Cognitive Anthropology. New York: Holt, Rinehart & Winston.

Varela, C. 1983. Cartesianism revisited: The ghost in the moving machine. Journal for the Anthropological Study of Human Movement 2(3):143–157.

———. 1984. Pocock, Williams and Gouldner: Initial reactions of three social scientists to the problem of objectivity. *Journal for the Anthropological Study of Human Movement,* 3(2):53–73.

Warner, T. 1990. Locating agency. *Annals of Theoretical Psychology* 6:133–145.

Williams, D. 1975. The role of movement in selected symbolic systems. 3 vols. D.Phil. thesis, Oxford University, Oxford, England.

———. 1979. The human action sign and semasiology. *Dance Research Annual X.* New York: CORD.

———. 1982. 'Semasiology': A semantic anthropologist's view of human movements and actions. In D. Parkin, ed., *Semantic Anthropology* ASA Vol. 22. London: Academic Press.

———. 1986. (Non)anthropologists, the dance, and human movement. In B. Fleshman, ed., *Theatrical Movement: A Bibliographical Anthology.* Metuchen, N.J.: Scarecrow Press.

———. 1991. *Ten Lectures on Theories of the Dance.* Metuchen, N.J.: Scarecrow Press.

Williams, D. and B. Farnell. 1990. *The Laban Script: A Beginning Text on Movement Writing for Non-dancers.* Canberra, Australia: Institute of Aboriginal Studies.

PART I

ETHNOGRAPHIC ESSAYS

Chapter 1 VISIBLE AND INVISIBLE IN HAWAIIAN DANCE

Adrienne L. Kaeppler

In Hawaiian dance it is often said that "the hands tell the story," and indeed this is true for some modern genres based primarily on pantomime. In more traditional Hawaiian dance, however, the most important element is poetry, and movements may allude to the surface meaning of the poetry, thereby making the text visible, or they may allude to the hidden meaning of the poetry, thereby enhancing the meaning of the invisible. The communication of this meaning is conveyed through culturally understood conventions that deal with human movement in time and space.

Dance is a socially constructed movement system, and such systems may be considered cultural artifacts. The movement dimension of these cultural artifacts consists of a series of movement motifs, which are rendered simultaneously and sequentially into a choreographed form. Through a specific choreography a sequence of motifs is given meaning, but this movement dimension is only one component of a larger social activity, which must be understood as a whole if one is to understand what or how dance communicates in a particular instance.

One of the most important traditional values in Hawaiian communication is indirectness. Known as *kaona,* "hidden meaning," to Hawaiians, the concept pervades Hawaiian life and brings an aesthetic, or evaluative way of thinking, to many cultural forms. *Kaona,* along with *no'eau,* "skillfulness" (cleverness, wisdom, knowledge, ingenuity), are the most important elements in all tradi-

31

tional cultural forms. Marshall Sahlins cites *mana* as the
"creative power Hawaiians describe as making visible
what is invisible" (1981:31). But as I have noted previously in the context of feathered cloaks (1985:120), I
believe that "*kaona* is equally important as a creative
power of understanding the invisible through the visible,
thereby gaining a more profound understanding of both
what is seen and what is unseen." This interrelationship
of the visible and invisible in traditional Hawaiian life can
be approached through an analysis of Hawaiian *hula*.

Dance is a cultural form that results from creative
processes that manipulate (i.e., handle with skill) human
bodies in time and space in such a way that the formalization of movement is intensified in much the same manner
as poetry intensifies the formalization of language. The
cultural form produced, though transient, has a structured
content that conveys meaning, is a visual manifestation of
social relations, and may be the subject of an elaborate
aesthetic system. Often, the process of performing is as
important as the cultural form produced.

In Hawai'i two socially constructed movement systems
traditionally had these characteristics and for the purposes of this paper may be considered dance. These two
movement systems are *ha'a*, a ritual dance performed as a
sacrament on the outdoor temples called *heiau*, and *hula*,
formal or informal entertainment performed for a human
audience. Although we have little firsthand knowledge of
ha'a, it is likely that *ha'a* movement sequences, like the
texts they accompanied, would have had a standardized
form that ideally was performed without deviation. *Hula*,
on the other hand, were composed in honor of people and
places and conveyed this information in an indirect way,
namely, through *kaona*, "veiled or layered meaning."
Kaona, especially in relation to words and their combinations, was thought to have a power of its own, which could
harm as well as honor. *Kaona*-laden texts were phrased in
metaphor and allusion, and the meaning had to be de-
duced from cultural knowledge.

Hula performances paid allegiance to the rank-based
sociopolitical system, which honored and validated social

distinctions based on descent from the gods. Specialists who were attached to the courts of high chiefs composed poetry, added music and movements, and rehearsed the performers for these dances of presentation. The audience brought to a performance a critical aesthetic evaluation of poetic composition, musical sound and appropriateness, movement allusion, and choreographic structure. It also evaluated the overall performance and its appropriateness for the occasion. Information was conveyed by the order of the dances, by the placement of individuals within the group, and by costumes—all of which imparted information about the rank of the performers and their genealogical lines.

Body movements enhanced the chanted texts by visual transient means—objectifying the text in *ha'a* and alluding to the text in *hula*. The integral association of visual and verbal modes of expression is basic to an understanding of Hawaiian cultural forms, and *kaona* is a key. Restating that sentence—the integral association of the visible and invisible is basic to an understanding of Hawaiian cultural forms, and *kaona* is a key. A poetic text was given its initial *kaona* by one or more word artists. Melodic contour could be added by the composer(s), by a specialist, or by the performer. A movement artist decides how the text should be conveyed in movement. In some cases the movements allude to the surface meaning of the text, suggesting or depicting certain words (usually nouns), through recognized movement motifs, such as flowers, birds, or other natural phenomena. In other cases the movement motifs refer to veiled or hidden meanings, making reference to genealogical lines, chiefs, and their deeds and thus enhancing the texts.

Using a series of Hawaiian dance texts that I published in 1976, let us examine how dance is used to enhance and obscure. The series of dance texts herein was in honor of King David Kalakaua (1836–1891). The first dance is the most important of the suite and I will discuss it after the others.

The second dance, "He aloha no na pua," a dance accompanied by the double gourd drum, *ipu,* is relatively

KAULILUA I KE ANU WAIʻALEʻALE (HULA PAHU)

1 Kaulilua i ke anu Waiʻaleʻale	Bitterly cold stands Waiʻaleʻale
2 He maka halalo ka lehua makanoe	The lehua blossoms, soaked with fog, hang drooping
3 He lihilihi kuku ia no ʻAipo	Around ʻAipo swamp the thorny shrubs grow
4 O ka hulu aʻa ia no Hau-a-ʻiliki	Pinched and made cold by the frosty dew
5 Ua pehia a ʻeha ka nahele	Pelted and bruised by the beating rain
6 Maui e ka pua, uwe ʻeha i ke anu	Bruised are the flowers that moan in the cold
7 I ke kukuna la wai o Mokihana	Touched by Mokihana's sunlight that shines thru the mist
8 Ua hana ʻia a pono a pololei	I can act in good faith and honor
9 Haʻina ia aku no ia ʻoe	As I declare this fact to you
10 O ke ola no ia o kiaʻi loko eia	That a pond keeper must receive his living from the pond
11 Kiaʻi Kaʻula nana i ka makani	Kaʻula looks on and observes the wind
12 Hoʻolono i ka halulu o ka Maluakele	Hearkening to the roar of the Maluakele
13 Kiʻei, halo ia Makaikeʻole	Peering and peeping at Maka-ike-ole
14 Kamau ka ea i ka Halau-a-ola	Keeping the breath of life in Halau-a-ola
15 He kula lima ia no Wawae-noho	A place loved and caressed is Wa-wae-noho
16 Me he pukoʻa hakahaka la i Waʻahila	Like branchy corals standing at Waʻahila
17 Ka momoku a ka unu. Unulau o Lehua	Torn and broken by the Unu-lau gale of Lehua
18 A lehulehu ka pono, leʻa ka haʻawina	So come the many little blessings that one enjoys to share
19 Keʻala mai nei ka puka o ka hale la-eia	For the door of the house is fragrant with humanity

HE ALOHA NO NA PUA (HULA PĀ IPU)

1 He aloha no na pua	I am fond of the flowers
2 Na pua ohelohelo	Flowers with rosy cheeks
3 Ohelo ai a ka manu	The berries picked by birds
4 Ka lehua ula i ka uka	And the red lehua of the upland
5 Nani wale hoi ka ikena	What a joy it is to see

6 I ka ua nui a o Hilo — The heavy rains of Hilo
7 A nui mai ke aloha — It makes love gush forth
8 Ua like me ka wai puna — Like a bubbling spring
9 He ihona no a he alu — Going down an incline
10 Hakalia i ka piina — Then up over a rise
11 Ka piina a o Poulua — The rise of Poulua
12 Elua o'u makemake — Where there are two things I admire

13 Ka wali a o ko kino — The suppleness of your body
14 Ka nahe a o ko maka — And the sparkle in your eyes
15 Haina mai ka inoa — The end of my song I sing
16 O Kalanikaulilua — In honor of the chief

EIA NO KĀWIKA (HULA PĀ IPU)

1 Eia no Kāwika 'ehe — Here is David
2 Ka heke a o na pua 'ehe — The greatest of descendants
3 Ka uwila ma ka hikina 'ehe — Like the lightning in the east
4 Malamalama Hawaii 'ehe — Brightening Hawaii
5 Ku'i e ka lono i Pelekane 'ehe — Report of him reached Great Britain

6 A lohe ke kuini o Palani 'ehe — And was heard by the Queen of France
7 Nawai ka pua iluna 'ehe — Whose offspring is this so high above
8 Na Kapa'akea he makua 'ehe — Kapa'akea was the name of his sire
9 Ha'ina ia mai ka puana 'ehe — This is the conclusion of our praise
10 No Kalani Kāwika he inoa 'ehe — In honor of King David

HOLO ANA O KALĀKAUA (HULA KĀ 'EKE'EKE)

1 Holo ana o Kalākaua — Kalākaua sails away
2 E imi i ka pono na moku — To seek prosperity for the islands
3 I Kahiki a ho'i mai — To Kahiki and return
4 I Kahiki a o pelekane — To Kahiki, land of the whites
5 Mai Kahiki a Wawae-pahu — From Kahiki to Wawae-pahu
6 I ka ohe kā'eke'eke — With the bamboo *kā'eke'eke* [stamping tubes]

7 I ka pahu kani a Lono — And the drum of the chief, Lono
8 O Lono-i-ka-makahiki — Lono-i-ka-makahiki
9 Ho'oheihei kani moana — It is beaten out at sea
10 Kani Hawea pahu ali'i — Hawea the royal drum

11 E o mai o kalani   Answer us O Chief
12 (O) Kalākaua no he inoa   To your name chant, O Kalākaua

LILIKOʻI (MELE MAʻI)

1 Ka ua i Lilikoʻi, Lilikoʻi e	The rain at Lilikoʻi, Lilikoʻi
2 Oheohe i luna la	It gathers high above
3 Puhaʻu i lalo e	Tumbles down below
4 Ku aku la ʻoe i ka uwehewehe kui kela la	You are pierced by the needle shuttling back and forth
5 Aia ihea? (Eia no ia la)	Where is it? It is here
6 Aia mahea? (Eia maʻanei la)	In what place? Right here
7 Eia nei, o kuli o lohe i neia la e-maumau e.	Say whether you are deaf or do hear this—hold on!
8 Hana kui kele ka ua i ʻOpae-ʻula la	Like a piercing needle is the rain of ʻOpae-ʻula
9 Mahiki i luna la	It leaves the sky
10 Haʻule i lalo e	And falls below
11 Ku aku la ʻoe i ka uwehewehe kui kela la	You are pierced by the needle shuttling back and forth
12 Aia ihea? (Eia no ia la)	Where is it? It is here
13 Aia mahea? (Eia maʻanei la)	In what place? Right here
14 E ia nei, o kuli o lohe neia la e-maumau e.	Say, whether you are deaf or do hear this—hold on!

straightforward. It praises Kalakaua with nature symbolism, comparing him to flowers and birds, using explicit body imagery such as "rosy cheeks," "the sparkle in your eyes," and the "suppleness of your body." The movements, too, are quite direct—the hands form flower shapes, the cheeks are touched, two fingers are held up to interpret "two," and movements made at eye level interpret "eyes."

The third text, also accompanied by *ipu,* states that the fame of Kalakaua has reached Great Britain and France, but the most important implications are genealogical: he is the son of the great chief Kapaʼakea, which is the reason that he should be so highly honored. Line 2, translated here as the "greatest of descendants," in literal translation means the "highest of all flowers." The movements do not refer to the genealogy itself but rather to the words that poetically allude to the genealogy (often flowers). The

literal translation of lines 9 and 10 is "this is in honor of
this flower, Heavenly David is his name."

In the fourth dance, "Holo ana o Kalakaua," the performer accompanies himself or herself with bamboo
stamping tubes (*ka'eke'eke*). The text refers to Kalakaua's
trips away from the islands to the United States to work for
a reciprocity treaty. The reference to Lono-i-ka-makahiki
is genealogical and refers to Kalakaua's great ancestor, in
whose honor the important Kumulipo chant was composed. This chant tells of the creation of plants, animals,
and men, and it establishes Kalakaua's relationship to
nature as well as to man. Lono-i-ka-makahiki in another
manifestation was god of peace and agriculture, and thus,
in addition to establishing Kalakaua's relationship with
the gods, this may be a reference to the peacefulness of his
reign.

The last text is a *mele ma'i*. This kind of dance is
traditionally performed last in a group of dances. *Mele
ma'i* was a special kind of name chant composed in honor
of a chief's sexual parts and, using nature symbolism,
alluded to these physical necessities for perpetuating the
royal lines. Movements often allude to nature symbols
rather than to the body parts, although today the references may be more explicit. It does not take much imagination to visualize the sexual connotations inherent in
this text.

Returning to the first dance, "Kaulilua i ke anu
Wai'ale'ale," this is a *hula pahu,* the most elevated of all
Hawaiian dance types because it is accompanied by a
pahu drum. The *pahu* was originally a sacred temple
drum used in conjunction with *ha'a*—the ritual dance
performed on the outdoor temples. *Hula* performed in
conjunction with *pahu* are seldom used in honor of chiefs.
Here, however, not only does Kalakaua have a *hula pahu*
performed in his honor, but also the text used is the most
sacred of the *ha'a* texts, originally performed as a sacrament—probably to Lono, god of peace and agriculture. For
use in honor of Kalakaua the text was given a different
interpretation and a new *kaona,* and this interpretation is
the one most often used today. According to received

opinion, the dance was composed for Kaumealani, a
Waialua woman chief, by her mother, and the *kaona*
refers to a passionate, yet disdainful woman. This opinion
contends that the chant was inherited by Kalakaua and
demonstrates not only that he descends from chief Waialu
but also that because of his elevated genealogy, he is
entitled to be honored with this sacred dance type (Kaeppler, 1976:213).

What was actually happening here was that Kalakaua
appropriated the text and changed not only its meaning
but also its status as part of a socially given category.
Visually, the movements did not change, but invisibly it
was used to culturally legitimize Kalakaua's rise to power
by invoking tradition. Although Kalakaua was an elected
king, he had descended from the high-ranking Kapaʻakea
(as noted in song 3, line 8). Appropriating this important
hula pahu served as status verification. Song 2, in addition to honoring Kalakaua's physical properties, promul-
gates this status fiction—taking the first word of the song
"Kaulilua" and making it into a descriptive name for
Kalakaua. Line 16 of song 2 translates as "the heavenly
Kaulilua."

This group of Hawaiian dances is arranged in the order
in which they would be presented, that is, the sacred and
more formal dances preceding the less formal and secular.
Only the first dance of the group retains the subtleness of
ancient Hawaiian *hula* in the allusive quality of poetry
and movement. The other dances are late-nineteenth-
century compositions in which the narrative potential of
Hawaiian dance has been exploited to make the dance
easier to understand for those who no longer understood
the poetic subtlety of the Hawaiian language, for by
Kalakaua's time, English had become a major medium of
communication. Kalakaua's genealogy, his physical person, and his fame are recounted, as is what he had done for
Hawaii to deserve its praise and honor. The final song, in
honor of his sexual parts, may be a wish for offspring to
continue the elevated genealogical line.

Finally, the dances visually pay allegiance to the sociopolitical system of the nineteenth century—a combination of indigenous Hawaiian concepts intertwined with ideas adapted from English monarchy, thus making invisible concepts visible and continually brought to mind. The movements, as aesthetic elements in their own right, enhanced the texts and invited the knowledgeable viewer to admire how the movements interpreted concrete things and yet referred to deeper meanings and more abstract concepts.

Poetry for a Hawaiian dance was probably composed in honor of a chief for a specific occasion and then became part of the repertoire of chants in honor of that person. In the hands of different choreographers the movements might be quite different, since each might allude to different words of the text, or to a different meaning of the same line, or to a different meaning of the same line if the poetry had been incorrectly heard or remembered (for most poetry existed only in the oral tradition). In fact, there was no one "correct" movement sequence for a *hula* text (although for a *ha'a* text there probably was), and part of the excitement of watching a *hula* was to discover how skillfully the choreographer had made the text visible, in a culturally satisfying way, by either enhancing or obscuring the meaning.

A dance and its poetry in Hawaii does not tell an integrated story for uninformed listeners. Instead, the dancer orally and visually relates invisible concepts that are intended for those who know the poetic and movement metaphors as well as the social and cultural context of the performance. A dance may appear to an uninformed audience to be fragmentary and inconclusive, whereas to a member of the society, the concepts are readily apparent. Only if one knows the social and cultural background will the visible and invisible emerge in all their dimensions to reveal the political acumen of the creator or, as in the case of "Kaulilua," the reinterpreter. The resulting products were passed from generation to generation to become chronicles of history and social relationships objectified in verbal and visual forms. Needless to say, although the products were visible, the aesthetic system by which they were evaluated was invisible, which brings me, then, to my final point.

In addition to meaning being invisible but accessible through *kaona,* the structure of the dance system is also invisible. In Hawaii, although the hands may help to convey the story, if one does not know the abstract movement conventions that the hands and arms are projecting as movement, the system remains not only invisible but also a mystery. The movements convey meaning essentially as conventional forms within a specific society. Dance movements may be signs or symbols in any combination that serves to convey various kinds of information in many contexts. In order to decode the messages, the observers (be they participants, human audiences, or the gods) must know or look for a pattern of structure or patterned sets (i.e., not isolated movements) that must be familiar if they are to be understood.

In order to understand movement as a cultural artifact with an internal structure and as part of socially given categories, the performer and the observer must have "competence" in an evolved Chomskian sense. Competence or knowledge about a specific dance tradition is acquired in much the same way as competence in a language is acquired. Competence relates to the cognitive learning of the shared rules of a specific dance tradition as langue is acquired in the Saussurian mode. Competence enables viewers to understand a grammatical movement sequence that they have never seen before. "Performance" refers to an actual rendering of a movement sequence— Saussure's *parole*—which assumes that the performer has a certain level of competence and the skill to carry it out. The concept of competence/performance has been refined by sociolinguists and discourse analysts. Dell Hymes, for example, posits rules for performance as well as grammar in what he calls "communicative competence," and Mikhail Bakhtin, noting that both parole and langue are controlled by laws, takes the "utterance" as a unit in his investigation of communication (Holquist 1983). Dance, like language, communicates, and therefore those who do not know the movement conventions will not have communicative competence and will not be able to understand what is being conveyed both visibly and invisibly. In addition, the movement and choreographic dimensions are often only components within a larger social activity; this, too, must be understood as a whole in order to understand what or how a dance communicates in a particular instance.

The aforementioned Hawaiian dances convey their messages, especially the veiled or invisible messages, only to those who have competence in the structure of the Hawaiian dance system and its sociocultural background and history. Meaning is transmitted by the way the movement units are combined, in addition to the traditional meaning of the movement motifs themselves. New sentences are generated from old grammatical structures. Dance creates new meanings by combining old forms in new ways. The product and process interact and may communicate or not depending on the message sender (i.e., the choreographer), the message (i.e., the dancer and product), and the receiver (i.e., the audience).

Dance—the movement dimension of activities or activity systems—conveys or communicates information as a symbolic medium that is quite different from spoken language but a significant part of uniquely human social and cultural systems. Dance, as a symbolic system that operates through conventionalization, creates meanings that can be undone or revised with relative ease and thereby can respond to changing contexts or circumstances. As biologically undetermined arbitrary forms, dances convey conventionalized information only to those who understand the cultural and social constructs of which they are a part. Only if one knows the cultural background will the dance communicate in all its dimensions.

The dance communication process is essentially social. Choreographers, performers, and viewers are socially and historically placed individuals. Communication involves decoding or making sense out of the process and product of cultural forms that manipulate human bodies in time and space according to the cultural conventions and aesthetic systems of a specific group of people at a specific time in specific contexts. An individual decodes the message according to his or her individual background and understanding of a particular performance and his or her own mental and emotional state at that time. Personal, social, and cultural, dance communicates as form and feeling in context.

Dance becomes visible as a product of human action and interaction in the context of a socially constructed movement system. The system itself is invisible, existing in the minds of people as movement motifs, specific choreographies, and meaningful imagery. In Hawaii, dance traditionally functioned to promote prestige, power, status, and social distancing. Today Hawaiian dance has an additional political dimension in that communicative competence in this cultural form is considered an aspect of social and cultural identity.

REFERENCES

Holquist, M. 1983. *Dialogism: Bakhtin and His World.* London and New York: Routledge.

Kaeppler, Adrienne L. 1976. Dance and the interpretation of Pacific traditional literature. In Adrienne L. Kaeppler and H. Arlo Nimmo, eds., *Directions in Pacific Traditional Literature: Essays in Honor of Katharine Luomala.* Honolulu: Bishop Museum Special Publication 62.

————. 1985. Hawaiian art and society: Traditions and transformations. In Antony Hooper and Judith Huntsman, eds., *Transformations of Polynesian Culture,* Memoir 45, Polynesian Society, Auckland, New Zealand, pp. 105–131.

Sahlins, Marshall. 1981. *Historical Metaphors and Mythical Realities.* Ann Arbor, Mich.: University of Michigan Press.

Chapter 2 SPACE, INTERSUBJECTIVITY, AND THE CONCEPTUAL IMPERATIVE: THREE ETHNOGRAPHIC CASES[1]

Drid Williams

SOME THEORETICAL CONSIDERATIONS

When I was a diploma student at the Institute of Social Anthropology in Oxford, Godfrey Lienhardt said to me, "The world [of anthropologists] is divided into two kinds of people: those who see similarities and those who see differences." At the time, I had no idea of the profound implications of his statement. I was still too naive to understand that he alluded to broad differences in anthropological ideology. Later, I came to understand Lienhardt's statement in terms best expressed these days, I think, by Dumont (1987), whose arguments about "hierarchy" (Dumont, 1970), "methodological individualism," and "methodological holism" have helped to form the broad outlines of this discussion.

My response to the issues generated by the tensions that exist between universalism and particularism, between "individuality" and "holism," was semasiology.[2] Because of the multilevel nature of its theoretical structure and its explicit inclusion of the notion of hierarchy, this theoretical framework eases the tension between universals and particulars; it permits investigators to negotiate between assumed "contradictions." Oddly enough, however, it is rooted in a preference for "differences." The kinds of anthropology that I reject are styles of analysis (which are particularly evident in Frazer's and, later,

44

Lomax's talk about dances) that emphasize similarities only. I also reject the kind of unqualified immersion into a single society (usually a "nonindustrialized" or "traditional" or "primitive" society), which seems to cause the anthropologist concerned to emerge from the experience either a total relativist or else so thoroughly identified with the people in question—so immersed in the specific and the particular—that a comparative viewpoint becomes impossible.

We are all familiar with theoretical complementarities such as whole/part, universal/particular, general/specific, similar/different, observer/observed. These are the oppositions with which we grapple constantly—more or less successfully—whether in the field or at home. They manifest themselves in questions about observer and observed and the notion of objectivity; in problems of translation, as Evans-Pritchard would have put it; or in problems in the analysis of events (Ardener 1973): "[p]aradigmatic-[s]yntagmatic structures," as he called them, expressed as relations between the identities and value systems of the anthropologist and his or her informants.

Mostly, one hears of these kinds of oppositions talked about as if they were dichotomies. *Either* one can be a "holist," *or* one can be an "individualist," but not both. *Either* one can ascribe to universals (and thus emphasize similarities in dances and sign systems, for example), *or* one can talk about "particulars," in which case one is forced, because of differences, eventually to become a total relativist. *Either* one can try to embrace notions of "objectivity" held by experimental scientists, thus treating one's informants as "objects," *or* one cannot think of anthropology as a "science" at all. In the current literature about semiotics there are even more glaring examples of false dichotomization: *la langue/la parole* and *signifiant/signifier,* for example, in which the language (the system) and "speaking" (the utterance) are separated and analyzed as contradictions, and in which the concept (*signifiant*) and the sound image or action image (*signifier*) are ripped apart and treated as if they were mutually exclusive.[3]

I long ago rejected such false dichotomizations of theoretical oppositions because the lesson that I learned from those with whom I was privileged to study anthropology (and which I think is also the ultimate lesson to be taken from Durkheim and Mauss) is this: specific dances or complexes of dances (or sign systems or ceremonies or whatever) cannot be made to coincide with each other in any simple or easy fashion. They are different, as the societies themselves of which the dances are a part are different, but we are not stuck because of that with having to make universal generalizations about a global village,[4] which, judging from some of the nonsense written about it, is nothing but a crazy patchwork of randomly produced cultural manifestations that are, in the end, unintelligible. In other words, if one restricts Mauss's conception of *le fait totale* to superficial interpretations of differences only, it is very easy to arrive at woolly metaphysical conclusions, to indulge in special pleading, or to avoid the issue entirely by immersing oneself in intense fieldwork situations in the hope that someday, somehow, the issue will put itself right.

I share Dumont's belief that there is a prior concept to be considered: specific complexes of specific societies must be seen with reference to the global society (not the same as the village concept) of humankind, which actually exists and which must be taken into consideration: "there is no sociological fact apart from the reference to the global society it concerns" (1987:2). What this means with regard to structured systems of human movement is this: different though specific danced, signed, or ritualized ceremonies may be, they have to be understood with reference to a universal framework that makes sense of the particularized facts. Otherwise, no useful comparison can be made between them. Moreover, I would want to say that one can speak of dances from a global or universalist point of view only when two or more dances, danced idioms, or body languages can be subsumed under a single formula—a single set of laws and principles that first identify the whole of which any single manifestation of a dance, a signing system, or any human action is a part, and second, provide a scientifically sound basis for comparison. From its beginnings, semasiology has provided such a set of laws and principles on a structural level and it may be able to provide, in the future, for adequate generalizations on a semantic level, which it does not now pretend to do because it would be scientifically irresponsible to make universal generalizations about the meanings of dances and sign systems until sufficient data are gathered and compiled.

The difficulties I had between the years 1972 and 1976, while in the process of constructing semasiological theory and methodology, were monumental. On the one hand, I couldn't deny the structural universals in the dance and human movement, which I knew existed but which are not empirically visible. On the other hand, I was intimidated by the constraints that older, more respectable styles of doing anthropology (mainly those based on hard-core empiricism and bequeathed by the past, as, e.g., functionalism and behavioral approaches) seemed to place on research into human actions. There were increasing complications too: the expressive range of movements of the human body is so complex that it soon became apparent that a mathematical description of structural principles—not only of the human expressive body itself but also of the space(s) in which it moves—was the only kind of description that would suffice.[5] I think it necessary to say that those descriptions have been offered to the anthropological community at great cost. They are still distrusted[6] by some and generally only incompletely understood, except by a handful of students, such as Farnell (1984), Puri (1983), Durr (1984), and Hart-Johnson (1984); an upcoming generation of Australians who are currently working with me at Sydney University; and some Americans working at Indiana University.

Yet I take some comfort out of the many misunderstandings: semasiological principles and the kind of anthropology they imply,[7] has been known to be one in which anthropologists stand on more radical intellectual grounds than they do in any anthropology that preceded it, and so far, it has proved to be the case that semasiology's theory and methodologies cannot be successfully watered down or chopped and changed so that they can be merged with other theories and methods, or attached to them like an extra appendage of some sort. It cannot be treated in these ways because it requires commitments to a different concept of objectivity for a start. Semasiology is part of an anthropology that proceeds from the premise that the observer cannot be abstracted from the process (Pocock (1994) and Williams (1976) convey the idea of a personal anthropology) and that assumes a different kind of objectivity (Varela 1984). From a semasiological stand-point, the notion of "us" and "them" is confronted di-rectly—or perhaps it is more accurate to say that the issue cannot successfully be avoided, because, from the start, it brings into conscious play the observer's own ideas and value systems. When a semasiologist asks, "Who are these people who behave in danced activities in such and such a way?" the question does not stop there: it includes another phrase. "Who are these people who behave in danced activities in 'X' way, and how does this behavior compare or contrast with ours, who seem to have other kinds of values and beliefs with regard to danced prac-tices?" (Williams 1982 offers a more thorough discus-sion).

Semasiology does not elevate economic, political, bio-logical, or environmental features of social life (to name some of the sociological possibilities) to dominant explan-atory positions, any more than nuclear physics does. It is not that kind of theory or method. Holding a semasiologi-cal point of view means that one always has to maintain a triple frame of reference: (a) there are the structural uni-versals, which are common to all human movement sys-tems anywhere and which are the gear, so to speak, with which every human being is equipped that defines the limitations and constraints under which they operate in a locally Euclidean space; (b) there has to be a reciprocal reference of comparison between participator/observer and the subjects of the action system under investigation (this includes searching for facts regarding the whole field, which correspond in their system with what we believe and for what corresponds on our side of the equation to what they acknowledge and understand); and (c) one has to keep in mind the particularities of the individual action system that is being studied, the forms of these particularities, and their inclusion into a human value system.

Always and everywhere, the structural universals[8] are embedded (one might say, "entangled" or "embroiled") in the human and the sociocultural. They are embodied in a sense in which one could say that the real definition of the substance diamond is embodied in any concrete example of diamonds.[9] The spatial set of universals consisting of the structure of interacting dualisms, that is, up/down (U/D), right/left (R/L), front/back (F/B), and inside/outside (I/O), form the basis for human value systems and ideologies. Johnson would call these "structures of imagination and understanding that emerge from our embodied experience" (1987:xiv). It is just here that the depth and multilevel nature of semasiological theory can best be comprehended.

Anthropologists are familiar with the seminal work of Hertz (cf. Needham 1973) and with the extremely valuable work of anthropological scholars on dual symbolic classification, most (but not all) of which has been based on one binary classification (right/left),[10] of the total structure of interacting dualisms. Dumont convincingly argues that oppositions such as right/left are hierarchical[11] in nature (1987:224–233), so much so that some of his remarks are reproduced here:

> The problem, as found in the literature and in the work cited, is essentially epistemological. The opposition is uniformly treated as a distinctive opposition, a simple "polarity" or "complementarity." But in actual fact the two terms or poles *do not have* equal status: one is superior (generally the right), the other inferior. Hence the problem as it has been historically posed: how is it that the two opposites [right and left] which we (groundlessly) assume to be equal are not equal in reality? In the language of Hertz, why is "preeminence" given to one of the two hands?
>
> What is lacking here is the recognition that the right-left

pair is not definable in itself but *only in relation to a whole,* a most tangible whole, since it is [part of] the human body (and by analogy, other bodies). The fact is familiar to the physicist, who sets up an imagined observer in order to be able to speak of right and left. How can "symbolic analysis" ignore this fact?

In saying that the right/left opposition refers to a whole we are saying that it has a hierarchical aspect, even if at first sight it does not appear to belong to the simple type in which one term encompasses the other and which I have referred to above as "hierarchical opposition." We are accustomed to analyzing this opposition in two component parts, as though it displayed at its base a principle of symmetry more generally encountered and, superadded unto it, an asymmetry of direction to which the value would be attached. This, it should be noted, is a manner of separating *fact* (the assumed symmetry) and *value* (the added asymmetry). Concretely, however, right and left *do not have the same relationship to the whole of the body.* They are differentiated at the same time both in value and in nature. And as soon as different associations and function are attributed to them, this difference is *ipso facto* hierarchical because it is related to the whole. Thus the function of the right will be more important in relation to the whole than the function of the left—more essential, more representative, etc. (Dumont, 1987:228)

Not only is the opposition right/left differentiated in value and nature, but its companion oppositions (up/down, front/back, inside/outside) are differentiated in value and nature as well, and there are no problems with assumed symmetries in these cases, because the human body does not even visually appear to be physically symmetrical on those oppositions. Yet the hierarchical properties of values attached to front/back, for example, with regard to concepts of time in our own culture are considered self-evident when front and a forward direction = future, and back and a backward direction = past, and the present is locatable by the presence of the individual in the here and now (Farnell 1988 gives the contrasting Assiniboine case). Their very self-evidence seems to condemn them to the domain of the unexamined. Likewise, up/down is a rich source of such considerations and so is inside/outside, the opposition that Hall (1966) explored in detail through proxemics in its manifestation as the near/far distinction.[12]

SPATIAL ORIENTATION

Dumont suggests, "Let us suppose that our society and the society under study both show in their system of ideas the same two elements A and B. That one society should subordinate A to B and the other B to A is enough for considerable differences to occur in all their conceptions. In other words, the hierarchy present in a culture is essential for comparison" (1987:7). We will, later on, turn to the specific conceptual spaces of three structured systems of human actions: the Roman Catholic post-Tridentine Mass (the Dominican rite), the ballet "Checkmate" (choreographer, Ninette de Valois), and the Chinese exercise technique tai chi chuan, but before doing that, some generalizations about spatial orientation are necessary.

In ordinary life, each individual's orientation to his or her personal, subjective space and to the physical spaces that are shared with others is usually taken for granted. Our received education with regard to spatial orientation tends simply to happen or to grow somehow, along with learning whatever spoken language one was born into and its associated codes of everyday behavior.

Whatever we grow up with is just "there"—as a kind of lived just-so story perhaps. Whatever it is that we learn (and then later amend through travel or study of various kinds, depending on our individual social and economic circumstances) is what we settle for, partly because nothing else is available and partly because spatial orientation has never achieved a very prominent place in Western education. Spatial orientation is so fundamental a feature of what we consider to be reality, however, that semasiologists believe it forms the core of intersubjective understanding. We also believe that spatial orientation is the

conceptual groundwork on which intelligent intersubjective relations with other people(s) are based.

To put the matter bluntly: talk of spatial orientation
(and any of the other deictic categories, i.e. direction,
reference, location, and force) means that we conceive of
human movements as acts—that we analyze them as
action signs, a phrase from our technical vocabulary that
is a marker for all of the notions about hierarchy, values,
and so on that have been previously discussed. To look at
human movements as action signs is to conceive of the
human body itself as a signifier—to conceive of the body
as a signifying body.[13] What this means is that we have to
conceive of human act/actions as embodied intentions[14]
and that we have to be able to see a lived space[15] as an
intentionally achieved structuring, something that has
been willed or is now willed by someone or by some group
of persons.

The spaces in which human acts occur are not simply
physical spaces. They are simultaneously physical, conceptual, moral, and ethical spaces. The people who generate and occupy these spaces are subjects in their own
natural language(s). What, in specific, concrete terms does
that mean? I will start by analyzing two prepositions that
are used by ballet dancers, because one of the conceptual
spaces examined later is that of the ballet.

AGENT-CENTERED SPATIAL ORIENTATION

The two prepositions are, in English, "over" and "under,"
translatable into ballet French as *"dessus"* and *"dessous,"*
respectively. Both written examples in Labanotation (Fig.
1 (a) and (b)) are of standard moves in the ballet dancer's
body language game. They are "steps," called *"pas de
bourrées,"* which are distinguished by the notions of
"over" and "under." We may well ask, "Over and under
what?"

In the written stretch (a) in Figure 1, the dancer is
stepping *over* his or her own supporting foot. In the
written stretch (b), the dancer is stepping *under* his or her

supporting foot. The point of the illustration is not to analyze the character of the ballet step itself; rather, the important point is that what we see here is merely one of hundreds of instantiations of the notion of using one's own body as a reference point. The terms "over" (*dessus*) and "under" (*dessous*) in this context are self-reflexive. The spatial orientation of a ballet dancer is different, not because the dancer has any special equipment that is not possessed by ordinary movers in the French-speaking or English-speaking body language games, but because the nature of complex body language idioms such as the ballet are built up using the semantic primitives and deictic categories of spatial orientation called reference and location.

A dancer's image of the actions to which ballet terminology (or the terminology of any other idiom of dancing) refers will inevitably include his or her own body, whereas the ordinary mover's images of movements tend to exclude his or her own body. Western dancers acquire agent-centered spatial orientations during the process of training. They acquire this through a process of transmission of the combined spoken and body languages pertaining to the idiom of dancing, which will be used throughout their professional life. Two other terms that illustrate practically how such transmission and such concepts are acquired in ballet dancing are *"en dehors"* and *"en dedans"*—"outside" and "inside," respectively. Agent orientation is built into these terms because of the spatial point of reference for the actual action involved, just as it is in the case of the *pas de bourrées.*

To an ordinary speaker of French, *en dehors* might simply mean "on the outside" or "outward"; *en dedans* might mean "inside" or "inward." These adverbs might mean "indoors" or "outdoors." Used as prepositions, they might mean inside (a room) or outside (a room or house). To the dancer, *en dehors* denotes a centrifugal motion outward and away from the central axis (more accurately, the center front plane) of the body. Conversely, *en dedans* is a direction of action toward the center frontal plane of the body. The spatial point of reference for the two terms is the central axis of the dancer's own body, and thus it is agent orientated and not external object oriented. In Figure 2 (a) and (b) below, notated examples of these actions are given as they are performed *à la barre.* Both actions illustrate, I think, what Fillmore means by the body as a reference object (1983:314), and I point to his work (and to Haviland's, 1986) simply to emphasize the fact that a danced idiom does not necessarily use different deictic components from those that are used in everyday life—they simply use them more "pointedly," so to speak.

It may be of interest to know that this type of spatial orientation gives rise to some interesting usages of the personal pronoun "I," which are usually unfamiliar to the ordinary speaker/mover but are taken for granted by many dancers. First, the dancer is often talking about self as that self exists in the dance—inside the action and generating it, not outside the action and watching it. Second, the dancer often refers to self not in the ordinary sense of a social persona but as self in relation to the role enacted in the ballet. This is a concept not entirely unfamiliar to ordinary speakers of English or Latin-based languages, although it is rarely thought of in such specific ways.

Consider, for example, the attribution of responsibility

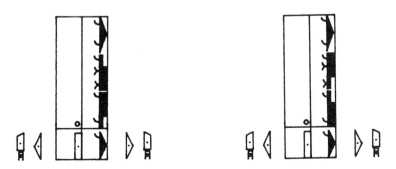

Figure 2.

involving actions, words, and the like that is implied by
the term *in loco parentis,* when one acts not in terms of his
or her own social persona (which may not include being a
parent at all) but in terms of the social persona of another.
Or, consider the abbreviation "pp," often found at the
conclusion of business correspondence next to a signature. In this case, "pp" means *per persona,* indicating that
someone has taken the responsibility for the contents of
the letter by signing the name of, say, an absent department head. One can also vote *in absentia persona.*

Even these comparatively trivial formulations of a concept of multiple selves present intricacies of our concept
of self that emphasize the points I would want to make.
Professional dancers are trained performers, and their
usage of the pronoun "I" often connotes the impersonality
of the 'self' directing the role played, as, for example, in
the case of Fonteyn talking about how she feels about
dancing the Swan Queen or some other role. It would not
stretch matters too far to say that very often, performers
use this impersonal I in other contexts besides the theater.
The dancer, describing a hypothetical situation through
the viewpoint of the I that controls performances, and the
ordinary speaker, describing the same situation in exactly
the same words (except for the substitution of the impersonal "one" or "you") are, in fact, often found to be
describing the situation from entirely different points of
view, although in neither case is it a "personal" point of
view. Their speech will reflect entirely different concepts
of what the situation is. It will also reflect different
concepts of their respective relations to the situation.

These are clearly not easy kinds of things to understand,
but then, human actions are themselves extremely complex: they are nonmaterial, and they are tied to the human
capacity for language use in important ways. This is
especially apparent to those of us who construct texts of
action sign systems.[16] All Labanotators use key signs
(✦,✧,⊞) to indicate general, nonsemantically specific
spatial orientation. These are called (1) the standard cross
of axes, (2) the body cross of axes, and (3) the constant
cross of axes. In general, these signs indicate whether or

not the actor(s) are oriented to the pull of gravity and to the space internal to the moved sequences by features of a room that are external to them, for example, the constant cross of axes, in which in a room, "up" is toward the ceiling, or to their own body, for example, the "body" cross of axes, in which "up" is where the head is, or in the usual way, for example, the "standard" cross of axes, in which up/down = the pull of gravity and the actor's "front" changes as his or her direction changes.[17] The key signs, used on their own, act like a key signature in music; that is, every spatial symbol in the subsequent text adheres to the key. This means that every forward directional symbol written is determined by the original key sign.

The use of the key sign, accompanied by other symbols (Fig. 3 [A], [B], [C], below) has a somewhat unconventional usage, which we call spatial orientation keys, where + = [S,W,E,N], for example, defines the paradigmatic features of an entire system (in this case, tai chi chuan).

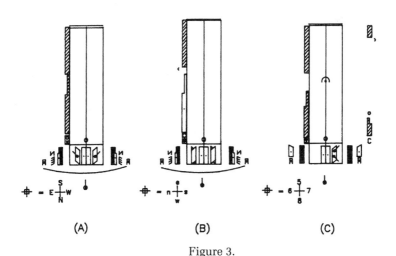

(A)   (B)   (C)

Figure 3.

THREE ETHNOGRAPHIC CASES

Conceiving of the key signs as spatial orientation keys, then, we see that stretch (A) in Figure 3 is the bow, which begins the short form of the exercise technique tai chi chuan. Stretch (B) is one of the bows (*inclinatio profunda a sacerdote et ministris*) that the celebrant performed during the High Mass. Stretch (C) is the bow the Red Knight performs to the White King on stage after failing to kill the Black Queen in the ballet Checkmate. They are all bows (in English) but it is clear, even to those who cannot read movement notation, that they are all quite different. We shall examine these differences in the light of what the key signs *followed by additional information* denote.

I stated that any human performed or lived space takes place in geographical, conceptual, moral, and ethical space(s). With regard to the Mass, the exercise technique, and the ballet, what does this mean? Structural elements of all of three systems are the cardinal directions of north, south, east, west.[18] We might express these directions as a set of geographical spatial elements this way: G = [N,S,E,W]. These elements are defined by the magnetic poles of the Earth's surface, lines of latitude and longitude, astronomical calculations, and such. We will refer to them as the "G" set of spatial elements. We may also say that the Labanotator's key signs, used by themselves, simply indicate that the written movements take place within this set of geographical elements and that the conceptual space(s) in which the movements take place are, for whatever reasons, being ignored. While it is true that any of the structured systems of action under consideration can (and must) be locatable in geographical space/time, there are additional spatial elements that have to be accounted for, because the G set explains nothing that happens internally in the rite, the exercise space, or the ballet. If these spaces are uniquely human spaces, occupied by beings who have signifying bodies, and if these action systems are lived spaces, then the "syntax" and "grammar" of the actions included in the systems and their distinctive spatial characteristics—already laden with meaning—are the (invisible) determining features of the (visible) perceivable actions that take place. Clearly, the "performers" in all three cases are operating in a conceptual space, the outlines of which must be known if the particular system is to be understood adequately.

Tai Chi Chuan

In Figure 3, stretch (A), we see that the same elements of N,S,E,W[19] are used, but they are ordered differently; that is, they are arranged so that the tai chi master faces south. North is conceived to be behind the master. West is to the right and east is to the left of the performer. We might say that in the context of tai chi, the spatial oppositions are thought of as G = [S,N,W,E].

In this chapter, I can attempt only a partial exegesis of some of the semantics of tai chi chuan, and thus a few rather dogmatic assertions about it will have to suffice: In China, for example, people practicing tai chi face the geographical direction south. When the exercise technique was introduced into the West, this caused so much confusion in classes that the directions were changed to accommodate the new group of students. That is, the American or English student of tai chi faces north, although this is not always geographical north.[20] The point is that Westerners are used to thinking of north as in front of them, as at the top of a map, putting north in front of them for the purposes of learning the movements. Whatever is the case, the performer of tai chi has to imagine himself or herself standing in the center of a compass that is lying flat on the floor or the ground, because many of the directions given are voiced in terms of the directions. For our purposes here, one is meant to imagine the tai chi master facing south, so that back, right, and left have corresponding directions. What is important here is the cultural rationale for this conceptual space.

The spatial orientation of Chinese forms of tai chi were meant to correlate with cosmological features of the arrangements of hexagrams in the I Ching (Williams 1975, vol. 2, gives a full explanation). The Chinese practitioner of this Taoist form of meditation faces geographical south.

The arrangement of trigrams in Figure 4 is called the Sequence of Earlier Heaven or the Primal Arrangement (Book of Changes:285). Part of the text regarding the arrangement is as follows:

> 3. Heaven and earth determine the direction. The forces of mountain and lake are united. Thunder and wind arouse each other. Water and fire do not combat each other. Thus are the eight trigrams intermingled.
>
> Counting that which is going into the past depends on the forward movement. Knowing that which is to come depends on the backward movement. This is why the Book of Changes has backward moving numbers.
>
> Here, in what is probably a very ancient saying, the eight primary trigrams are named in a sequence of pairs that according to tradition, goes back to Fu Hsi—that is to say, it was already in existence at the time of the compilation of the Book of Changes under the Chou dynasty. It is called the

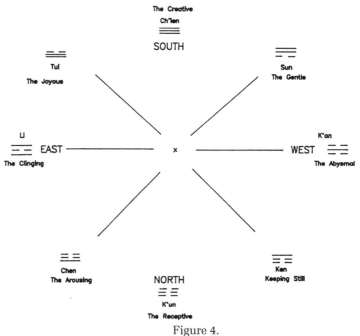

Figure 4.

Sequence of Earlier Heaven, or the Primal Arrangement. The different trigrams are correlated with the cardinal points, as shown.

Ch'ien, heaven, and K'un, earth, determine the north-south axis. Then follows the axis Ken-Tui, mountain and lake. Their forces are interrelated in that the wind blows from the mountain to the lake, and the clouds and mists rise from the lake to the mountain. Chen, thunder, and Sun, wind, strengthen each other when they appear. Li, fire, and K'an, water, are irreconcilable opposites in the phenomenal world. In the primal relationships, however, their effects do not conflict; on the contrary, they balance each other.

When the trigrams intermingle, that is, when they are in motion, a double movement is observable: first, the usual clockwise movement, cumulative and expanding as time goes on, and determining the events that are passing; second, an opposite, backward movement, folding up and contracting as time goes on, through which the seeds of the future take form. To know this movement is to know the future. In figurative terms, if we understand how a tree is contracted into a seed, we understand the future unfolding of the seed into a tree. (Book of Changes:284–286)

The three primal powers in this system are heaven yang, earth yin, and humanity (in-between, but standing on earth). The yang is light, and in performance practice of tai chi, a foot, for example, that has no weight on it is a light, or yang, foot. A foot that has weight on it is a heavy, or yin, foot. The distribution of weight is constantly shifting and changing. The only time the weight is really in static equilibrium is at the beginning and ending of a whole form, as shown in the beginning position in Figure 3, stretch (A).

The point that is relevant to explorations of meaning and the notion of the visible and invisible is this: there is nothing visible on a tai chi master's body that tells an investigator that he or she is standing inside the perimeter of a compass and that the compass is also attached to some of the central cosmological thinking of Chinese people, yet, the movements themselves, even the weight distribution of the body—everything—is dictated by the conceptual space of tai chi chuan, and that in turn is linked in a specific way to the "G" set of elements in the visible, manifest world. This is why I have emphasized the notion of the conceptual imperative in this chapter and why I have also stressed the notion of hierarchy, but we shall now move on to the second example of conceptual spaces; the Dominican post-Tridentine Mass.

The Latin Mass

The exercise space of tai chi, that is, $E = [S,N,W,E]$, consists of actual geographical elements of space, rearranged so that the actor faces south and in so doing also enters the cosmology that accompanies the arrangements of the directions as given in the I Ching. The celebrant of the Mass, in contrast, is standing in a conceptual space, that is, $L = \{e,w,n,s\}$, which also consists of the cardinal directions $[N,S,E,W]$, but there is a noncorrespondence with the geography of these directions.

That is to say that Dominican friar-preachers always face (liturgical) east when they celebrate Mass, but the altar (which *is* liturgical east) is not always or in every church located in the east geographically. The missa major is thus a case of an embedded space, so to speak, although it is possible to find instances in the world where liturgical and geographical east do correspond. Figure 5 illustrates the point. Blackfriar's chapel in St. Giles Square in Oxford, England, is a case of noncorrespondence. St. Peter's basilica in Rome is a case of correspondence.

We may say, therefore that $G = [N,S,E,W]$, but $L = \{e,w,n,s\}$. The reason the initial key sign of a constant cross of axes is used for stretch (B) in Figure 3 is that the Mass had to be written from the standpoint of all of the moves by the ministers taken from the focal point of the high altar,[21] simply because the high altar in the missa major *is* liturgical east. In this rite, priest, brethren, and congregation all faced liturgical east. Why east and not some other direction as the highest-valued element of the canonical

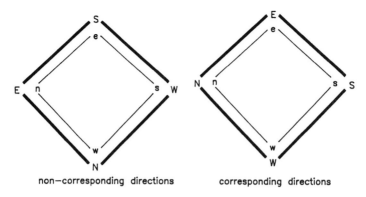

non—corresponding directions   corresponding directions

Figure 5.

directional set? The following texts from Psalm 67 (Douay) reveal the answer:[22]

Verse 5: Sing ye to God; sing a psalm to his name: make a way for *him who ascendeth upon the west* . . .
6: God who maketh men of one manner: *to dwell in a house* . . .
34: . . . who mounteth above the heaven of heavens, *to the east*

"Ascendeth upon the west" in the first text refers to the oppositions east/light/dawn in contrast to west/dark/sunset. This is, of course, a theological metaphor by which the Divinity is associated with light, illumination, and understanding in contrast to the darkness of ignorance, confusion, and absence of understanding. The "manner of dwelling in a house" can be taken to mean a structured space, and verse 34 is a positive statement of the negative formulation in verse 5.

It is important to note that in the third and fourth centuries, before people knew that the Earth was round, there was a much more literal association between liturgical east and geographical east. There is evidence that people expected that the literal Lord would appear from the geographical direction of east. In the missa major, however, liturgical east is established by the fact that, at the consecration, the priest is *in persona Christi* and the Lord therefore "comes" via the consecrations and subsequent communion from the altar, which is why the high altar was liturgical east in the semantic and conceptual space of the High Mass. It is thus that the priest, the altar, and the actions of breaking, blessing, pouring, and distributing are irreducible elements of the rite regardless of its formal exteriorization, but with apologies for these brief remarks, we must now get on with an examination of Checkmate and stretch (C) in Figure 3.

Checkmate

The constant cross of axes is used for the bow from Checkmate because no matter what ballet is being performed, it takes place within a conceptual spatial schemata for the ballet dancer's body language game, which consists of a system of numbering the walls and corners of a classroom (hence, a proscenium stage). The Cecchetti system is the numbering system indicated at the beginning of the stretch in Figure 2.[23] The ballet dancer's conceptual space is diagrammed in Figure 6.

The space is taken from a proscenium stage and is hierarchized, neither in terms of geographical directions nor in terms of concepts relating to them, but in terms of

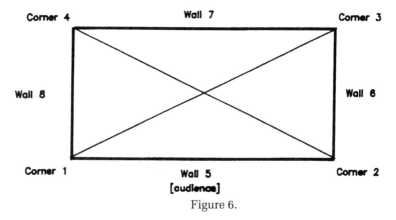

Figure 6.

an audience relationship (wall 5), which orients the dancer to the audience. It is an embedded space like that of the Mass, but it does not have the same metaphorical or historical properties of associations with east and the other directions. The history of this space really began with ballet masters and it was adapted for use in the classroom. Numbers are used because with each specific ballet, the metaphorical properties of this more abstracted conceptual space of the stage changes in accordance with the themes of the particular dance. The ballet dancer's conceptual space, that is, BD = {5,8,6,7}, is an abstract space, which organizes the balletic idiom of dancing and orients the individual dancer to a real or imagined audience. Specific ballets are then performed in this space, and with each of these, the numbered walls and corners assume different metaphorical properties.[24]

In the written stretch in Figure 3 (C), it happens that the dancer is not bowing to the audience but bowing to the Red King, who happens at the time to be up center stage.[25] The King's "throne" is located in front of wall 7, and in bowing to him, the Red Knight's back is to the audience. The important point for readers to understand is this: given a conceptual space like that of the ballet dancer, we must ask, "From whence comes the mandates for the overall conception of the particular ballet (Checkmate) that provides the semantic properties of the ballet as a whole?" The answer is, "The choreographer," and it is of sufficient importance to this discussion that the entire statement of Ninette de Valois about this ballet must be reproduced:

> It was Sir Arthur Bliss who brought it [the ballet] to me. He brought me the complete book—the complete ballet. That is why when I heard about the Black Queen and the strange things she does, I thought, "this is to do with this particular moment [in history] obviously." He brought it to me and he wanted it done in a Chinese way, but I said no. I was against this: a great flamboyant set and the [Red] King carried on under a canopy. It just wouldn't do.
>
> I told him, "we can't play a game [of actual chess] so we've got to, in my opinion, symbolize its relation to

life—what this means." So we discussed it and decided that the pages [the Red pawns] represented the mass mind [in the sense of the collective mind], which changes with every atmosphere. They start their dances with a chic little court dance—very smart, and that is an introduction to the entrance of the Red Knights, who challenge each other, but as knights—in a gallant way. It's a real challenge, not just a "fight," and the pages reflect their mood throughout. Then you have the entrance of the Black Queen, which starts trouble—the aggression of the woman. You see, we saw the Black Queen—in fact all the black figures at the end—as revolutionary figures led by this woman, out to disturb the peace of everything. So you can see how it happens. The [Red] King, with his sort of decrepit entrance, represents a sort of dying imperialism. He couldn't stand up to it. This is emphasized by his frailty, and this woman, that is, the Red Queen, is much stronger than he [the Red King] is, although she is no match for the Black Queen. The Red Queen is the one who holds him, who eggs him on, who leads him. If you see the ballet, of course, you can see the whole thing.

The Bishops represent the Church, which the Black Queen and her people flaunt. In the first "check," the Church is disposed of—just pushed off, and that's that. Both the Red and Black Castles represent war, so when you see the Castles dance you will see they are enticing the dancers—the little pages—inciting them to war. They lead them on and they change their mood to aggression. The pawns, Black and Red, are the "mass" figures all the way through. They do exactly what is happening, between, shall we say, the politicians of today. They are reflections of revolution or of imperialism—it doesn't matter. This is how I see it all. And, of course, in the end, the revolutionary side wins. He [the Red King] is killed.

As far as the presentation of it went, I try and keep everything as much "along" the stage as possible, so that you get a feeling throughout the whole pattern of the work that there is something pushing—like a destiny. To me a chess figure [and she picked up a salt cellar and moved it]—the hand takes hold of it and does *that*. The actual figure itself has no power. It's destined to move; it is fate that it moves that way. So they move along in this way [indication by gesture], not in regular chess patterns, but because something is moving them. It's not the hand, of course, but something of which the hand is a symbol is putting them *there,* etc. It's fate. It's the fate of all of them—the fate of the figure. It's all very symbolic really, if you think of it in relation to life. We don't know what makes any of us do all these things. On a chessboard, we see a hand doing it. We don't see what's making us do it, but the feeling is the same feeling as if you don't know where you're going. None of us know where we're going. This is what I feel about it.

You asked about [the figures of] Love and Death. Love and Death is a struggle, I suppose, between right and wrong—let's face it. I've called it Love and Death, but I suppose it could be "life." Life is love, you see. Life is love and war is death. This is why the symbolism of "love" is more accurate, but it comes to the same thing. You can think of love as life if you like—I don't think it matters.

The figures of the Prologue being on the right or left have no significance—after all, they turn their chess board around several times between them showing that the board can be moved in any way. And besides, let's be practical about it, you could not do the whole ballet with the pieces on either side of the stage.

It is true that the symbolism in the ballet lies in life itself. I never saw it any other way, and I know Sir Arthur didn't either. I remember saying to the Pawns only the other day, "Now remember, you are the mass mind; you react to every change on this board—every change in the atmosphere, whether it's church, whether it's war, whether it's chivalry, you're the ones who have to react." And the destiny in front of them is, of course, love and death or life and death.

There *is* a symbolic reversal of the sexes of the figures. It wasn't a deliberate thing on my part: it would just happen. The queens are the strong pieces on the board, although when the Red Queen stands up to the Black Queen, it is only to plead with her through love. The Red Queen very much represents sympathy, but it's no good—revolution comes and sweeps it all away. I just see it as what is happening in the world today. I always say to them [the dancers], "More *along* the ground than *up;* imagine that you are being moved by a hand or by destiny."

You asked about the Red Knight: he stands for chivalry. He stands for what the army stands for when we suddenly had to do something about Mr. Hitler. More practically speaking, he stands for chivalry and death—but in a different way. He is prepared to sacrifice himself. And chivalry wins, in a sense, because of the way the woman has seduced him, you see. Chivalry means he won't kill her. He can't kill her. There is no ruthlessness in the chivalric figure as there is in their opposite numbers. They've passed that stage. The knight is too civilized for that. They've passed the stage where they're able to stand up to anything, I think. When he turns around to apologize to the king that he can't do it, she [the Black Queen] immediately takes her opportunity . . . same as the terrorist bombs, isn't it? Revolution is ruthless, and to me, it's the ruthlessness of a woman when she is out for what she wants. She starts by leading him on. She's got to weaken him, and that's the way they do it. In the days of chivalry and imperialism, you know, the foreign office wouldn't permit a woman spy. They thought it was unsporting. As for the wider symbolism of the audience being players, I leave this up to them. (Transcribed from field tapes, 1974)

SUMMARY OF SOME SIGNIFICANT DIFFERENCES

Tai Chi	The Mass	Checkmate
1. Uses actual geographical space and directions with south the dominant facing. Tied to an ancient Chinese cosmological system based on the I Ching and is a form of Taoist meditation.	1. An embedded liturgical space, using cardinal directions but not necessarily corresponding to a geographical set. In the Mass, the high altar is liturgical east. The rest of the set derives from Christian theological concepts.	1. An embedded space based on the performer/audience relation, wherein geographical directions are irrelevant. The spatial arrangement of the ballet is based on a chess game and the choreographer's usage of the game as an allegory.
2. The initial bow is to the Tao. The movements are smooth and flow-	2. The bow is a profound acknowledgment of a monotheistic Di-	2. The bow is to another character in the ballet and is an apology in the

ing, with no break or pauses occurring throughout. The aim is the control of the chi (energy) in the body. Also used as a self-defense technique. It is from the Shao Lin, or "soft" school of movement.

vinity. The moves are entirely ordinary in the sense that they could be performed by anyone. The celebrant is a mediator between the congregation and the tripartite Divinity. The moves are performed in a dignified manner.

context of a code of honor that is central to the plot of the dance. Like tai chi, the moves stem from a specific idiom of body language and could not be performed by everyone.

3. The conceptual space of the exercise technique is based on a compass; the actor stands in the center. There is no relation set up with another group as an "audience" or "congregation." The technique uses actual geographical directions.

3. The conceptual space of the Mass is based on a scheme of assigned cardinal directions. The celebrant is a mediator, and the whole liturgy is a public act of worship related to an institutionalized religion.

3. The conceptual space of the dancers in "Checkmate" is twofold: (a) the scheme that pertains to the stage, and (b) the scheme of moves of each character in relation to others. The dance is an entertainment.

There are many more differences that could be mentioned, of course. My purpose here is to illustrate the distinction that semasiology makes between structural universals and semantic particularities. We mean to point out, as well, that the set of geographical elements, namely, $G = [N,S,E,W]$, is handled differently in each of the conceptual spaces of the systems under examination. Moreover, the structures of these conceptual spaces are paradigmatic to any of the empirically visible moves that take place in each system. It is this kind of evidence that provides the underpinnings for the assertion that an adequate understanding of rites, rituals, ceremonies, dances, exercise techniques, and the like has to include a thorough understanding and subsequent exploration of the conceptual spaces in which the system under examination exists, because we believe that, with regard to systems of human actions, the "visible" (the empirically perceivable) is dependent on the "invisible," the facts of L = {e,w,n,s} in the missa major, for example, which are *not* directly perceivable to an onlooker.

We have seen, too, that different values are placed on elements of the cardinal directions in two of the systems we have looked at. East is the more valued direction in the liturgy of the Mass, but south is more valued in the context of the Taoist exercise technique. Why is preeminence assigned to east? Following Dumont, we might say that what is important here is the recognition that the east-west pair is not definable liturgically in itself, but only in relation to a whole, which includes north-south as well. This pair bears the following values; north = right, which equals the Gospel side of the high altar, and south = left, which equals the Epistle side of the high altar. The celebrant's left hand corresponded to the Gospel side, his right hand to the Epistle side of the altar in the old Dominican Mass, making out of the full set L = {e,w,n,s} a coherent and certainly tangible whole, since not only the body but also church architecture, the arrangements of objects, and much else depended on it.

In saying that these similar sets of oppositions thus far have a hierarchical aspect, we believe that we are simply pointing out the folly of separating fact (the assumed equalitarian nature of the cardinal directions) and value (the added, valorized asymmetries of sociocultural weightings) that are placed on the directions. Concretely, in the spaces internal to the systems we have looked at, east-west, north-south, and right-left do not have the same relationship to the human body either. In tai chi, south is in front of the body; therefore, west = right, and east = north in this context. That the practitioners of each system subordinate different elements of the same set, assigning to the elements different meanings, should provide sufficient evidence for us to realize, perhaps, one of the ways in which cultural differences occur in all human conceptions, which is simply to say that hierarchy is present in all human cultures and that it is essential for comparison.

Semasiologists must ask themselves, "Are the tai chi master, the Dominican friar-preacher, and the ballet dancer doing the same kinds of things when they bow? They are all bowing, but in how far is this act the same in different contexts?" Questions like this lead to an important difference between natural science and social science, which pertains to the notion of judgments of identity. The Dominican's act of bowing is a religious matter, the tai chi master's act is religious in some sense, but more accurately described, I think, as cosmological, because there is no notion of a Divinity involved. The ballet dancer's bow pertains to a specified code of honor that is dominated by the notion of fealty to a human monarch.

> [John Stuart] Mill's view is that understanding a social institution consists in observing regularities in the behaviour of its participants and expressing these regularities in the form of generalizations. Now if the position of the sociological investigator (in a broad sense) can be regarded as comparable, in its main logical outlines, with that of the natural scientist, the following must be the case. *The concepts and criteria according to which the sociologist judges that, in two situations, the same thing has happened, or the same action performed, must be understood in relation to the rules governing sociological investigation.* But here we run against a difficulty; for whereas in the case of the natural scientist we have to deal with only *one set of rules,* namely those governing the scientist's investigation itself, here *what the sociologist is studying, as well as his study of it, is a human activity and is therefore carried on according to rules* [italics are mine]. And it is these rules, rather than those which govern the sociologist's investigation, which specify what is to count as "doing the same kind of thing" in relation to that kind of activity. (Winch, 1958:86–87)

The simple identification of physical regularities (we call them the *kines*) of movement is not enough. The identification of the regularities of gross physical movements is child's play compared to the task of making judgments of identity regarding human actions in their sociocultural contexts, and it is because of this that the investigator's relationship to the performers involved in the sign systems under investigation cannot be a simple one of "observer to observed," as if they were some species of animal, plant, or mineral.

It seems reasonable to assume that some other set of universally valid features of human movement than those offered by kinesiology and anatomy is necessary if the aim is to proceed from a scientifically valid basis for cross-cultural comparison and generalization. In other words, in order to talk about bows or religious rites or dances, it is necessary to know something about the structural characteristics of the expressive human body and the space(s) in which it moves. These structures are not the dances, rites, or exercise techniques themselves, but structures that constitute the rules of the rules of dances, of rites, or of any set of human actions whatsoever. They are the dimensions of the structure of interacting dualisms—also thought of as the semantic primitives of human action sign systems, namely, U/D, R/L, F/B, I/O, which, combined with locational, directional, demonstrative, deictic, and ostensive evidential features of a spoken language are the metarules that govern empirically observable actions.

The point of my rather sketchy analysis of the conceptual spaces of three ethnographic examples of action sign systems has been to illustrate clearly the difference between empirically perceivable, transitive structures (the visible) and nonempirically perceivable, intransitive structures (the invisible). Such universals as I have pointed to are the gear, so to speak, that all moving human beings possess and that any investigator needs to know in order to carry out cross-cultural comparisons of human movement systems effectively. Haviland implies that McNeill (1979) and McNeill and Levy (1982) "seem to suggest that the conceptual structure that underlies gestural production is in some ways also the deepest structure that underlies spoken language as well" (Haviland 1986:fn. 16, p. 26). If that is the case, then the conceptual structures of human actions (also called semantic primitives) postulated by semasiology must be those to which McNeill and Levy refer.

NOTES

1. This paper was prepared for a panel entitled The Visible and the Invisible: Meaning in Systems of Human Movement [Session 4-019] at the annual American Anthropological Association conference in Phoenix, Arizona, 16–20 November 1988.
2. A neologism in social anthropological usage, which designates a style of movement analysis that could have been called semiotics, had it not been redefined by status holders such that it was changed from the original definitions given by Locke and Saussure (Williams, 1986a, gives further discussion).
3. In 1983, Roy Harris translated Saussure's "Course," in a supposedly "improved" translation. He confused matters considerably by translating *significant* and *signifié,* respectively, as "signal" and "signification." Needless to say, perhaps, semasiologists do not agree with his novel (and unjustified) interpretations.
4. I speak disparagingly of this notion in Williams (1986).
5. See Williams's introductory article to the special issue on semasiology (1981).
6. See, for example, Gell's criticism (1977) and Williams's rebuttal (1978).
7. A view of the kind of anthropology that I have in mind and that Ardener had in view, i.e., semantic anthropology (Parkin, 1982).
8. Stated in semasiological theory as "the degrees of freedom of the semasiological, i.e., expressive, body; "the law of hierarchical motility," "the structure of interacting dualisms," "the paradigmatic-syntagmatic scale of relations," and such (Williams, 1975, gives a complete discussion).
9. The real definition of the substance "diamond" lies in the tetrahedral structure of its carbon atoms.
10. We may well ask, "Why has the opposition 'right/left' held the apparently privileged position that it has in anthropological research?"
11. Semasiology cannot do without the notion of hierarchy, nor, in my view, can any adequate account of human actions (Williams, 1975a, gives my use of the term in ethnographic description, and a previous reference to Dumont). Dumont (1987:279) gives a definition of the term, with which I would concur, i.e., HIERARCHY: To be

distinguished from power, or command: order resulting from the consideration of value. The elementary hierarchical relation is that between a whole (or a set) and an element of that whole (or set)—or else that between two parts with reference to the whole. It can be analyzed into two contradictory aspects belonging to different levels: it is a distinction within an identity, an encompassing of the contrary. Dumont adds that "hierarchy is thus bidimensional," a proposition with which semasiologists would agree, but, based on our work on the body, dances, sign systems, and the like, we would want to say that hierarchy is thus *at least* bidimensional, and it probably includes much more.

12. Valuable though Hall's work has proved to be, it nevertheless represents a kind of destructuring; that is, from a semasiological standpoint, proxemics focuses on only one binary opposition out of a possible four, and nowhere does Hall's methodology attempt to relate his findings, even to one other dimensional set, far less the whole that is implied by the concept of a structure of interacting dualisms.

13. The notion of a signifying body means the body of a human being—a body that belongs to a creature who can generate significations and symbolic actions. It refers to a creature who possesses the nature, powers, and capacities to speak, to construct, and to use meaningful systems of actions for the purposes of expression and communication with others. Semasiologists call this signifying body the "semasiological body." In Western medicine, by and large, the body is considered separate from the mind and it is seen as a kind of machine—a network of purely physical processes, having functions, true, but basically mindless functions. The behavior of this body in that context is believed to be best understood by understanding the nature of its individual physical parts. Classical physics and mechanics tend to see the body in the same way, and the notion of a real body (without a mind) is a product of classical deterministic physics. The notion of the body that must be developed in semasiology is very different, because in terms of any analytical procedure, the body has to be seen as a signifying body that exists in a kind of field consisting of a timeless state of no energy, as a superposition of possibility in a mathematical framework of all theoretically possible moves that it could make, with equal probabilities of realization, until an actual move or act takes place, at which

point a choice has been made in a field of complementarities or processes, which manifest themselves as
empirically visible acts. Although the body has equal probabilities of realizing actions out of a theoretical field of
possibilities, not all possible actions are realized, and one
of the determining factors here is the hierarchical system of
values the particular culture places on spatial dimensions,
movements, etc.

14. This is a difficult and complex concept that I do not know
how to articulate very well at this time. I can only indicate
the direction of my thinking and thus will share this
paragraph, leaving readers to draw their own conclusions:

Quantum physics shows that there are two major ways of
dealing with the manner in which consciousness is involved in physical processes. With the first, consciousness
exists outside all physical events; it enters whenever an
observer makes a choice. It then acts by "forcing" the
quantum system to enter into one or another possible real
situation. The outcome of this "forcing" is the appearance
of something physical, such as the location of a particle in a
measuring instrument. With the second, known as the
parallel-world theory, consciousness does not do this; instead, the observer's consciousness "splits" when an observation takes place. That split is unnoticed by the observer
because the observer also splits; one observer sees and
records the particle at one location; the other sees and
records the particle at another location. Each observer
remains unknown to the other until yet another kind of
observation occurs. (Wolf, 1987:257)

15. A "lived space" means, quite simply, a humanly constructed
space. Such a space could be someone's lounge or the whole
house, a classroom or a university, a warehouse, a train
station, a stage in a theater, a camp in the bush, or what-you-
will, including imaginary spaces, such as those of Tolkien's
Shire. The notion always bears the connotations of a space
that has had a human construct imposed upon it.

16. There are important distinctions hidden behind the phrase
"construct texts of action sign systems," which must seriously be considered: two notators of movement (A and B),
who possess the same level of skill in usage of a movement
script may record the same rite, say, a Catholic Mass.

Notator A, in constructing a text, does so utilizing knowledge of the whole system and the spatial referents that cause all of the individual actions to hang together as a coherent whole. Notator B, on the other hand, may simply record the movements of the participants in the Mass without knowing anything about the conceptual spaces of the rite. Both will produce movement texts; however their values as documents will be different because notator B's text will consist only of kines: moves devoid of meaning. This kind of text may be useful analytically, as the basis for a kinological examination of the rite, but it is a reduction and should be recognized as such. In contrast, notator A constructs a text of the rite, which includes all of the invisible features of the conceptual space(s) of the rite and their significances.

17. I ask notators' indulgence for the oversimplified explanation of these complex concepts, but the length of the chapter prevents further explanation. Suffice it to say here that we use the key signs both in conventional ways internal to a movement text and in the rather more unconventional way that is described here, because we add what we call spatial orientational keys to systems where they are clear, as in the ethnographic examples provided, and where they govern all of the moves in the system. The spatial orientational key, if there is one, is semantically paradigmatic to all other directional keys in the text.

18. Semasiologists think of these (plus the Earth's gravitational pull, which adds the up/down dimension) as intransitive, structural directions. Expressed as spatial dimensions, i.e., F/B (which may face anywhere), R/L (which is defined contingent to the facing direction), and U/D, they are the "semantic primitives" of human conceptual spaces. Regardless of how they are conceptualized (and this can be as differently as in the three examples given), the dimensions themselves (i.e., F/B, R/L, U/D plus I/O) are paradigmatic to any human actions which take place anywhere, at any time in the world.

19. For tai chi, the elements really *are* the same, which is why uppercase letters are used, and readers will see why later, when the liturgical space of the Mass are given as {e,w,n,s}. A different notation is used because the orientational elements used in the Mass are not the actual geographical directions, but an embedded set.

20. Thus, strictly speaking, a tai chi exercise notated in the West would be an embedded space, i.e., E = {n,s,e,w} in oppositional terms, or E = {n,e,s,w} considered as clockwise directions around the perimeter of an imaginary compass.

21. The celebrants see their actions as being toward or away from the focal point of the altar rather than being judged from their own bodies or the space of the physical church. Additional information for the Mass was therefore also stated in the Glossary of the text for the Mass indicating that throughout the text, front is judged from the focal point of the altar. A focal point description is an alternative form of a constant-cross-of-axes description in conventional Laba-notation terms.

22. This psalm is not found in the King James version of the Bible, and, as far as I am aware, it is not to be found in any Protestant version of the Bible.

23. The Vagonova and RAD (Royal Academy of Dancing, UK) spatial elements are numbered differently, but they use the same diagrammatic scheme as the Cecchetti system does.

24. As, for example, where upstage left becomes "the forest" and downstage right becomes "the village" in "Swan Lake."

25. This example is meant to make the usage of the paradig-matic spatial orientation keys and the ordinary use of crosses of axes very clear: the bow in stretch (C) is not written according to a constant cross but a standard cross, as the Knight is bending forward toward the King.

REFERENCES

Ardener, E. W. 1980. Some outstanding problems in the analysis of events. In Foster and Brandes, eds., *Symbol as Sense.* London: Academic. [Paper first given for Decennial Conference, ASA, Oxford, England, 1973].

Crick, M. 1976. *Explorations in Language and Meaning. Towards a Semantic Anthropology.* New York: Halsted.

Dumont, L. 1970. *Homo Hierarchichus.* London and Chicago: Weidenfeld and Nicolson, with University of Chicago Press.

———. 1987. *Essays on Individualism. Modern Ideology in Anthropological Perspective.* Chicago: University of Chicago Press.

Durr, D. 1984. The structure of ballet-dancing, with special emphasis on roles, rules, norms and status. *M.A. thesis,* Anthropology of Human Movement, New York University, New York, New York.

Farnell, B. 1984. Visual communication and literacy: An anthropological enquiry into Plains Indians and American Sign Language. *M.A. thesis,* New York University, New York, New York.

———. 1988. Where mind is a verb: 'Sign-talk' of the Plains Indians re-visited. *Paper for AAA Conference,* Phoenix, Arizona, November.

Fillmore, C. 1983. Commentary on papers of Talmy and Klein. In Pick and Acredolo, eds., *Spatial Orientation: Theory, Research and Application.* New York: Plenum.

Gell, A. 1977. On dance structures: a reply to Williams. *Journal of Human Movement Studies,* 1979(5):18–31.

Hall, E. T. 1966. *The Hidden Dimension.* Garden City, N.Y.: Doubleday.

Hart-Johnson, D. 1984. The notion of code in body language: A comparative approach to Martha Graham technique and sign language. *M.A. thesis,* Anthropology of Human Movement, New York University, New York, New York.

Haviland, J. B. 1986. Complex referential gestures. Draft manuscript. Center for Advanced Study in the Behavioral Sciences, Stanford University, Stanford California.

The I Ching [Book of Changes]. 1961. 2nd ed. C. F. Baynes, trans. Preface: R. Wilhelm, New York: Bollingen/Pantheon.

Johnson, M. 1987. *The Body in the Mind. The Bodily Basis of*

Meaning, Imagination and Reason. Chicago: University of Chicago Press.

McNeill, D. 1979. *The Conceptual Basis of Language.* Hillsdale, N.J.: Lawrence Erlbaum.

McNeill, D., and E. Levy. 1982. Conceptual representations in language activity and gesture. In Jarvella and Klein, eds., *Speech, Place and Action.* Chichester, UK: Wiley.

Needham, R., ed. 1973. *Right and Left. Essays on Dual Symbolic Classification.* Chicago: University of Chicago Press.

Parkin, D., ed. 1982. *Semantic Anthropology* (ASA 22). London: Academic.

Pocock, D. 1994. The idea of a personal anthropology. *Journal for the Anthropological Study of Human Movement.* 8(1):11–42.

Puri, R. 1983. A structural analysis of meaning in movement; the hand gestures of Indian classical dance. *M.A. thesis,* Anthropology of Human Movement, New York University, New York, New York.

Varela, C. 1984. Pocock, Williams, Gouldner: Initial reactions of three social scientists to the problem of objectivity. *Journal for the Anthropological Study of Human Movement* 3(2):53–73.

Williams, D. 1975. The role of movement in selected symbolic systems. D. Phil. thesis, Oxford University, Oxford, UK.

———. 1975a. The brides of Christ. In S. Ardener, ed., *Perceiving Women.* London: Mallaby.

———. 1976. An exercise in applied personal anthropology. Dance Research Journal 11(1). New York: CORD, New York University.

———. 1978. On structures of human movement: a reply to Gell. *Journal of Human Movement Sciences* 6(4):303–322.

———. 1981. Introduction to the Special Issue on Semasiology. *Journal for the Anthropological Study of Human Movement* 1(4):205–225.

———. 1982. 'Semasiology': A semantic anthropologist's view of human movements and actions. In D. Parkin, ed., *Semantic Anthropology* ASA Vol. 22. London: Academic Press.

———. 1986. (Non) anthropologists, the dance and human movement. In Fleshman, ed., *Theatrical Movement: A Bibliographical Anthology.* Metuchen, N.J.: Scarecrow.

———. 1986a. Prefigurements of art: A reply to Sebeok. *Journal for the Anthropological Study of Human Movement* 4(2):68–80.

Winch, P. 1958. *The Idea of a Social Science and Its Relation to Philosophy.* London: Routledge & Kegan Paul.
Wolf, F. 1987. *The Body Quantum.* London: Heinemann.

Chapter 3 WHERE MIND IS A VERB: SPATIAL ORIENTATION AND DEIXIS IN PLAINS INDIAN SIGN TALK AND ASSINIBOINE (NAKOTA) CULTURE

Brenda Farnell

Many Nakota speakers, who live on the Northern Plains of North America, accompany their speech in everyday action and interaction and in storytelling performances with gestures that belong to a system known as the Plains Indian Sign Language or Plains Sign Talk (PST). PST was formerly a lingua franca among the Plains tribes.[1] Today, only a few people are sufficiently skilled to use sign talk without speech, and most often, speech and signs occur together, interweaving meaning between both media, in action that is as complex as it is beautiful.

In this chapter, I first discuss the existence of a "rhetoric of demise" with regard to PST, which, while not entirely incorrect, has served to make continued use of the sign language largely invisible to outsiders. The contemporary use of PST in conjunction with speech, however, also presents an interesting theoretical problem for linguistic anthropology given the generally accepted distinction between verbal and nonverbal communication. A brief examination of signed and spoken data addresses this problem by showing how some key symbolic forms provide semantic resources that are common to the use of both spoken language and signed language in Assiniboine culture. In addition, deictic devices that organize space/time in language are shown to be shared by both media, and not restricted to spoken language. An actor-centered theory is suggested that seeks to embody the notion of deixis and so overcome the problematic Cartesian division between language viewed as non-material product of mind separate from a moving body.

A RHETORIC OF DEMISE

One of the criticisms some Native Americans have of the anthropological record is that it consistently tells them that they and their traditions are dying out: "Why does no one talk about the changes in the white man's culture that way?" they ask. "You don't live like your great-grandparents did either." Their complaint is justified and insightful. When American ethnologists began to document the ways of life of Native American peoples during the nineteenth and early twentieth centuries, the general assumption was that those cultures were doomed to extinction or assimilation given the inevitable onslaught of "progress."

Whether ethnologists aligned themselves with assimilationists or actively engaged in assisting Indian peoples to retain their lands and way of life, an understandably pessimistic outlook prevailed. The drastic economic, political, and social changes that were being imposed on indigenous peoples a century ago (and since) created a rhetoric that was predominantly one of loss and regret, among Indians and ethnologists alike. In that climate, documentation of precontact and prereservation culture became a priority, and these writings often presented an idealized and normative view of pre-contact aboriginal cultures, frozen in time. When current conditions were included, the focus tended to be on the Indian as victim, and little attention was paid to the remarkable flexibility of indigenous peoples and their accommodation to ongoing cultural change that had, in fact, long been a feature of Plains Indian life. Unwittingly perhaps, ethnologists contributed to the anti-Indian political rhetoric of their own society: if the only good Indian was not a dead Indian, then the next best thing in terms of a more comfortable political accommodation to racist government policies was at least a dying Indian culture. The Indian-as-victim metaphor left out of the record the strategies of resistance, the imaginative assimilations of new ideas with older practices, and ways that traditional symbols and practices were being actively reinterpreted to accommodate new meanings (Fowler 1987).

Ironically, however, the assumption that customs were "dying out" has, in unexpected ways, provided some distinct advantages for later scholars. For example, Gen. Hugh L. Scott, retired army veteran of the Plains wars and amateur ethnologist, became convinced that PST—that unique gestural lingua franca of the Plains—was dying out. So in 1930 he persuaded the U.S. Congress to authorize the making of a film record as soon as possible, thereby providing one of the earliest and the most extensive film records of Plains sign talk in use.[2] That the U.S. Department of Agriculture should pay for the project could have been a public relations gesture designed to lessen the antagonistic relationships between Indians and that agency over Indian land rights. At Browning, Montana, in September 1930, representatives from thirteen different tribes, all of whom spoke different languages, arrived to take part in the making of the film so as to record for posterity that the sign language was indeed a lingua franca.

In the film, General Scott is not wearing the uniform of the army but that of the Boy Scouts of America. Although fascinated by, and knowledgeable about PST, Scott nevertheless believed that its ultimate value and only hope of survival lay in its potential application as an international communication system for that most Anglo-Saxon of boys' institutions—the Boy Scouts of the world—who, of course, appropriated and romanticized many elements of a supposedly Indian forest lore and brotherhood. Had it not been for this odd combination of preservationist, political, and altruistic motivations, the film of the sign council and its accompanying film dictionary of signs would never have been produced.

Twenty years later, in the 1950s, it was anthropologist Alfred Kroeber who noted that PST was falling into disuse, and he urged Carl Voegelin to find a student who could undertake a linguistic study of it before it was too late (Kroeber 1958). Consequently, La Mont West Jr. embarked on a pioneering study of the language from the perspective of descriptive linguistics. West moved around the Northern Plains at a rapid pace during the fall of 1956, collecting data from twenty-five reservations and ninety-seven sign talkers in only fifty days, including travel time. Many of West's informants were elderly, and certainly the sign language as a lingua franca was in decline by the 1950s because English was gradually taking over the intertribal function. But it cannot have been dying out quite as rapidly as was assumed to be the case, for it is otherwise doubtful that West could have accomplished his project with such ease and speed. I suspect that the impression of impending extinction came from the fact that the contexts in which PST was still used were no longer quite so visible to outsiders. As a public intertribal language it had been clearly visible at events where non-Indians were present: at treaty councils, in trading contexts, for public oratory, and among Indian army scouts who were often drawn from tribes speaking several different languages (Dunley 1982). The historical record focuses on these contexts and the impression is given that quite separate languages are involved—as if speech switches off as the sign language switches on. Ignored were contexts in which signs continued to be used among people who *did* speak the same language and for whom the sign talk was an integral part of their linguistic repertoire.

West's work was pioneering because sign languages were not considered by linguists and educators at that time to be real languages—a battle that is still going on in the education of the Deaf today.[3] In conjunction with a long-standing cultural bias against the body generally, sign languages were considered to be simple codes, probable precursors to spoken language in the evolutionary scheme of things. Indeed considerable interest had been shown in PST by nineteenth-century anthropologists such as E. B. Tylor, precisely because they seemed to provide indisputable evidence of a primitive state. The predominance of iconic or representational gestures in sign languages was viewed by some as evidence of an earlier stage of development when language was a direct representation of nature prior to the development of arbitrariness in the spoken language sign.[4] The possibility that the so-called "savages" might be more sophisticated than Europeans because of their systematic skill in the linguistic use of both movement and sound, was certainly ignored.

In 1984, when I explored the possibility of turning my library study of PST into field research, the general opinion among Plains scholars was that this long-standing and distinctive language was now dead—a "lost" tradition, along with the buffalo hunting economy and buckskin dress of bygone days. Fortunately, I was encouraged (and stubborn enough) to go and see for myself, and I started with a visit to an elderly Assiniboine woman from Fort Belknap, Montana, who apparently "waved her hands around a lot" when she was telling stories. I was delighted to recognize from the nineteenth-century documentation that she was indeed using the sign language as she talked, and we later began to work together making video recordings of her stories and other vocabulary in both signs and spoken Nakota.

I thought I must have found the only remaining sign talker on the Plains, but I began to notice that other Nakota speakers in the community also frequently accompanied their speech with gestures belonging to that system. Upon mentioning this observation, I was told, "Of course, it's part of the language," and my remark was considered to be rather obvious if not altogether stupid. This alerted me to the consideration that the conception of a "Plains sign language" as a distinct and primarily intertribal language, is grossly misleading. It may be a product of what Roy Harris (1981) has called "the language myth": the artifactualization of languages as "fixed codes." Instead, there exists, in the Assiniboine case at least, a continuum, moving from an informal use of gestures that accompany or replace speech in everyday interactions, to more formalized contexts such as storytelling performances (and signed songs and hymns). In former times, and where deafness exists today, the continuum extends to the use of a widely conventionalized intertribal system that can exclude speech altogether. People draw on an available repertoire of gestures that can be used with or without spoken language according to individual knowledge, personal preference, skill, and context. In Assiniboine storytelling, both speech and gesture are an integral part of the narrative sense and gestures are not simply dramatic enhancement or a repeat of the spoken narrative (Farnell, in press). In addition both kinds of utterance are considered to be "talking" (hence the use in English of the term "sign talk"), and some use the English lexeme "word" to refer to either a vocal or a gestural utterance. Assiniboine people often use signs and speech simultaneously and do not privilege speech over gestural talking. On one occasion, for example, when I asked for the spoken equivalent of a gestural utterance by saying, "How would you say that in Nakota?" the reply was, "Like I just showed you." Obviously, there is a very different conception of "language" going on here, one that combines body and mind in ways that confound Cartesian dualistic thinking.

If this was a "lost" tradition, then I was led to ask, "Lost to whom?" The stereotypic silent but visible and stoic-faced Plains Indian so beloved by Hollywood, displaying his primitive grandeur by talking in signs had gone, and so, it was assumed, had the language. PST had become invisible to non-Indians, in part because of this change of contexts but also because that same Cartesian bias prohibits such gesturing with speech from being valued by the dominant culture. Waving one's hands around when talking is, for the most part, viewed as a sign of a deficiency—an inability to express oneself adequately in words, or a marker of lower class or undesirable ethnic origin. The French and Italians, for example, are stereotypically thought to be prone to such excesses of gesture in response to overly active passions, interpreted on the whole by those of Anglo-Saxon and derived cultures as evidence of less rational, more emotional and therefore uncontrolled (read "immoral") behavior.[5]

NAKOTA AND THE EMBODIMENT OF MIND

Examination of PST and Nakota reveals some fundamental distinctions between Assiniboine and Euro-American ways of thinking about language and the body. For example, when I asked how to say in Nakota that someone has a good mind, I was taught the phrase *"tawac'į wasté."* When I asked how to say this in signs, I was taught to move a pointed index finger from the heart away from the chest with the finger pointing straight forward, and then to add the sign GOOD, a flat hand with the palm down moving from the center of the chest diagonally to the right (Figure 1.).[6] Two things are important: first, in contrast to gestures used by speakers of English and American Sign Language (ASL)[7] there is no reference to head as a place where mind is located, and second, emphasis is on the movement not on a location. Later, I learned that in order to say "She thinks clearly," one would use the same word in the phrase *"tayą t'awac'į"* and the sign was almost the same. Consistent with an apparent lack of distinction between verbs and nouns, well described by Siouan linguists (Boas and Deloria 1941), mind in Nakota acts more like a verb than a noun;—an action not an object. *Wac'į*, "to think," seems to be a verb about thinking but one with a very wide semantic range. According to Lakota scholars it can be used in the sense of intention, willpower or one's will and unbounding consciousness.[8] Deloria (1940) defines the term for Lakota speakers as both a noun meaning mind and reason and as a prefix added to active verbs that indicates a willingness, desire, will, or disposition to do: an intention or plan. In Nakota also, *t'awacį mneha*, for example, means strong-willed, and *t'awac'įknuni* undecided. *Wac'į* is one of four Nakota verbs relating to thinking and one in which remembering seems to be involved.

The phrase *"t'awac'į wasté"* seems to indicate a general disposition: "It means they really like what you're

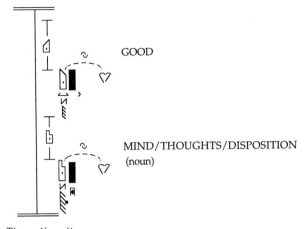

GOOD

MIND/THOUGHTS/DISPOSITION
(noun)

a) Tʻawacʻį wašte.
"She/he has a good mind."

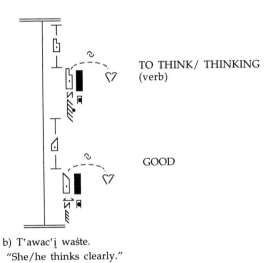

TO THINK/ THINKING
(verb)

GOOD

b) Tʻawacʻį wašte.
"She/he thinks clearly."

Figure 1. Assiniboine/Nakota embodiment of "mind."

doing" and "a good person in every way" were other meanings given to me. The Lakota Sioux use the phrase to mean a generous person (Raymond Bucko S.J., personal communication; also Buechel 1983). In other words, as the sign language emphasizes, mind is not a place but a disposition toward others: a capacity of a whole person, not a place in the head separate from a body.

Notions of personhood in Assiniboine and other Plains cultures involve the complex combination of a strong sense of agency (emphasizing personal autonomy in decision making for example) without resort to individualism because of the emphasis placed on kin relationships. People are defined and define themselves fundamentally in terms of social relationships, and so it is not surprising that the sign moves from the heart toward the space of relationship, linking the space between speaker and hearer.

The possessional prefix *"t'a"* is also involved in this social view of mind. It is a prefix denoting separable possession unlike those prefixes used with kinship terms, for example, which denote inseparable possession. Your mother and grandfather are always and inseparably yours, whereas your thinking and thoughts (*mit'awac'i*), while certainly yours, are separable from you in the sense that they can be shared.

Such data provide evidence of some fundamental philosophical differences in conceptions of mind/body between Nakota speakers and English speakers. This provides a basis from which to explore two spatial concepts that provide semantic and syntactic resources for both spoken Nakota and PST.

SIGN TALK AND SPATIAL CONCEPTS

Many investigators of native North American peoples have noted the importance of two spatial concepts—the circle and the four cardinal directions. Though this idea has been discussed in the context of traditional religious symbolism (e.g., Neihardt 1972, Brown 1953, Walker 1980), exactly how these concepts are formed and expressed with body movement as well as spoken language, and how they are used in the lived experience of cultural members has not been articulated. The Assiniboine both share in this widespread Plains symbolism and impress their own distinct variations upon it.

A brief glimpse into the lived experience of the shape of the circle in terms of human relationships and the sense of loss due to the altered shape of contemporary living spaces is possible through the following statement by one of my Nakota teachers, Mrs. Emma Lamebull:

> After the white people came they said, everything changed, you know, they're sitting there [the old-timers] telling stories, they said everything changed, they said. Long ago they said, everything we did in a circle, like in a tipi we always sat in a circle and looked at each other's faces. When we ate we sat in a circle. When we talked and visit each other, tell stories, we sat in a circle, and when we looked at each other [we] could tell when this person was feeling bad, what his feelings were 'cause you could see their faces. And after the white people came, well then they took our kids to school and instead of looking at each other, they're looking at the back, at the back of heads—you don't see their face no more, you don't know if they're feeling bad or, if they don't feel good you can't comfort them because you can't see their faces. And then the teacher stands up there, teaching you, and instead of trying to make you learn lessons, they teach you your lessons but they learn you how to compete—they learn you to be higher than this one—you study harder and you get A's and they do things for you because they learn you how to compete. Even these animals, we learn to, they learn their children to kill them when they need it—when they need to eat. When the white people came they turn that into competing—they wanna see who killed the biggest elk or the biggest buffalo or the longest fish, you know, and . . . they get recognized for doing the biggest things they killed you know, they don't think of the animal itself, what they're doing to them, and they learn the people how to compete against one another. And you see they turned our kids, teaching them like that and they said it's sad the way some kids they don't even care now, or pay attention. It's hard to make them mind because now they

went and bought homes like this one and they said, their
brother's got TV and he's got his own room, sister's got TV
and she's got her own room, parents got their own room—
no more circle, they broke the circle.

Thus the circle was and still is, though perceived as
diminished through architectural and social change, a
powerful form for the organizing of social relations and
interaction in a very practical sense. It symbolizes not
only community and caring but also a face-to-face non-
competitive ideal social world. In storytelling, for example, Mrs. Rose Weasel often begins with a large circular
gesture saying:

Žeįś,   oyate   ka   t'ipi   hųśta,   kan.
That one, tribe/people there they live(d) it is said, over
there.
Those people, over there they lived, it is said, over there.

or

Wi   ne   eyaś   kahąkeya   t'ipi   hųśta.
Lodge this just over there they camped, it is said.
There was a lodge; just over there they lived, it is said.

In both cases Mrs. Weasel literally describes the camp
circle (Fig. 2 gives a transcribed example), but moreover
the metaphor of the circle creates the social space within
which the characters will interact and the story will
unfold. The circle also circumscribes the limits of the
signing space: clearing or setting the spatial stage.

DEIXIS IN NAKOTA AND PST

In the two Nakota sentences used as examples there are
three different ways of saying "there" and two other
indexicals (ne and že, "this" and "that") all of which
contribute to the fairly complex deictical system that
organizes space/time in both the spoken language and the
gestural system.[9]

Linguists have drawn attention to the ways in which spoken languages use such deictical devices, but on the whole they have neglected to pay attention to the embodiment that accompanies the use of these terms (Hanks 1990).[10] Yet the zero point of the deictical coordinates can be viewed not merely as the here and now of a speaker but as the body of the person. Time/space is measured from the here and now of the embodied person as mover and speaker in a space that is simultaneously physical and social. Deictical terms refer to such embodied notions of time/space *at the same time* as they relate the speaker to the speech situation.

The Nakota deictic space falls readily into three horizontal zones (Fig. 3). Demonstrative pronouns, for example, express proximal, distal and extra distal areas, or "here, there, and there visible so that it can be pointed at" (Boas and Deloria 1941:2). If we set aside standard spoken language classifications into categories such as demonstratives, pronouns and adverbials and categorize according to spatial criteria, we see that in Nakota deictic space these three zones are remarkably consistent. Proximal space is marked by a series of words all of which begin with *ne* and all terms dealing with near space use this root. Likewise all gestures referring to near space either with or without vocal accompaniment are performed closest to the body itself. Distal or "there" space consistently uses terms beginning with *że*, and PST signs correspondingly refer to and reach into a space farther from the body than the *ne* space. The extradistal, or far but visible, space uses *ka,* although PST signs relating to this group do not necessarily reach out of the comfortable "signing space" in front of the torso during performance, because this is a relative rather than an actual positioning. Figure 4 shows the consistency of this arrangement in spoken language terms when applied to demonstratives and adverbials of space/time. Given this consistency it is not surprising to find that these three zones of horizontal space are maintained in the gestural system, although it would be a mistake to assume that this implies a naive realism in the deictic system, that is, that "here" and "there" only refer

ka

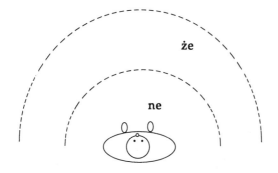

że

ne

ne - near space/time (here/now)

że - farther space/time (there/then)

ka - far and visible space/time

Figure 3. Deictic co-ordinates shared by Nakota and Plains Sign Talk.

HERE (near space and time)		THERE (medium distance away)		YONDER (far but visible space)	
ne	this, this one	zéi	that, that one	ka	(that) over there
nejs	this, this one	zéjs	that, that one (it)	kejs	that over there
nen	here	zen	there	kan	over there
néc'i	here, over here, this	źéc'i	there	kák'i	over yonder
néc'iya	this way, towards	źéc'iya	that way, in that direction, over there	kakiya	yonder, towards yonder place
néc'iyataha	this place over here, through here, from (over) here	źéc'iyataha	from (over) there (ya/u—going/coming) there	kakiyataha	from yonder, over there in that direction
néc'en	here, over here, thus, this way, like this, in this manner	źéc'en	then, so, after, that	kák'en (ken)	over there
netam	over here, this way	źetam	over there, that way	katam	over that way
néc'etuh	so, this way	źéc'etu	like that	kana	those there
néc'a	then (near time), this kind one like this, similar to	źéc'a	that kind, thus		
		źéc'a u	so it was, (thus + to be)		
néna	these here (pl. of ne)	źéna	those		
netamya	go this way	źetamya	go that way		
netam u	come this way	źe u	thus, (use) that kind)		
netaha	from here (this time/place)	źéc'enźeha	then		
nétu	right here	źeha	that, then		
nétun(a)	near here	etaha źeha	from then, after that		
apa ne(n)	today, this day	źehata	then, after that (time)		
éstena nen	soon	źehac'eha	then, in those times		
n(e) iyuha	all of these	źetaha	from there (that time/place)		
nehakam-nikte	I'm going this far	źena (k'o)	those (too)		
		źehakam-nikte	I'm going that far		

Figure 4. Deictical Terminology in Nakota

to zones of relative proximity in physical space (cf. Hanks 1990).

The Nakota spoken language, like English, often combines space and time, and this too is paralleled in gesture. Thus, *étu* or "close," refers to both near space and near time, and the sign is performed in near space and moves towards this zero point of the deictical coordinates—the here and now of the body itself. The same gesture is used with the word *ésten* meaning "soon/right away." Likewise the word *t'éhạ,* "far away," refers to a long time or far distance and there is one gesture that can apply to both. In this case, however, the *ka,* or far space, is not used, perhaps because *t'éhạ* refers to invisible rather than to visible distance. The same gesture is also used with the word *wanạkas* meaning "a long time ago," and in storytelling this often functions in a similar manner to the way "once upon a time" is used to begin European stories.

A shortened version of this gesture is often used as a past time or completed action marker. Nakota is a language that does not use verb tense and verbs mark only two categories of time: present or completed action and potential action. Thus we do not find any equivalent to the time line in ASL, wherein past time signs use the space behind the line of the body, present time signs are located at the body, and future time signs are in front, consistent with the way in which the English language locates time spatially (Baker and Cokely 1980).

This deictic organization extends to involve the four cardinal directions. They are referred to in Nakota as *t'atetopa* the "four winds" or *t'atéoyétópa,* "the four tracks of the winds." In Assiniboine religious thought it is from the four winds that various kinds of spiritual assistance or power comes. Each term would appear to connote a general direction *from* which certain things *come toward* a person in contrast to the Euro-American conventional picture of the four directions as lines moving *outward* from a given point, as shown by the pointing arrows on most geographic maps (Fig. 5). An additional difference lies in the conception of the cardinal directions as four quarters—that is as a circle sectioned into four quarters. Each direction therefore comprises an area in contrast to the single line of Euro-American convention.

Wíhiŋap'e, "east," refers to the sunrise, literally "sun comes up," and is the direction from which the grandfather spirits come. In the prereservation era, when extended family groups were scattered to hunt, it was the direction in which the tipi would often be faced, so as to greet the morning sun with prayer. Wiyotạ(hạ) is translated as "south" but refers literally to the "sun in the middle" and also means "noon." South is a particularly salient direction for the Assiniboine: the door of ceremonial structures such as the sundance lodge and sweat lodges face the south, for example. Wiyohpe, "west," refers to "sun going down." It is the home of the eagle who "lifts prayers to heaven" and the "thunderbirds" responsible for lightning and thunder and much more. It is also the direction in which departing souls are said to go when they leave this home on earth. Waziyata, "north" refers to "where the snow comes from," the home of the old man who, some Assiniboine say, "lives in the cold and makes the cold and rarely takes pity on anyone."

Like the deictic terms discussed earlier, spatial concepts also coincide with notions of time passing as reckoned by the movement of the sun across the sky (Fig. 6). A day is marked by the circular passage of the sun from E-S-W, and the passage of the year is marked by "winters" with their northern connection.

What is particularly interesting about Assiniboine use of the cardinal directions is that, although these terms as described above exist in the spoken language, they are rarely if ever used in everyday contexts. Consultants who were fluent speakers of Nakota had to search their memories for the names of the directions, conceiving of these words being appropriate in only three contexts: religious concepts involving the four winds; the four seasons and passing time; and far distant places and peoples. Another term for "south," for example, was mastamak'oc'e, literally, "hot country," which might be used of someone traveling to Arizona, but not for someone traveling south within the reservation or the state of Montana. Two

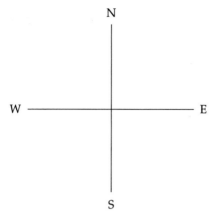

Euro-American cardinal directions

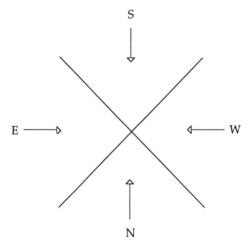

Assiniboine/Nakota cardinal directions

Figure 5. Two different cultural conceptions of the cardinal directions.

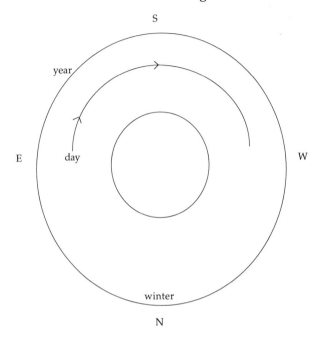

Figure 6. Time in space in Nakota and Plains Sign Talk.

variant terms for "north"—*Waziyam* and *Wiyohąpa*—
refer to places where other Assiniboine people live, on the
Red Pheasant Reserve and the Santaluta/Regina area, both
in Canada. To ask, "Did you come from the North?"
(*Wiyohąpa etahą yahi*) refers to coming from Canada. The
spoken language terms themselves therefore do not seem
to involve either local geographical space or immediate
orientation space. How is it then that information about
such local space is organized?

I found that despite this lack of vocal reference in
everyday contexts, the cardinal points nevertheless provide a constant frame of reference that all use, whether
they speak Nakota or English only and regardless of
whether they know the sign language or not. It is through
indexical spoken expressions and gestures that this frame
of reference is utilized. Today, even though few people are
fluent in the sign language proper, there remains a use of

gesture that is coincident with it and that undoubtedly stems from a very different view of language from that held by Euro-American people. For example, I found that both speech and gesture have become equally important when giving route directions, whether spoken Nakota or spoken English is used.

In asking how to get from the Agency buildings on the Fort Belknap reservation to the nearby town of Harlem, I received the following reply in English from an Assiniboine person: "You go out of here this way, turn this way again and you'll come to the highway. Go this way again, over the river and you're gonna go that way into town." Obviously if one were to take notice of only the spoken component involved in this utterance, the information is somewhat ambiguous. Of equal importance in understanding these directions, however, is the accompanying gestures of the arms and hands, as shown in the movement text in Figure 7.

This is in marked contrast to a non-Indian Montana resident who said, "Well, go out of these doors to the parking lot, then take a left past the Headstart building till you get to the road, and take a left again. You'll get to Highway 2. Go west on 2 about three miles and Harlem's right there on your right. There's a sign right there says Harlem." The only gestures accompanying this were a hand directed towards the doors in question (𝄆) and a raised hand at the end (𝄇), indicating the road sign, as if placed in front of the speaker.

In contrast to the Assiniboine case, the Euro-American example encodes directions by making reference to landmarks such as doors and signposts, buildings, and a numbered highway, as well as directional terms such as left and right. In the route directions given by an Assiniboine person, indexical expressions such as "here," "this way," and "that way" are accompanied by gestures that point to the actual geographical directions involved. In this manner, the indexicals and gestures provide information just as accurate as that encoded in the Euro-American case, but in a different manner.

Assiniboine people always seem to know where the

actual cardinal directions lie, even if they are deep inside
a multiroomed building and in a room without windows
(which was the case when these directions were given).
Consequently, when Assiniboine people give directions,
the cardinal points provide a constant frame of reference,
which everyone uses, even though the actual words
"north," "south," "east," and "west" are not used. This
implicit awareness of geographical direction means that
people draw upon a map that is constant, regardless of
which direction the speaker happens to be facing at the
time. In this way, spoken indexical expressions plus the
gestures of hands that point to actual geographical directions are sufficient, and no one (except perhaps the anthropologist) gets confused.

Even in situations when visual field is restricted, such
as driving in a car, I found that an Assiniboine passenger
will gesture and say "go this way" or "go that way" rather
than use American English alternatives that do not require
a gesture such as "take a right here" or "go east until you
get to the highway," or British English alternatives such as
"turn right at the Red Lion," and "take the Scarborough
road." The intimate social space of a reservation community permits the use of indexicals and gesture well
beyond this kind of general spatial orientation and extends into the frequent use of pronouns and demonstratives so that proper names of places and people are
avoided whenever possible.

In the context of storytelling, this geographical frame of
reference is frequently retained. When working with Mrs.
Weasel on one occasion on the sign vocabulary in one of
her stories I was puzzled as to why signs for "morning"
and "afternoon" were performed as in Figure 8a when on
another occasion they had been performed as in Figure 8b.
Although the hand shape (first finger and thumb create the
shape of a circle, other fingers curled) and arm action (a
curving arc of the whole arm, upward or downward, the
whole sign being an iconic representation of the sun's
rising in the sky and then lowering) remained the same,
the space in which the rising arc was traced by the arm
varied. On the first occasion Mrs Weasel raised her arm on

her right side and lowered it on her left side; on the second occasion the sun rose directly in front of her and set behind her. The puzzle was solved by realizing that in the first instance Mrs. Weasel had been sitting in a room and facing northwest, so east was on her right side and west to her left, whereas on the second occasion she had been facing east.

This spatial orientation makes a difference in the transcription of those signs if they are to reflect accurately the ethnographic context; what is constituent to the signs is not the forward-middle or side-middle direction of the arm in relation to the torso, but that the arm goes toward geographical east (Figure 8c).

CONCLUSION

The theoretical value of these observations lies in the exposure of a deeply rooted Cartesianism in our definition of language as traditionally constituted, reflected by the view that there are two separate systems involved in the human organization of space, time, and the body, one having to do with the movement of the body, a physical realm of sensory-motor organization and doing in the world; the other having to do with sound and speech and a mental realm of thought and reflection on the world. Such a conception may indeed be an accurate picture of the Western folk model of the person, but it is surely no longer acceptable as a cross-cultural analytic model. It creates dualities between mind and body, speech and action, reason and emotion, conception and experience, verbal and nonverbal, symbolic and instrumental, and a host of others, all of which may be misleading or irrelevant to understanding the organizational principles in the knowledge systems of other peoples.

Mead (1933), Wittgenstein (1958), Goodman (1984) and others involved in a social constructivist view of mind have argued that mind is best conceived of as the sum total of ways in which knowledge can be organized through language and other semiotic practices. Such a definition,

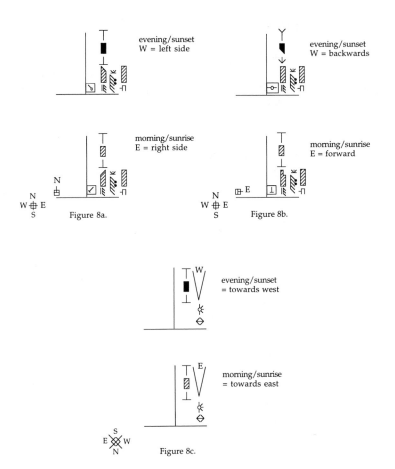

evening/sunset
W = left side

evening/sunset
W = backwards

morning/sunrise
E = right side

morning/sunrise
E = forward

Figure 8a.

Figure 8b.

evening/sunset
= towards west

morning/sunrise
= towards east

Figure 8c.

Figure 8. Assiniboine/Nakota spatial orientation.

it seems, would accommodate Assiniboine conceptions of language and mind much better than the Cartesian legacy. The Assiniboine data on spatial orientation also show that although such knowledge is usually tacit—that is, not normally expressed in words—it is nevertheless organized. Such cultural resources illustrate some of the integral connections between gestural and spoken languages such that we could reasonably posit a core of deictic features of this kind that will be common to both speech and action in any language community. Through these "semantic primitives" (Williams, this volume) we can perhaps gain entrée into our own and other cultural epistemologies and metaphysics through a view of language as inseparably constituted *with* action and not independently *by* action.

NOTES

1. See Clark 1885, Mallery 1880, 1881. La Mont West attempted a dialect survey across the Northern Plains in 1956 and concluded that there was a "standard" dialect known by fluent and well traveled sign talkers, as well as regional variations. This is certainly a reasonable suggestion. West's conclusions, however, are based upon statistics drawn from problematic descriptions in the 19th century documentation plus his detailed work with one Arapaho consultant, not upon his own survey (West 1960). Sign talkers among the Assiniboine today recognize dialect variations that belong to neighboring groups.

2. The film of the council and Scott's film dictionary are housed in the National Archives, Washington D.C., Video and Sound Branch, nos. 106.3, 106.4, and 106.5.

3. The use of an upper case letter with the word "Deaf" is a convention recently established by deaf and hard-of-hearing Americans who identify themselves as members of the Deaf Community, a distinct sub-culture whose language is ASL.

4. Ardener (1989:18) suggests that Saussure's complex notion of the arbitrariness of the linguistic sign was clearly designed to answer adherents of the view—supported by Tylor—that all language had a representational origin.

5. See Herzfeld 1987:137 for discussion of Tylor's view of gesture as a sort of "expressive incontinence" and further discussion in Farnell, in press.

6. I have attempted to use word glosses (in upper case letters) and descriptions of signs for those readers unable to read the Labanotated texts enclosed in the figures. This is not easy because descriptions in words are always inadequate as well as lengthy, and photographs or pictures are only static, hence the need for the script, of course. See Farnell 1984 and Williams and Farnell 1990 for discussion of the notion of literacy in relation to movement.

7. ASL is an acronym for American Sign Language, also called Ameslan, which is the sign language used by Deaf communities in America. Linguistic research into ASL has blossomed over the past thirty years since the pioneering work of William Stokoe at Gallaudet University. Stokoe was the first to insist and demonstrate that ASL as a sign language

was a real language in every sense of the word "real," and not a primitive substitute for speech (see Stokoe 1972).

8. Ray De Mallie: Personal communication and Buechel's Lakota grammar (1983:72).

9. The word "deixis" is a technical term in linguistics, used to handle those features of language that are relative to the place and time of the spoken utterance. They include personal pronouns and adverbials of time and space such as "here" and "there," and "now" and "then," as well as demonstratives and tense. "Deixis" is a Greek word meaning "pointing" or "indicating," which is somewhat ironic given the exclusion of the act itself from Western definitions of language and language-in-use. For introductions to deixis in general see Lyons 1977, and Buhler 1934.

10. Recent work on deixis in linguistics and psycholinguistics can be found in collections edited by Jarvella and Klein 1982, and Pick and Acredolo 1983. Important exceptions to this general neglect of the body in deixis are Sherzer 1973, McNeill and Levy 1982, McNeill 1985a and 1990 and Haviland 1986 and 1993. See also Bellugi and Klima 1982 on ASL and deixis. Hanks 1990 also aims to accomplish an embodiment of deixis in his masterful study of Mayan deictics.

REFERENCES

Ardener, E. W. 1989 [1971]. Social anthropology and language. In M. Chapman, ed., *Edwin Ardener: The Voice of Prophecy and Other Essays.* Oxford, U.K.: Basil Blackwell.

Baker C., and D. Cokely. 1980. *American Sign Language: A Teachers Resource Text on Grammar and Culture.* Silver Spring, Md.: T. J. Publishers.

Bellugi, U., and E. S. Klima. 1982. From gesture to sign: Deixis in a visual gestural language. In R. J. Jarvella and W. Klein, eds., *Speech, Place and Action: Studies in Deixis and Related Topics.* Chichester, U.K.: John Wiley & Sons, 297–313.

Boas, F., and E. Deloria. 1941. *Dakota Grammar.* Memoirs of the National Academy of Sciences, vol. xxiii. Washington, D.C.: U.S. Government Printing Office.

Brown, J. E., ed. 1953. *The Sacred Pipe: Black Elk's Account of the Seven Rites of the Oglala Sioux.* Norman, Okla.: University of Oklahoma Press.

Buechel, E. 1983 [1939]. *A Grammar of Lakota.* Saint Francis, S.Dak.: Rosebud Educational Society.

Bühler, K. 1934. *Sprachtheorie.* Jena, Germany: Fischer.

Clark, W. P. 1885. *The Indian Sign Language.* Philadelphia: L. R. Hammersley.

Deloria, E. 1940. Lakota-English lexicon. Manuscript, American Philosophical Society Library, Philadelphia, Pennsylvania.

Dunley, T. W. 1982. *Wolves for the Blue Soldiers.* Lincoln, Nebr.: University of Nebraska Press.

Farnell, B. 1984. Visual communication and literacy: An anthropological enquiry into Plains Indian and American sign languages. M.A. thesis, New York University, New York, New York.

———. In press. *Do You See What I Mean?: Plains Indian Sign Talk and the Embodiment of Action.* Austin: University of Texas Press.

Fowler, L. 1987. *Shared Symbols, Contested Meanings. Gros Ventre Culture and History 1778–1984.* Ithaca, N.Y.: Cornell University Press.

Goodman, N. 1984. *Of Mind and Other Matters.* Cambridge, Mass.: Harvard University Press.

Hanks, W. 1990. *Referential Practice: Language and Lived Space among the Maya.* Chicago: University of Chicago Press.

Harris, R. 1981. *The Language Myth.* New York: St. Martin's.

Haviland, J. B. 1986. Complex referential gestures. Draft manuscript, Center for Advanced Study in the Behavioral Sciences, Stanford University, Stanford, California.

————. 1993. Anchoring, iconicity and orientation in Guugu Yimithirr pointing gestures. *Journal of Linguistic Anthropology* 3(1):3–45.

Herzfeld, M. 1987. *Anthropology through the Looking Glass: Critical Ethnography in the Margins of Europe.* Cambridge, U.K.: Cambridge University Press.

Jarvella, R. J., and W. Klein, eds. 1982. *Speech Place and Action: Studies in Deixis and Related Topics.* Chichester, U.K.: John Wiley and Sons.

Kroeber, A. 1958. Sign language enquiry. *International Journal of American Linguistics* 24:1–19.

Lyons, J. 1977. *Semantics, Vol. 2.* London and New York: Cambridge University Press.

Mallery, G. 1880. *Introduction to the Study of Sign Language among the North American Indians as Illustrating the Gesture Speech of Mankind.* Washington, D.C.: U.S. Bureau of Ethnology.

————. 1881. Sign Language among the North American Indians. *BAE Annual Report* 1:269–552. Washington, D.C.: Smithsonian Institution.

McNeill, D. 1985. So you think gestures are nonverbal? *Psychological Review* 92(3):350–371.

————. 1990. *Hand and Mind.* Chicago: University of Chicago Press.

McNeill, D., and E. Levy. 1982. Conceptual representations in language activity and gesture. In R. J. Jarvella and W. Klein eds. *Speech, Place and Action: Studies in Deixis and Related Topics.* Chichester, U.K: John Wiley & Sons, 271–295.

Mead, G. H. 1933. *Mind, Self and Society.* Chicago: University of Chicago Press.

Neihardt, J. G. 1972 [1932]. *Black Elk Speaks: Being the Life Story of a Holy Man of the Oglala Sioux.* New York: William Morrow.

Pick, H. L. Jr., and L. P. Acredolo, eds. 1983. *Spatial Orientation.* New York and London: Plenum.

Sherzer, J. 1973. Verbal and nonverbal deixis: The pointed lip gesture among the San Blas Cuna. *Language in Society* 2:117–31.

Stokoe, W. 1972. *Semiotics and Human Sign Language.* New York: Humanities.

Walker, J. R. 1980. *Lakota Belief and Ritual.* R. J. DeMallie and E. A. Jahner, eds. Lincoln, Nebr.: University of Nebraska Press.

West Jr., La M. 1960. The sign language: An analysis. Ph.D. dissertation, Indiana University, Bloomington, Indiana.

Williams, D., and B. Farnell. 1990. *The Laban Script: A Beginning Text on Movement Writing for Non-Dancers.* Canberra, Australia: Australian Institute for Aboriginal and Torres Straits Islander Studies.

Wittgenstein, L. 1958. *Philosophical Investigations.* English text of 3d ed. G. E. M. Anscombe, trans. New York: Macmillan.

Chapter 4 SOCIALITY, SOCIAL INTERACTION, AND SIGN LANGUAGE IN ABORIGINAL AUSTRALIA[1]

Adam Kendon

It has been noted by many observers of Aborigines that, at least in the central arid regions of the Australian continent, some form of sign language, more or less elaborate, is in widespread use. Among the Warlpiri, Warumungu, and other groups of the north-central desert, highly elaborate forms of sign language are found. These are used by women, mainly as alternatives to speaking when women are observing speech taboos during mourning and male initiation ceremonials. On the northerly fringes of the central desert; in northwest-central Queensland, Cape York; and in the Western Desert, signing is also used by men—in some regions mainly by men, usually in connection with their initiation rituals.

Notwithstanding these ritual uses of sign language, some form of sign use in daily life is widespread, not only throughout the regions mentioned but elsewhere as well, including Arnhem Land and the Kimberleys, where no complex sign languages have been reported. Whereas speech taboos almost certainly account for the more complex forms of these sign languages, the widespread use of signs in daily interaction throughout much of Aboriginal Australia calls for a more general explanation. In this chapter I suggest that there is a link between the kind of sociality found in Aboriginal society, the special character of Aboriginal face-to-face interaction, and the presence of sign use.

Aboriginal sociality has been especially well described by Sutton (1978), Sansom (1980), and Myers (1986) for Aboriginal society in Western Cape York, in the urban fringe camps of Darwin, and in the Western Desert, respectively. Their accounts have much in common, and it seems likely that the kind of sociality they describe is characteristic of Aboriginal society generally. The special characteristics of Aboriginal face-to-face interaction have been described by Harris (1977, 1980); Von Sturmer (1981); Malcolm (1982); Eades (1982); and Liberman (1982, 1985), as well as by Sutton, Sansom, and Myers. These characteristics appear to fit well with the special communication requirements that Aboriginal sociality imposes, and they provide a context for the proliferation of communicative styles often noted among Aborigines. I suggest that because signing is silent, less intimate, and informatively less complex than speech, it is particularly suited for the indirect, semiexplicit communication that is so often required in Aboriginal interaction.

The hypothesis presented herein is thus that signing is widely used in Aboriginal society because its special properties as a mode of communication suit it to the communicative tasks Aborigines face daily among themselves.

This hypothesis does not claim a causal relationship. Face-to-face interaction in other hunter-gatherer societies, such as the !Kung San, is reported to have many features similar to those described for Aborigines (cf. Liberman 1985:103). However, as far as I know, the !Kung do not make extensive use of signs. What I am suggesting is that if people, for whatever reason, resort to signs as a means of communication, if the society they live in conducts interaction in the way to be described here for Aborigines, then the practice of using signs will be favored and may spread. This does not mean that the development of signing in a society is an inevitable consequence of particular modes of interaction.

In the North Central Desert, as elsewhere in Australia, Aborigines lived in small groups of variable size and composition, usually of two or three families, each with a

man and his wife or wives and children, but often including other relatives as well. Most recent work shows that
these groups are aggregates of individuals who are associated with one another through ties of kinship and affec-
tion, as well as ties to country. Sansom refers to these
groupings as "mobs," following the usage of English-
speaking Aborigines in the Northern Territory. Myers
refers to them as "bands."

Myers speaks of bands as having an egocentric structure; they arise through dyadic ties between members and
endure just as long as particular individuals prefer to
remain associated with one another. In order for a collection of individuals to stay together as a band, to "run
together," in the terminology of Sansom's fringe dwellers,
the interpersonal ties that make this possible have to be
continuously negotiated.

In the practice of daily interaction, thus, people must
continually compromise with one another if they are to
sustain relationships. Yet, inevitably, no one is willing to
compromise all the time. People have strong needs, opin-
ions, and desires, and further, although autonomous in
the sense that people regard themselves and others as free
agents, they are nevertheless bound to one another by
obligations of all kinds. People are therefore limited in
several ways in the degree to which they can accommodate to one another. As has been noted by a number of
observers, Aborigines interact with one another in what
appears to be a very polite, indirect fashion; they avoid
putting themselves forward and attempt not to impose
upon others with direct orders or requests. There is a
continual endeavor to establish and maintain congeniality. This appears to be because, if congeniality is not
maintained, resort may be had to interpersonal quarreling,
often of a violent nature. Furthermore, people may readily
become jealous of one another, and there is a continual
underlying suspicion of each other's intentions. In interaction, thus, individuals must be highly diplomatic, continually negotiating with one another and attempting to
achieve satisfaction of their own needs and desires at the

same time as they try to ensure good relations and continued cooperation with others.

A further important feature of everyday Aboriginal
sociality is its highly public character. People live out
their lives in continual copresence. Individuals are almost
never alone and there is almost no privacy. This means
not only that everything that one does may be open to
observation by others but also that others have a right to
observe what one is doing, so that to attempt to conceal
one's activities may give rise to resentment and suspicion.

The aggregate character of Aboriginal sociality, the
negotiable nature of interpersonal relations, the continual
need to maintain personal autonomy and equality in the
face of generational hierarchy, the need to sustain related-
ness and identity, and the highly public character of daily
life impart great complexity and delicacy to Aboriginal
interaction. Accordingly, it may perhaps not seem so
surprising that, among Aborigines, there is much interest
in the techniques of interpersonal communication and
that many different modes of communication have been
elaborated. The special avoidance languages and the mys-
tic languages taught to male initiates are but the most
well-known and obvious examples. In addition, in many
parts of Australia, people may speak several different
languages, not so much because they need to do so to
make themselves understood in different places, but because these languages serve as a means of expressing the
multiple social identities that they can lay claim to
through their network of kin relationships. Commanding
a range of different languages provides the individual
with a range of communicative codes that facilitate the
maintenance of a complex and delicate range of social
relationships.

Let us turn now to consider sign language. As a silent,
visual mode of communication, produced by actions of
the hands and arms, it has a number of properties that
seem to make it more useful than speech for certain kinds
of communication.

First of all, we may note that if signs are to be transmitted, they must be seen. This means that, in respect to the signer, the recipient must be oriented in an appropriate way. This does not mean, necessarily, that the recipient must gaze directly at the signer, but it does mean that some kind of definite orientation is required. Receipt of speech, on the other hand, does not require any definite orientation. This means that it is easier for the transmitter of visual information to know who its recipients are. A signer, thus, may more readily see who may be a recipient than a speaker and so exercise greater control over who may receive signed messages than a speaker can over who may receive spoken messages.

This ability to control who one's recipients are is further enhanced because signs may be varied in where they are made. Although in Aboriginal sign languages signs are typically performed within a fairly restricted space in front of the signer, more or less at shoulder level, this is not an absolute requirement. Signs that are not articulated in relation to a specific body part may, in fact, be produced in a variety of locations. Thus many signs may be done above the head, over the shoulder, down low, to one side of the body or the other, and even behind the signer's back. This means that a signer can sign in a particular location, using the body as a screen, so that signs can be observed by others selectively. It is therefore possible for a signer and a recipient to collaborate in the establishment of an exclusive communication channel more easily than can be done with speech. Given the highly public nature of everyday interaction in Aboriginal society, it may well be that signing proves a useful alternative when one desires to conceal one's communications from others.

Signing makes it possible for articulated messages to be transmitted over longer distances with less effort than if speech is used. Although the human voice can be heard over quite long distances, due to turbulence of the medium and echo, its articulate character is quite quickly lost. This is not so with sign; hence it may serve as a convenient and relatively effortless means of communication over distances that would be much more difficult to cope with using the voice. Furthermore, since signing is silent, it can be used when a raised voice or shouting would otherwise be necessary. Raising the voice is generally frowned upon among Aborigines, especially if relatives are about for whom respect must be shown; hence the use of signs for communicating at a distance may be favored for reasons of etiquette as well as economy.

The dispersed and open arrangement of Aboriginal camps, in which people tend to place themselves so that they can both be seen and be able to see others (Tonkinson and Tonkinson 1979, White 1977) would also appear to favor the use of signs as a means of articulate communication between people who are visible to one another but separated by some distance. Use of signs for brief exchanges over distances of many yards may indeed be observed, both among seated people in camp and among people who are moving about. For instance, at Yuendumu, a Warlpiri settlement some 300 kilometers northwest of Alice Springs, it is not uncommon for women who can see each other, often at distances much too great for casual spoken interchange, to use signs to exchange information about where they are going and what they have been doing. Sign is quite often used between people as they pass to and fro in the settlement, to indicate the purchases made at the store or what was caught on a hunting expedition.

Another point is that signs may be varied in the degree of explicitness with which they are performed. When performed in a minimal fashion, many signs may be hard to distinguish from casual physical acts. It is possible, thus to disguise them as actions that have no particular explicit communicative character. Speech cannot be performed as an ambiguous activity in the same way. It is not possible to speak in such a way that a hearer might not be certain whether an utterance had been engaged in or not. This graded character of signing makes it a useful modality for handling interaction situations in which communication must be indirect. It makes it possible to communicate in a tentative fashion, so that messages can easily be denied, if necessary. This makes signing highly suitable in many circumstances of Aboriginal interaction. It has been noted by several observers, for instance, that people rarely ask each other direct questions and often may not make requests for goods or services directly. Sign may sometimes be used instead of speech as a way of making known one's needs, for it can be used as a way of doing this in a casual, indirect, semiexplicit fashion.

The indirect, highly diplomatic character of much Aboriginal interaction reflects the great importance that is attached to self-effacement in many situations. As already noted, Aboriginal people have great respect for each other's personal autonomy, and individuals try to avoid any suggestion that they are putting themselves forward. At meetings where matters must be decided, for instance, when people express their views, they tend to do so in an impersonal manner, with as little indication as possible of their own involvement in the position being expressed. Thus signs may be used in such circumstances, for in this way people are able to express their views without being directly noticed as doing so. As has been reported to me from the Western Desert, at community meetings many cross-conversations in sign may be carried on, often with the result that the chairman is able to announce a consensus on a matter that has never been explicitly discussed in words. It seems that there is considerable reluctance to wrangle over things verbally. It is much more acceptable for people to put their varying viewpoints in sign.

Signing may be used in such situations at times not only because it may be conducted in a highly indirect fashion and provide a means of communicating without drawing attention to the communicator but also because it is a less intimate, less personal mode of communication, with a more objectlike character than speech has. Signs that do not require a bodily location, for instance, may be held away from the body and may thus, to some extent, be distanced from the self. This cannot be done with speech. The voice, issuing as it does from inside the body, has a more intimate connection with the person, as if it is a manifestation of the person's invisible essence or soul. Signs formed by the hands, however, can be treated almost like physical objects. They have an objective, depersonalized character. It is probably for this reason that signs are often used when reference is made to sacred matters, which must be spoken of with respect or, as Sutton (1978) has reported, when making reference to persons who deserve the greatest respect. Sign seems to be the least personal way of referring to someone.

Finally, signing probably has a more neutral character because the information it conveys is less complex than that conveyed in speech. In speech almost anything can be said in many different ways. Even within a given dialect, the words chosen, the voice quality used, the pattern of stress, the rapidity of speech, and the like all may vary. The particular choices that a speaker makes in respect to all these different aspects convey information at many different levels, both in regard to content and in regard to the speaker's attitude toward the recipient or recipients, toward the self, toward the interaction in which the utterance takes place, and toward the relationship that obtains between the interactants. In Aboriginal sign languages, signed utterances probably do not have the same degree of complexity. These sign languages have relatively small lexicons, so there are fewer choices in how a thing may be said. In addition, because these sign languages are not fully acquired until adulthood, and since they are almost never an individual's only means of linguistic communication, signers may not control it as subtly as they do speech. In this we may expect a difference between native deaf signers and users of alternative sign languages such as we are dealing with here. These considerations suggest that, in using sign, Aborigines have fewer choices of expression and thus cannot convey nuances of meaning to the same degree as is possible with speech. The more neutral character of sign that follows from this means, again, that sign is a more suitable medium for impersonal, neutral utterances that are so often demanded in Aboriginal interaction.

For these various reasons, signing appears to be a medium of communication well fitted to many of the interactional circumstances of Aboriginal life. It can be used with a great deal of discretion, making private exchanges possible even in quite public circumstances; it can serve usefully as a mode of communication for people who are much of the time visually copresent but often at considerable distances from one another; nevertheless, it can be varied in the explicitness of its performance and so is useful as a vehicle for tentative communications; it has a less personal, more objective, and neutral character and may thus be suitable for conveying messages in a more anonymous, objective style. For all these various reasons, it would seem, signing is a valuable communicative modality within the context of Aboriginal interaction. In this way, perhaps, we may understand why it is that sign use and sign languages have developed so widely among Australian Aborigines.

NOTE

1. This chapter is adapted from "Aboriginal Interaction and Aboriginal Sign Language," chap. 14 of my *Sign Languages of Aboriginal Australia: Cultural, Semiotic and Communicational Perspectives.* Cambridge, UK: Cambridge University Press, 1988. Full references and acknowledgments will be found therein.

REFERENCES

Brandl, M. M., and M. Walsh. 1982. Speakers of many tongues: Toward understanding multilingualism among Aboriginal Australians. *International Journal of the Sociology of Language* 36:71–81.

Eades, D. 1982. "You gotta know how to talk. . . .": Information seeking in South East Queensland Aboriginal society. *Australian Journal of Linguistics* 2:61–82.

Harris, S. G. 1977. Milingimbi Aboriginal learning contexts. Ph.D. dissertation, University of New Mexico, Albuquerque, New Mexico.

———. 1980. Culture and learning: Tradition and education in north east Arnhem Land [an abridgment by J. Kinslow-Harris of a Ph.D. thesis by S. G. Harris]. Darwin, Australia: Northern Territory Department of Education, published for the Professional Services Branch.

Liberman, K. 1982. Some linguistic features of congenial fellowship among the Pitjantjatjara. *International Journal for the Sociology of Language* 36:35–51.

———. 1985. *Understanding Interaction in Central Australia: An Ethnomethodological Study of Australian Aboriginal People.* Boston: Routledge, Kegan Paul.

Malcolm, I. G. 1982. Speech use in Aboriginal communities: A preliminary survey. *Anthropological Forum* 5:54–104.

Myers, F. R. 1986. *Pintupi Country, Pintupi Self: Sentiment, Place and Politics among Western Desert Aborigines.* Washington, D.C.: Smithsonian Institution.

Peterson, N. 1986. Australian territorial organization. *Oceania Monograph* 30.

Sansom, B. 1980. *The Camp at Wallaby Cross: Aboriginal Fringe Dwellers in Darwin.* Canberra, Australia: Australian Institute of Aboriginal Studies.

Sutton, P. J. 1978. *Wik: Aboriginal Society, Territory and Language at Cape Keerweer, Cape York Peninsula, Australia.* Ph.D. dissertation, University of Queensland, Queensland, Australia.

Tonkinson, M., and R. Tonkinson. 1979. Modern housing for sedentarized nomads. In M. Heppell, ed., *A Black Reality: Aboriginal Camps and Housing in Remote Australia.* Canberra, Australia: Australian Institute of Aboriginal Studies, 196–206.

Von Sturmer, J. 1981. Talking with Aborigines. *Australian Institute of Aboriginal Studies Newsletter* 15:13–20.

White, I. D. 1977. From camp to village: Some problems of adaptation. In R. M. Berndt, ed., *Aborigines and Change: Australia in the '70s.* Canberra, Australia: Australian Institute of Aboriginal Studies. 100–105.

Chapter 5 WHERE WORDS HARM AND BLOWS HEAL

Gaynor M. Macdonald

WIRADJURI FIGHTING

This chapter is about an Australian Aboriginal people known as the Wiradjuri. Traditional Wiradjuri country is in central New South Wales, the most highly developed state in Australia, where Aboriginal people have had two hundred years of direct control by Europeans and where there are few visible signs of the Wiradjuri precontact culture. My fieldwork centered on Cowra, a town of 8,500 people serving a rich agricultural region. It is 300 kilometers (200 miles) west of Sydney and has an Aboriginal population of about 250, half of whom live in town and the others on a small reserve of 32 acres. I traveled extensively during eight years through the 100,000 square kilometers of Wiradjuri country, with its twenty different communities and a total Aboriginal population of approximately 12,000. I was interested in exploring what it means for Wiradjuri people to experience themselves as Aboriginal in that contemporary, urbanized context.

I had observed fist fights in pubs before and initially took little notice. My interest was aroused as I listened to the way in which people spoke about them. Wiradjuri people, or Kooris, as they call themselves, fight a lot and value fighting as an activity despite that it is against the law in Australia. As I got to know Kooris better, I realized that the fights I observed were not random or attributable simply to too much alcohol. It became evident that to understand a fight situation one had to understand the

124

relationship between those involved and their personal histories. Some fights that initially seemed to have no explanation were accepted as being predictable behavior by others with this information. It was through my observations of fights that I came to understand many of the dynamics of Wiradjuri life.

There are no typical fights; each has its own dynamic. However, there are certain ground rules expected in a fight, which assist in drawing broad distinctions between fighting and assault. A fight may be "proper," indicating that it adheres to the ground rules, or "dirty," as when weapons are introduced or someone is kicked when down. "Casual" fights refer to occasional sparring with no risk of physical injury. Assaults take place between Kooris and Gabba (white people) or between Kooris from different parts of the country—in other words, between people who are not expected to know or share the ground rules. Although there are nonfighters, everyone is expected to be able to fight with relative physical and social equals at some time in their life. The usual age range of fighters in "proper fights" is between 16 and 35 years. Men, women, and children may all fight when occasion demands. It is rare to find someone who is not prepared to fight if pushed far enough. This is as true of women as of men.

THE FORCE OF AN INSULT

The most commonly stated reasons for fights between Kooris can be grouped into three main explanations: insults, jealousy, and "standover tactics." This chapter focuses on insults; however, all three share the main characteristic of insults in that they attempt to redefine a state of affairs and to challenge people in some way.

The old saying that "sticks and stones may break my bones but words will never hurt me" is not part of Aboriginal socialization as it is in Western society. Words are effective and explosive weapons, and insults delivered in public are taken seriously. An insult is an imposition—a redefining of the ways things should be—as when someone is called "a slut," "a dog," or "a Gabba-luva" (a person whose allegiances and values are closer to those of white people than to those of Kooris). These are certain to provoke an angry response. They each suggest that the person so named is outside social life and unfit for inclusion: they exclude the individual from the right to be social.

Most Kooris react quickly to insults directed at themselves and their kin. It may be legitimate for a woman to laugh at her mother's idiosyncrasies or to criticize her own children, but she may become very angry should others take it upon themselves to do the same thing. If a child is acting up and is criticized by the adults around, the mother may feel she has been shamed by the suggestion that her child is no good or that she lacks control over her child. She may react in various ways: telling others to mind their own business, challenging them to fight or apologize, berating the child, or upholding the right of the child to do its own thing. Her response would depend on the context and how she perceived herself within it.

Kooris do not exercise an option to ignore insults unless they can be made benign, as when the insulted person interprets the remark as humorous. A sincerely offered apology may be acceptable, especially if there is no particular history of conflict between the people involved. A serious insult, or an apology not accepted, will certainly lead to verbal abuse and often to a fight.

Insult is a manipulation of the meaning of the person: a redefinition of the self or of significant others (such as kin or leaders one supports). To be redefined is to be devalued, at least symbolically—to be made to count for little. It could be seen as a way of testing people, to see how they will react when "put down"—when they are made to appear socially inadequate or deviant. Can they prove otherwise? When it is evident that the insult has made an impression, there is a sense, however fleeting, of superiority over the person insulted, which creates a subtle imbalance in the social order. A person insulted may need to make his or her presence felt: this threat to one's social integrity requires some form of confrontation in order to repudiate the insult and restore one's status. The repudiation does not—or need not—focus on the content of the insult but it must challenge the impudence of the insulter.

Hence, insults reduce the self and the capacity of the self to act. They are debilitating. Restoration of the persona requires refutation of the insult. Until then, an insulted person is in a state of shame as a state of being, not just in reference to feelings or emotions. To shame is to destroy, to maim, to create an imbalance in a relationship, to be disempowered. No one could be completely without shame and still remain a valued and involved member because the state of shame suggests that one is socially unacceptable, even less than human. In fact, this is the suggestion in the insult "you're just a dog." This is not only about honor and reputation; this is about being. Shame *must* be repudiated. One "who's got no shame" may leave oneself without kin, resources, or options. People should not tolerate even being ignored; that in itself is shameful and debilitating. One thing that continually characterizes white people from a Koori point of view is that they "just let you walk all over them," "they got no shame," they can be "taken for a ride," they don't "stand up for themselves"—unlike the Koori, who "wouldn't let no one stand over me."

Being in a state of shame can be understood as being somewhere on a continuum, the end point of which is total social denial—the death of social relationships. This, to Kooris, is devastating. It means loneliness and ostracism. Many of their favorite songs are about loneliness, and their stories are often of people and places now gone, which are fleetingly recaptured in the telling. The still-loved physically dead are constantly brought alive in storytelling and their graves tended regularly. The substance of life is social relationships, even with those who have died. The cruelest death is the death of the social self, when one is not even remembered. I recall a very moving time when a Koori woman asked me to promise to attend her funeral. Not to have people at one's funeral is the ultimate sign of social death. Retaliating against shame is thus a reclamation of sociality and harmony, a fighting back to restore relationships and dignity.

Fighting restores the individual back to social life. In doing so, it also acts as a means by which the society as a whole protects itself from another form of death: the threat to *social* life as it is experienced at any given time that stems from the exposure of contradictions in the social order. The protagonists in a Koori fight could be seen as victims, sacrificed to a particular ideology of social harmony and stability. But, as I shall explain, this feature of the fight has to be denied in order that it be effective.

I came to appreciate this particular characteristic of fighting after discussing with some Kooris the plan of a white agency to introduce Kooris to workshops on dispute resolution techniques as a means of helping them to talk over their problems and conflicts and hence stop them from fighting. The suggestion was initially met with laughter and comments, which indicated Kooris did not value "talking things over" and did value many fights. Why, then, in many situations, do Kooris prefer to fight rather than talk things out?

An examination of Koori notions of self and society helps to illuminate this choice of blows rather than of words. One of the strongest underlying themes or ideologies of Koori social life is that Kooris are close, committed to each other and to sharing with each other. This is the impression they wish to leave with newcomers or outsiders. One thing they want to avoid all the time is "washing out dirty linen in public," allowing outsiders to see problems, conflicts, and tensions. To do so would encourage intervention from outside, undermining Koori leadership and the ability of the community as a whole to manage its own affairs. Kooris stress the fact that theirs is an egalitarian society in which no one is boss of anyone else; that Kooris are autonomous and self-determining individuals; that they do not differentiate one mob of Kooris from another; that they, unlike white people, share their material resources; and that Koori families are very close. Kooris are, of course, aware that their social lives are not that harmonious. None of these claims is borne out in practice—at least not all the time or even in a majority of cases. But conflicts and contradictions, even when they are well understood by Kooris, are not part of publicly acceptable discourses. Ideas, attitudes, and practices that deny the dominant ideology are knowingly and unknowingly suppressed by participants in the society.

Because they reveal contradictions, the tensions that emerge from time to time have to be dealt with if they are not to be damaging. If life is to go on with some semblance of normality and continuity, a game, as it were, has to be entered into in which the contradictions can be denied or redefined. There are several ways in which such contradictions emerge: some of these are more obvious than others, such as when people do not do the right thing by, say, refusing to share or by standing over others. One way is through insults hurled by one individual at another, whether calculated to cause harm or said in the heat of the moment.

There are very few fights that surprise Kooris. For the most part they are predictable. It is known which individuals and families fight with which others from time to time, and this can be demonstrated over generations in some cases. If there are newcomers, it is possible to predict the range of people with whom they might clash. This is not about personality problems or infringement of rights associated with difficult individuals, but with oppositions and factions that reflect the structure and history of the community. To settle a dispute between individuals might seem relatively easy—it is a matter of leveling up scores when someone's persona is threatened. But when a dispute can by understood only in terms of generations of conflicts between certain social groups or between insiders and newcomers, it touches on contradictions in the social order that may be very damaging when revealed openly. To concede, for instance, that a family is on the outer is to challenge the claims of egalitarianism among Kooris. This admission would demand a response: for instance, that the ideology of equality be recognized as false or that this family be treated differently—as equals.

In either case, the implications for a small-scale community could be enormous.

The contradictions in social life are kept invisible in favor of an ideology of "communitas" in an unchanging and knowable universe. It is important to keep the ideology intact. This was evident in concerns about white people's knowing about intracommunity conflicts—airing the dirty linen. The appearance of everything being in control is important, or else leaders, for instance, lose their credibility, resources may stop flowing, people may vote with their feet, and the prestige and government funding gained from looking strong and united may disappear.

What is significant then is that insults bring to the surface within the community certain tensions and contradictions that are better left alone. They represent the irresolvable. These words (or actions) that shame individuals suggest implicitly that all is not well in this community, that maybe people don't want to share, maybe they don't care enough for their children, maybe some are too powerful. But Kooris have always known this. Their myths—full of conflicts—once reminded them of the various facets of the spiritual and human condition. Now events like fighting and fight stories do. Kooris are taught to accept that people are the way they are—and that's that. Some things need to be lived with. It does no good to air them. In fact, it may do a great deal of harm. It is one thing to recognize that contradictions and inequalities are part of the human condition. It is quite another to suggest that somehow they could be resolved or done away with. That implies a new social order: that means death of the known order and of its power structures. The choice is a certain kind of repression and censorship, served well by the recourse to physical responses to insult and injury.

Insults do not create oppositions; they merely bring them to light, at least partially. But the harmony that is the ideological superstructure loses its force to control and to legitimize certain powerful individuals if the weakness of the underpinnings is revealed. The contradictions must be kept invisible. To try and resolve them is dangerous:

full of unseen and unforeseeable consequences. Kooris tackle the contradictions in their society head-on at one level, but only by making them tolerable, not by trying to resolve or dissolve them. They do not assume a utopia is possible or even desirable. Conflicts are part of the stuff of life. They need to be controlled, that's all. All that is necessary, as Kooris say, is to "keep things square" or "even" (Myers 1976:523–524). The insult-fight sequence is an important way in which tensions can be expressed and managed without disturbing this ideology of harmony and cooperation.

The question I am most frequently asked by non-Kooris is, "What do they fight about?" This question can be approached from various angles: the reasons given by fighters themselves before or after a fight; those given by onlookers; or underlying and unstated causes, which can be inferred after longer acquaintance with participants and with the community generally. However, it is the question itself that is interesting: it assumes that fights must have explicable causes, and it implicitly suggests that these causes will then justify or facilitate the appropriate evaluation of a fight. Kooris do not share this attitude, and statements concerning the precipitators of a fight are rarely given spontaneously. Kooris are reluctant to delve into the personal lives of others. There is little soul-searching in discussion, analyses of people's motives, or suggestions as to how people might change (also Hiatt 1965:111, on the Gidjingali, and Harris 1987/1977:4, on the Yolngu). Although they will talk about a fight, they seldom discuss a fighter's motives and may deliberately prevent or sidetrack others who might seem to be asking too much. A very frequent response to this irrelevant or nosy question about motives is, "I wouldn't know, probably nothing at all." Articulating the perceived cause of a fight involves a commitment: a recognition of involvement, of concern, or of criticism, which someone may not be prepared to divulge either in present company or at all.

To sort out conflict or antagonism by "talking it over" presents a difficulty in a system in which motive is not attributed or discussed. Motive involves a recognition of factors that lie below the everyday surface, invisible, potentially dangerous. Motive suggests that one is moved by something other than oneself. This may not be problematic within the Western philosophical tradition, which separates mind, body, spirit, self, other. It is more of a problem if people are seen holistically and as non-changeable, as is true of Kooris. To be influenced by something other (presumably including one's own unconscious) is to be out of control. The notion of motive is part of a different concept of self. It implies a self that is subject to external forces, not able to self-determine, a self that changes.

Because no underlying motives for the insult can be sought, an action that settles and restores without the necessity for an inquest into causes is required. It is important that the response that must repudiate the insult be such that it does not reveal further the unstated and nonvisible factors of which the insult is the visible tip. One might say that invisible problems require invisible responses. To make the invisible visible is to invite disorder and disruption—and possibly death, at least of the known order—into relative order and harmony, into life as it is known. The visible tip—the insult that threatens to reveal the contradictions—must be brought under control.

Fighting rather than talking avoids a confrontation with established meanings. It is a substitute for the words that would come dangerously close to the invisible; a ritual containment in which the incident and its resolution are regarded as a closed sequence. Even if it involves long-standing hostilities between protagonists, these are not necessarily mentioned except perhaps just to acknowledge "that one's bin brewing long time." Kooris do not feel a need to go beyond the sequence in order to explain it.

But the injury—the wound—must be squared up with injury. Fighting becomes an appropriate non–socially threatening injury with which to respond. Unlike spoken language, which reveals too much, fighting can operate at one remove from the complex of intrigues, ideologies, beliefs, jealousies, conflicts, hierarchies, and inequalities in social life, concealing them from scrutiny through its implicit form of censorship.

Because the insult is implicitly recognized as being about deep-seated conflicts, beyond the immediacy of the fighters' concerns, "solving" them through a direct airing, a confrontation, or a heart-to-heart chat is not an issue. What is important is to be able to live without their becoming unnecessarily divisive. The fight is able to make a statement about the insult without revealing underlying stimulants; it can affirm the reciprocal nature of social life and allow it to continue. The fight weaves the protagonists back into sociality and allows for the reestablishing of the orderly form of daily relations; it ritualizes and redirects unacceptable or disturbing aspects of the social experience, acting as a censor in its repression of ideas and activities that might threaten the social order and the status quo. It can do this because its meanings are multi-layered and ambiguous and because meaning signification is in the process itself rather than in any cause or end result. Any aspects of the fight—the relationships between the protagonists, or between them and other individuals, or between them and the society as a whole—can be emphasized, played down, ignored, or denied, consciously or unconsciously. Koori fighting is thus a form of implicit censorship by which the society prevents invisible contradictions from becoming visible and damaging. Almost any insult has the potential to make visible certain aspects of social life that may be harmful for the life of the community as a whole. The fight is able to make these invisible again, concealing what should remain unseen.

By fighting rather than talking, Kooris bypass underlying tensions which might encourage further divisiveness and destroy relations between individuals and groups whose identity and survival are dependent on their interdependence. Although Kooris frequently differentiate themselves from others, they are not disassociating themselves—the other is necessary in the whole process of self-definition. The paradox is that, in fighting to reassert one's sense of self, separate from the other, one is at the same time confronting the social, which is exercising a control over self. Confrontation is therefore reinvolving. In it Kooris recognize their existence as part of a social whole on which they are dependent. This applies as much to a minor dispute over a card game as it does to a fight that ends in bloodshed. In fighting to assert one's "right to be," one is also fighting for the right to be a member of the community rather than be excluded on the basis of shame or failure. A fight leads to social involvement—a fighting individual is involving himself or herself *as part of* the group rather than walking away. Fights establish or maintain communication rather than impede it. They deny the destructive power of an insult and place value on relationships. They are assertions of sociality. The fact of fighting among Kooris acknowledges tensions and allows the resultant conflicts to be expressed and set aside, at least temporarily. This constitutes it as a technique necessary for the maintenance of sociality.

This is also why a "dirty" fight often leads to another fight. The "dirty" fight has not effectively restored harmony, and the threat of social disorder exists while that state of affairs continues. The alternative response might be to ostracize an offender or shame the offender to the extent that he or she is rendered powerless to further threaten the social order—because no one will take any notice of him or her. Some people overdo it. They want to fight all the time and be highly visible. They are socially redefined. They have to be, or the system will lose its significance: too much egocentricity threatens sociality. Such people are described as "too ready to fight," as having "just a big mouth," or as being "off their head," implying they are out of control and beyond accountability in conventional social terms. Thus their insults or baiting can be ignored for the most part without loss of honor on the part of the receiver of the insult. In this way, troublemakers can be rendered relatively ineffective.

The conflicts and oppositions in Koori social life over time are remembered in fight stories, which today take on the form of modern myths, told and retold. To those who understand the history of events and relationships, these stories are full of meaning as well as explanation. In the same way, actual fights are as rich in meaning. There are hardly ever fights that could be called spontaneous, that have no background in the histories of the protagonists and their kin. The fight stands for their immediate griev- ances but also for the underlying factors that have prompted those concerns, however spontaneous and spe- cific to the present moment they may seem to the on- looker. The fight meanings transcend the particular mo- ment and point of contention, and the fighters come to symbolize oppositions in the community more generally, both expressing and censoring conflicts. This is why a good fight will always attract a large audience and why today's good fights become tomorrow's good stories.

REFERENCES

Harris, S. G. 1987. "Milingimbi Aboriginal learning contexts." Ph.D. dissertation, University of New Mexico, Albuquerque, New Mexico.

Hiatt, L. 1965. *Kinship and Conflict. A Study of an Aboriginal Community in Northern Arnhem Land.* Canberra, A.C.T., Australia: Australian National University Press.

Myers, F. 1976. "To have and to hold: A study of persistence and change in Pintupi social life. Ph.D. dissertation," Bryn Mawr College, Bryn Mawr, Pennsylvania.

Chapter 6 SOCIAL COMMENTARY IN AFRICAN-AMERICAN MOVEMENT PERFORMANCE

LeeEllen Friedland

When jazz was the mainstay of American popular music—roughly from the 1920s through the 1950s—tap dancing achieved tremendous recognition and visibility in mainstream American culture. Infused with many elements of traditional African-American aesthetics and repertoire, tap dancing became the visible, physical embodiment of the innovative artistic scene that characterized the jazz era and provided exposure for a corps of black tap dancers. As rhythm and blues and, later, rock and roll, eclipsed jazz in the 1950s, however, significantly fewer black tap dancers were featured performers in nightclubs and theaters. Consequently, this venerable African-American vernacular dance style became increasingly invisible to an American public accustomed to seeing expert adult artists performing on stage with big bands. It nonetheless remained a very visible and vibrant part of everyday life in American black communities, particularly among urban black children.[1] This chapter explores various aspects of the invisible/visible theme in relation to African-American children's movement performance.

When I began fieldwork in the black community of Philadelphia in 1979, dancing was a highly visible phenomenon among all age groups, but especially among children and adolescents. In every neighborhood throughout the city, kids belonged to informal dance clubs that specialized in a fast-stepping, soft-shoe style of exhibition dancing (in contrast to social dancing) that had clearly

136

descended from the older black tap dance styles chronicled by theater dance historians.[2] Black vernacular dance was alive and well, although no longer the same as the dance of the swing and big band eras. It was called "disco" in the late 1970s and early 1980s and later became a partner to rap music and the aesthetic milieu of hip-hop.[3]

During this period too, black vernacular dance was largely invisible to the mainstream American public—and historians—whose attention was directed toward the concert stage. This myopia was intensified by the focus on famous black adult dancers who, because of their extraordinary talent and perseverance, enjoyed some success outside the black community. Knowing that these performers had learned to dance as children in a traditional African-American aesthetic milieu, many observers assumed that those dancers represented the black dance tradition at its best.[4] Clearly, these observers (including theater dance historians) were using a model with which they were comfortable. They focused on the stars of stage and screen, on adult virtuoso performers in a fiercely competitive environment in which only the best made it to the top. It can be argued that these tap dancers, seen in terms of a hierarchical model of success derived from ballet and other Western theatrical dance forms, were viewed as black Baryshnikovs.[5] As children they had been brilliant students of their art—perhaps even prodigies—and as adults they attained the pinnacle of physical skill and artistic expression.[6]

Acceptance of this Baryshnikov model obscured the fact that within African-American communities the most intense involvement with exhibition dancing is achieved in children's culture, most particularly during the adolescent years. In fact, the professionalization of black vernacular dancing during the heyday of jazz music had provided a nontraditional context, one based largely outside the black community. It had allowed adult dancers to refine their performance skills beyond the level traditionally allowed by the leisure time normally available to an adult.[7] Thus, while many commentators assumed that professional tap dancing represented the pinnacle of the

African-American dance tradition, it was actually a customized repertoire selected primarily from one of three movement genres that make up that tradition, as will be described later.[8]

This faulty assumption arose again more recently during the mid-1980s when the mass media heightened visibility of break dancing for the mainstream American public.[9] As with the repertoire of professional black tap dancers, the repertoire popularized by break dancers represented only a minute portion of the African-American dance repertoire popular in black communities at the time. More than this, however, break dancing highlighted a portion of the repertoire that had relatively low status and prestige in the native aesthetic hierarchy, according to dancers raised within the broader community-based tradition.[10] Black youngsters in Philadelphia, as native participants in this tradition, initially judged break dancing in relation to traditional aesthetic criteria and did not find it particularly impressive. Nonnative audiences, however, saw break dancing as something entirely new. It was considered an exciting and authentic "minority youth" performance genre that generated tremendous enthusiasm and a demand for more performances.[11]

Movement performance in African-American culture is part of a complex of interrelated communicative and expressive systems that constitutes a whole world of artistic performance.[12] This aesthetic milieu consists of: (1) body movement; (2) sound, including several different types of music and a broad variety of rhythm and percussion playing; (3) visual forms, including drawing and wall writing, costume, and hairstyle; (4) language, including mastery of certain ways of speaking, and certain verbal art forms such as raps, ritual insults, toasts, and related poetic and narrative types; and (5) "attitude," which includes aspects of social behavior and ethics, creativity, and aesthetic worldview.[13]

All these interrelated communicative and expressive systems—movement, sound, visual arts, language, and attitude—are explored by young African-Americans in the pursuit of "style." Style is the means by which an individual progresses in the spiritual quest for aesthetic communication. The social prestige of being recognized as an artist in the culture, and in the community, can be achieved only through the cultivation of "style."[14] After tending to the necessities of food and shelter and the social relationships and obligations of the family network, involvement in this aesthetic world is one of the dominant preoccupations of urban black children.

The self-contained children's play culture found in Philadelphia's black community is largely invisible to outsiders who rarely sustain extended contact with children, either outside an institutional environment such as school or without requiring children to interact with the adult world in some way. Indeed, some elements of this world are often invisible even to black adults who are hard-pressed to keep apace of the complex layers of internal references to popular culture icons. There are quick-changing fashions in everything, from the brand names of sneakers to toys and cartoon characters. There is also a fluid system of naming practices—in itself a form of game—for types of play, new dances, and the mimetic components of the movement repertoire.[15]

BEING RHYTHMIC

Most children begin their career in artistic movement performance by responding to musical patterns of rhythm and melody. Children of only two or three years of age soon learn that dancing is a behavior that garners praise and encouragement from older children and adults. Initially, such efforts are dominated by fundamental physical skills such as maintaining balance unaided on two feet and trying to move specific body parts independently. Later, children become astute at copying socialized movement forms and utilize short movement motifs, such as those that might be incorporated into longer motifs in social dancing. Motifs might include rhythmic weight shifts or torso movements, arm gestures, foot tapping, or hand clapping and are usually learned by watching older children and adults in social dance contexts.[16]

Though these movement motifs serve as the building blocks of a young child's performance repertoire, they also play a distinct role for older, more highly skilled children and adults. For older dancers, these movement motifs constitute a genre of short, undeveloped (in relation to other, more extended movement patterns), and nonnarrative rhythmic responses to musical rhythms. There is no indigenous label for this genre, but kids maintain that it is *not* dancing as such but is "just moving your body" or "moving to the music" (Friedland 1983:28).[17] It is best characterized as "being rhythmic," a performance that creates a dialogue between two expressive systems—sound (music or percussion) and body movement.

This performance genre is generally learned in informal contexts, because it is often a fleeting rhythmic comment in the midst of otherwise ordinary activity, such as listening to the radio or to taped music. Young children who are just starting to be integrated into older children's play culture have ample opportunity to observe appropriate contexts for, and variations of, "being rhythmic." These fleeting comments can suggest more developed games that play with rhythm or even instigate full-fledged dancing.

DANCING

This second movement genre can be subdivided into the areas of social dancing and exhibition dancing. Social dancing is the consummation of the impulse expressed in being rhythmic; it is the context in which the full rhythmic interaction between body movement and musical contours is developed (Friedland 1983:31). It is also the form through which dancers express themselves personally and pursue social interaction, usually with a partner of the opposite sex. Social dance forms are quite fluid in the sense that they continually go through a process of absorbing new influences and recycling old movement patterns.[18]

Children as young as three to five years old begin to learn the contemporary repertoire from older children and adults, but generally lack the understanding necessary to perform dance moves with the intent of cultivating social relationships or personal expression. Six- and seven-year-olds, who have already become full participants in children's play culture, start to become more excited about the challenge of keeping current with the ever-evolving social dance repertoire, but the potential for personal and social expression in dance performance is still not the most compelling feature for young children. Rather, these children begin to appreciate the important status attributed to the multifaceted world of artistic performance in general, and they crave the prestige and recognition that are bestowed by the community on those who exhibit artistic prowess.

Children between the ages of eight and eleven become more aggressive participants in the world of artistic performance and often begin to innovate and contribute to the repertory. They begin to have a better sense of the cultivation of personal style and a more sophisticated understanding of the cultural meanings invested in specific movement styles and images. Though the younger children in this age group do not necessarily consider flirting a standard component of social dancing, they are well aware of its potential, and they pursue social interaction with their dancing partners on a level acceptable to the peer group.

Most eight- to eleven-year-old children become consumed by involvement in an aesthetic world, variously named by different generations as "jazz," "bop," "soul," "disco," and "hip-hop." They are star-struck by popular black music performers and the allure of attaining an artist's status in their own peer group, in children's culture generally, and in their community. Social dancing becomes a type of currency during playtime; children will practice new dances, trading distinctive dance moves like baseball cards, in search of the right new component to increase the cumulative value of their collection.

Children in this age group also become active teachers of younger children. Whereas three- to five-year-olds are for the most part still copying without understanding, and six- to seven-year-olds are often still tentative in their aesthetic judgements, the eight- to eleven-year-olds are vigorous defenders of the aesthetic faith: artistic performance is important, exciting, vital. This is also the age group in which children begin to explore other, related artistic specialties. Those interested in visual arts start to keep notebooks of drawings and wall-writing (or graffiti) designs. Such children become forthright exponents of different verbal art genres, and some start to write elementary raps that are often preserved in a special notebook. Though many develop a keen interest in the complex electronic musical mixing skills of the deejay and pay close attention to the technical workings of the related audio equipment, they are generally considered too young to be permitted access to that equipment.[19] Those who sustain a serious interest in learning the arts of the deejay must wait until they are older and win the trust of a mentor.

Twelve is usually a transitional age, bridging the gap between child and teenager, the latter holding the preeminent position in children's culture. Teenagers find increasing social opportunities through social dancing and become more competitive and proprietary about individual repertoire and performance. It is much less common for teenagers to inject social dance forms into playtime; dance becomes reserved for moments of personal expression that are increasingly confined to dance parties and similar mixed gender social contexts. Girls are more likely to occasionally perform social dances in play contexts— sometimes as a brief interlude during other activities to show particular liking for a song playing on the radio, sometimes in a dance with other teenage girlfriends to show solidarity or display feminine and artistic qualities, and sometimes to demystify a new social dance form for younger children. Teenagers are usually the most active innovators of new social dance forms. This is one feature of keeping up-to-the-second with the contemporary, popular black music performance scene. They keep a sharp eye out for new dance ideas, which can be collected from a variety of sources, including kids from other neighborhoods, black musical performers seen on television or in films, and even adults, who might demonstrate an "antiquated" motif popular in their younger years that will be reinterpreted and renamed by current teenagers. Innovating new dance moves or styles is serious business, and many dancers aspire to lofty status in the local avant-garde.

Exhibition dancing contrasts with social dancing in several ways. It is considered a specialty, not learned by everyone but performed as a theatrical display with a marked differentiation between performer and audience. The core of the exhibition repertoire consists of fast stepping, performed in tap shoes by older generations of dancers but more commonly done in soft shoes, such as sneakers, by more recent generations of dancers (though there are some who used tap shoes through most of the 1980s). In the black community generally, adults sometimes perform fast stepping as a brief display in the midst of social dancing or in other contexts in which individual dancers challenge each other in artistic competition. Children of all ages are eager and appreciative audiences for such performances and will often pick up ideas to incorporate into their own dancing or movement play. Children who show special interest in learning fast stepping might seek out an adult performer as a mentor and then practice each new piece of repertoire until the opportunity arises for another infusion of knowledge.

It is teenagers, however, who become the most direct intermediaries between the older tradition bearers in the community and children's culture at large, because, among all age groups of children, they possess the highest level of performance skills and leadership abilities. Frequently, one individual acts as a catalyst in this transmission process, often someone who has pursued an apprenticeship with an adult dancer and has made a specialty of fast stepping throughout the teenage years. Exhibition dancing is traditionally considered a male form, though females participate freely, according to personal interest. It is extremely rare, however, for a female dancer to serve in a leadership role.

As an older teenager approaches "retirement" from the performance world of children's culture, he or she generally recruits younger dancers who show some ability or flair for the fast-stepping repertoire and tutors them. Usually such a dance leader also choreographs routines for the recruits, using fast-stepping sequences interspersed with theatrical slides, dramatic gestures, and the use of props such as sticks, canes, or hats. The leader may incorporate acrobatic or mimetic components from movement play that most children already know. In addition, the older dancers in this select group recruit younger children, who start with the fundamentals or sometimes bring to the corps a certain specialty such as tumbling. Even very young children of, say, four or five years of age are sometimes recruited for exhibition dancing if they seem eagerly disposed toward it. Experienced exhibition dancers soon learn that very young performers are sure to please any crowd, because they look "cute" trying to execute their moves.

Clubs are sometimes formed around such confederations of youngsters devoted to exhibition dancing, generally when there is a reliable core of dancers who are fluent with a repertoire of specialized routines. Within the community, the clubs tend to function in an informal way, meeting whenever and wherever a quorum of members congregates, often appropriating someone's porch or a corner of the playground. The clubs are generally run by the oldest dancer (who is usually also the head teacher and choreographer) with the assistance of older dancers, who help with organizational tasks and oversee the youngest children. Normally there is no input from, or supervision by, adults. The clubs do not have much impact on the traditional informal networks of learning and teaching exhibition dancing in children's culture, but they do provide a vehicle for controlling membership, so only the better dancers participate. Troublemakers, no matter how good they might be, are excluded. Older dancers also help to organize appearances at more formal venues such as talent shows, and any traveling outside the community—usually to downtown locations where the prospects of making money from passing the hat are fairly good.

MOVEMENT PLAY

The third movement genre used in artistic performance I have called movement play. It is by far the most prominent movement genre used in children's play activity. Movement play is distinguished by the presence of social commentary that is expressed solely through movement performance. There may be verbal commentary accompanying movement play that contributes to the overall message, but it is not considered integral and is not very common. There is a vast variety of forms within the genre. To the casual outside observer, many of the forms appear as nothing more than kids fooling around in a playground. The repertoire includes general acrobatic stunts (the corpus from which break dancing developed), mime and mimicry, and highly stylized and distinctively African-American forms such as popping. "Popping" is an umbrella term covering moves such as "the moonwalk" (which singer Michael Jackson made famous to non-black audiences), moving in slow motion, and moving like a robot by using body parts in a highly segmented manner so that most of the body is held perfectly still while one or two body units move in isolation and freeze abruptly in the next position. In one variation of this, the isolated body part moves into its next position and the connecting joint is made to snap, or "pop," as the limb is frozen still. All of these forms, and many others, are used in performing social commentary that is quite explicit.

In the everyday contexts of children's play, forms of movement play provide an almost endless variety of

activity. Most young children delight in the mimicry of
things familiar to them and readily adopt this kind of
movement game. But because effective imitations require
a considerable amount of skill, it is usually not until
children reach the age of eight that they are able to do
justice to a subject. Mimicry is something of a specialty for
the eight to eleven age group; they seem to find intense
satisfaction in the narrative and improvisational features
of this type of play. Children practice these moves with
great concentration and often check their progress in a
mirror. Some forms of the pop, on the other hand, are so
difficult to perform well that children from eight to eleven
often specialize in just one type until they master it, before
trying another. Many of the more demanding forms are left
to highly skilled teenagers, who are happy to capture
special attention for performing less common and relatively esoteric physical feats.

Unlike the other two movement performance genres—
being rhythmic, and dancing—movement play is not usually influenced significantly by musical patterns of
rhythm or melody. This does not limit its status in performance, however. In addition to fueling games and challenges during playtime, movement play is also incorporated into fast-stepping sequences to build a dramatic
climax or highlight a novel routine. A brief examination of
the performance of social commentary in movement play
illustrates the richness of this narrative component of the
African-American dance tradition.

SOCIAL COMMENTARY IN MOVEMENT PLAY

There are four main types of social commentary expressed
in movement play and each is configured in some way by
an opposition between the visible and the invisible. Social
commentary can occur when cultural movement forms
are annotated. Performing a sequence of everyday movements in robot style or slow motion is an example of this
because by distorting the usual time frame or anatomical
sequence, the performer is saying, "Look at this more

closely. How is it different from everyday life? Don't you see something you usually take for granted?''

Annotation also occurs when a performer exaggerates a current, popular social dance form. There are several potential layers of meaning and commentary contained in such an act. First, social dancing is a subject of vital interest among children and adolescents, for even when there is no interest in flirtation, social dancing is one of the most satisfying ways to relate to music. Social dance forms divide and multiply quickly, and an essential part of being stylish and a good dancer is keeping up-to-date with every innovation and variation. That knowledge is generally confined to children's culture, because children maintain an intense artistic community that is quite distinct from that of adults. It would be easy, therefore, for a movement reference to a current social dance form to become immediately visible to other black kids but remain invisible to black adults.

Also, social dance forms are often derived from motifs that can be pinpointed to a specific source. A dance step might be associated with a certain song or singer, as when a movement motif is borrowed from a music video or television variety show performance. A motif may be suggested by the content of a song's lyrics, as was recently the case with Da Butt, a dance popularized in a song of the same name that jumped onto the black music charts after being featured in Spike Lee's film *School Daze* (1988). In addition, a social dance form can be closely associated with either the individual who first performed it or with someone who becomes known for doing it particularly well. When a performer exaggerates a social dance form in movement play, the commentary may be visible only to those who are sufficiently stylish or hip to be current with the black popular culture database. In that case, adults could certainly be in the know also. Commentary referring to a local individual's predilection for a certain step, however, would be visible only to the small community of children who regularly dance and play together.

Annotation can also be seen in the use of movements characteristic of specific age and gender groups in Afri-

can-American culture. Perhaps the most intense illustration of this is found in a move that youngsters call "the
gigolo."[20] To do the gigolo, one must allow one's entire
body to be overtaken by an inner trembling: head, torso,
arms, and legs all tremble in helpless abandon. (The name
"gigolo" has more to do with jiggling than with any other
meaning of the word.) This type of trembling is generally
reserved for religious contexts and is usually a marker of
spiritual possession and trance behavior. It is also most
commonly exhibited by older black women and virtually
always in church. The social commentary implied by
using the gigolo in movement play is entirely invisible to
an average white audience. They would not have enough
knowledge about black age and gender group repertoire,
nor about black religious behavior, to comprehend. The
primary commentary visible to other black children is that
of thumbing one's nose at adults, especially older black
women, with whom the trembling is most closely associated. Black adults generally see not only age and gender
comment but also the risque nature of extracting an
explicitly sacred movement from its religious context.
The specific religious denomination to which black adult
audience members belong is also a factor in the interpretation of the gigolo. To some, especially black Catholics, for
example, the gigolo may be tinged with ridicule, since
trance and possession behavior are often frowned upon by
their official religion. By far the most intense reaction to
the gigolo comes from older black women who immediately recognize that the commentary is directed at them.
Normally, most children would not dare criticize or be
disrespectful to their elders, but when this is done within
the ritual of performance, youngsters are safe from repri-
sals or discipline. Older black women, of course, realize
the clever defense in this public transgression. The commentary relates to sacred/secular distinctions especially
visible to older black women, who are reminded that such
trembling movements are indeed part of the cultural
movement repertoire of mortals and not infused exclusively from a spiritual source. Despite the suggestion of

criticism, black women usually respond to the gigolo with loud and enthusiastic howls of laughter.

A second type of social commentary in movement play occurs when icons of popular culture are imitated. In this case, a performer imitates a sequence of movements from a popular celebrity's performance. The goal is to reproduce the famous star's moves accurately rather than to exaggerate them in any way. To an audience that recognizes the faithful rendition of a movement trademark, the editorial comment is quite visible. Depending on the larger narrative sequence in which such an imitation is placed, the commentary might be positive, negative, or neutral. The fact that youngsters select such telling movement examples is testimony to their extraordinary skill in precisely articulating the movement features that best capture the essence of a character or personality.

A common example of a popular culture icon imitated through movement in the 1980s is singer Michael Jackson, although it is interesting to note that he is not portrayed with his famous "moonwalk," because that was already common property in the local repertoire before he performed it on television, in 1982. Instead, Michael Jackson is invoked through his distinctive pelvic tilt and thrust, which is done with a particular body attitude, rotated leg and arm gestures, and sharply angled hand positions. The singer Prince is also imitated through general body attitude, head tilts, and facial expressions, as well as with the occasional illustrative gestures he sprinkles in the performance of certain songs.[21] Actor Bill Cosby is imitated with a performance of a short dance he did in the original introductory segment to his weekly television series "The Cosby Show" (which was set to Latin music). Cosby's dance was itself a parody of age and gender group repertoire in which he held his torso very stiff, slightly bent forward from the waist, with arms rotated from the shoulder, wrists flexed, and hands held stiff in a slightly cupped position. Cosby superimposed this exaggerated body attitude of an old man onto an attempt to wiggle his torso in a manner characteristic of a young man trying to "be sexy."

The kids adopted this motif from Cosby's dance for a social dance they called "The Huxtable," after Cosby's TV character, Dr. Cliff Huxtable.

A third type of social commentary occurs when local personalities are mocked. Developing an individual style is very important to youngsters looking for status in the world of artistic performance and this often makes it easy to pinpoint someone's movement signature or trademark. In movement play, a performer mocks someone else's movement style, either by exaggerating it so that it looks foolish or by doing it accurately while performing (or imitating) some other, incongruous or embarrassing task, such as going to the bathroom. This type of commentary is, of course, invisible both to anyone who is not familiar with the individual targeted for mockery and to anyone who is less articulate about specific movement features.

Social attitudes also can be ridiculed in movement play. Some related examples have already been mentioned, but this type of commentary is always negative in nature, since it is directed at a general social or cultural concept rather than an individual. Respect for elders is one such general concept and might be ridiculed through a movement narrative showing how an old man is so stiff he can not perform the simplest task and then looks like a fool. Homosexual men might be parodied with stereotypically effeminate gestures and facial expressions that are usually highly exaggerated. No narrative comment is necessary in this case, because simply broaching the subject through movement performance is in itself a scathing attack. In this urban black community there is no public sympathy for homosexual men. It is interesting to note that there is no parallel movement stereotype for homosexual women; they are a nonissue. Another common theme for ridicule is the manner in which men and women try to present themselves as irresistible to the opposite sex. Usually this is parodied through a narrative sequence that shows that despite the outer trappings of beauty, the person is actually ugly or, at least, foolish.

Commentary directed toward respect for elders would generally be visible to a broad audience of all age groups, both black and white. Commentary regarding homosexual men would, likewise, be visible to a general audience. The portrayal of an attitude that implies sexual attractiveness would generally be visible to a broad audience, but the specific commentary regarding ideals of beauty versus ugliness is usually invisible to white audiences. For example, a white audience usually equates ugliness with being fat, whereas a black audience typically judges beauty on the basis of grace and coordination, and does not necessarily consider excess fat a detriment.

CONCLUSION

This discussion has only scratched the surface of some visible/invisible aspects in African-American movement performance, but two things seem clear. First, an examination of the community-based movement performance tradition in Philadelphia's black community has provided a glimpse of how children's play culture provides a forum for the perpetuation and ongoing development of dance and movement forms, which may or may not become visible to the mainstream culture. Second, it is clear that the visibility of social commentary in movement play is dependent not only on visible visual data about body movement but also on invisible conceptual data that can be portrayed both figuratively and literally through movement performance. This study also highlights the complexities of mapping the visible and the invisible in movement performance; it is as much a matter of "seeing" social relationships and aesthetic values as it is of observing a dance step.

NOTES

1. See Friedland 1983. Children's dancing is also discussed in Jones and Hawes 1972, Hale-Benson 1986, and Hazzard-Gordon 1990.
2. See, for example, Stearns and Stearns 1964.
3. See Friedland 1983, 1984; Hager 1984; and Banes 1985. The transition from disco to hip-hop in Philadelphia's black community is discussed in some detail in Friedland 1984a.
4. See, for example, Charles "Honi" Coles's account of neighborhood competition in Philadelphia in Stearns and Stearns 1964:306.
5. The reference here is to Mikhail Baryshnikov, the famous Russian-trained ballet dancer, resident in the United States, who is considered by many to have achieved a pinnacle of perfection in technical skill.
6. This model of the black tap dancer is also presented in the film, *No Maps on My Taps,* produced by G. Nierenberg, 1979.
7. In Philadelphia's black community, for example, it is common for dancers who have pursued special skills in exhibition dance performance to have "retired" from the spotlight in children's culture by the time they edge into their twenties. Extensive discussion of the development of black vernacular dance style in American popular entertainment can be found in Nathan 1962, Stearns and Stearns 1964, Toll 1974, and Emery 1988 [1972].
8. The three categories of movement performance native to Philadelphia's black community are described in detail in Friedland 1983.
9. National clamor over break dancing resulted from the intense popularity of the film *Flashdance* (released in the summer of 1983), in which there was a brief scene showing break dancing on a Pittsburgh street. The status of break dancing was further enhanced when the film's female protagonist used a distinctive move—a back spin—as the choreographic climax in her ultimately triumphant audition for a prestigious dance company. Sally Banes's article "To the Beat, Y'all" (1981) was the first published article to bring break dancing to the attention of a large, nonparticipant audience. See Banes 1985.

    Before the impact of *Flashdance,* interest in break dancing outside black communities was confined largely both to New York City, where local media coverage advertised the form to a general public, and to two special interest groups that included break dancing in their programs and performances: the New York City avant-garde who featured break dancing, rapping, and graffiti in downtown performance spaces; and folklife specialists who incorporated break dancing into folklife programs such as the Folklife in the Bronx Conference (spring 1981). Similar folklife programs in Philadelphia, such as the Atwater-Kent Museum concert series (summer 1980) and the Children's Folklore Series at the Folklife Center/International House (fall 1981) featured related traditional African-American movement performance forms.

10. In general, portions of the movement performance repertoire that require primarily athletic or acrobatic skills are considered to be of lower status than those moves that require more refined physical skills, such as those used to create music-related rhythmic patterns, as is done in fast stepping. When athletic and acrobatic moves are integrated into fast-stepping sequences, they are considered part of the larger whole and acquire higher status. In break dancing, however, the athletic and acrobatic moves are isolated and highlighted.

11. See Friedland 1984a.

12. The interrelationship of expressive systems in African and African-derived artistic performance is discussed in Keil 1966, Szwed 1966, Armstrong 1971, Thompson 1974, Chernoff 1979, Keil 1979, Drewal and Drewal 1983, Thompson 1983, and Dobbin 1986.

13. For discussions of body movement see Friedland 1983, 1984, and Banes 1985. Contemporary music styles are examined in Hager 1984, George 1988, and Keyes 1990. Studies of visual arts include Castleman 1982, Hager 1984, Flinker 1985, Romanowski and Flinker 1985, and the film *Style Wars,* produced by Silver and Chalfant 1985. The performance of verbal art is discussed in essays in Kochman 1972, Folb 1980, Bell 1983, and Shuman 1986. "Attitude" is discussed in most of the aforementioned works and in Rose 1987.

14. For discussion of "style" see the works cited in note 13 on expressive systems in artistic performance and Hebdige 1979.

15. Examination of the interrelationship between movement performance and other expressive systems is outside the scope of this chapter.

16. Movement genres and their interrelationship with music are discussed in detail in Friedland 1983.
17. Descriptions are based on fieldwork conducted in Philadelphia's black community from 1979 through 1984. Comparative fieldwork was also conducted with black and Hispanic adolescents in New York City in 1983–84, and with black adolescents in Washington, D.C., in 1987–89 and 1993.
18. See Stearns and Stearns 1964 and Hazzard-Gordon 1990.
19. "Mixing" consists of a variety of techniques for playing sound recordings; creating new, nonrecorded sounds by distorting prerecorded sounds; and integrating (or "mixing") the varied sound output. Deejays use electronic sound systems that consist of two turntables, speakers, an amplifier, a mixer, headphones, and sometimes synthesizers. The name "deejay" or "DJ" is descended from the abbreviation for "disc jockey." The full term has fallen into increasing disuse since the early 1980s. See Friedland 1984b and 1984c, Hager 1984, and Keyes 1990.
20. Names like "the gigolo" are fluid and subject to change in response to new images. These names often do not stay in use very long. In general, movement forms outlast their names and can sometimes go for periods without having a specific name. Names also have a life of their own and can be recycled endlessly. The name "the gigolo" was current in Philadelphia from the late 1970s through the mid-1980s, an extraordinarily long tenure.

    In contrast, kids did "the moonwalk" long before Michael Jackson first performed it on television, and prior to that point called it "the worm." As soon as "moonwalk" became associated with Jackson's performance, the name was adopted immediately. Soon after, the name "worm" was bestowed upon another move that looked like an imitation of a worm. The latter move, although already in the repertoire, had not previously been known by a specific name.
21. For example, note the gestures in Prince and the Revolution's performance of "I Would Die 4 U" in the film *Purple Rain,* produced by R. Cavallo, J. Ruffalo, and S. Fargnoli 1984.

REFERENCES

Armstrong, R. Plant. 1971. *The Affecting Presence: An Essay in Humanistic Anthropology.* Urbana, Ill.: University of Illinois Press.

Banes, S. 1981. To the beat, y'all. *Village Voice* April:22–28.

———. 1985. Breaking. In N. George, S. Banes, S. Flinker, and P. Romanowski, *Fresh—Hip Hop Don't Stop.* New York: Random House, Sarah Lazin.

———. 1986. Breakdancing: A reporter's story. *Folklife Annual 1986*:8–21.

Bell, M. J. 1983. *The World from Brown's Lounge: An Ethnography of Black Middle-Class Play.* Urbana, Ill.: University of Illinois Press.

Castleman, C. 1982. *Getting Up: Subway Graffiti in New York.* Cambridge, Mass.: Massachusetts Institute of Technology Press.

Chernoff, J. Miller. 1979. *African Rhythm and African Sensibility.* Chicago: University of Chicago Press.

Dobbin, J. D. 1986. *The Jombee Dance of Montserrat: A Study of Trance in the West Indies.* Columbus, Ohio: Ohio State University Press.

Drewal, H. J., and M. Thompson Drewal. 1983. *Gelede: Art and Female Power among the Yoruba.* Bloomington, Ind.: Indiana University Press.

Emery, L. Fauley. 1988 [1972]. *Black Dance in the United States from 1619 to 1970.* Reprint. Pennington, N.J.: Princeton Book Company, Dance Horizons.

Flashdance. 1983. D. Simpson and J. Bruckheimer, producers. Paramount, Polygram Pictures (film).

Flinker, S. 1985. Fashion. In N. George, S. Banes, S. Flinker, and P. Romanowski, *Fresh—Hip Hop Don't Stop.* New York: Random House, Sarah Lazin.

Folb, E. A. 1980. *Runnin' Down Some Lines: The Language and Culture of Black Teenagers.* Cambridge, Mass.: Harvard University Press.

Friedland, L. 1983. Disco: Afro-American vernacular performance. *Dance Research Journal* 15, no. 2:27–35.

———. 1984a. Mass media and vernacular tradition: Street dancing in the global village. Paper presented at annual meeting of the American Folklore Society, San Diego, California, October.

————. 1984b. Scratch DJs on the wheels of steel: Musical performance and audio technology in Afro-American dance events. Paper presented at annual meeting of the Society for Ethnomusicology, Los Angeles, California, October.

————. 1984c. Street dancing, rapping and DJ mixing: Traditional African American performance and contemporary culture. In *Smithsonian Festival of American Folklife Program* 43–45.

————. 1986. Black music in a big city: Radio as a medium of cultural influence. Paper presented at annual meeting of the Popular Culture and American Culture Societies, Atlanta, Georgia, April.

George, N. 1985. Rapping. In N. George, S. Banes, S. Flinker, and P. Romanowski, *Fresh—Hip Hop Don't Stop.* New York: Random House, Sarah Lazin.

————. 1988. *The Death of Rhythm and Blues.* New York: Pantheon.

Hager, S. 1984. *Hip Hop: The Illustrated History of Break Dancing, Rap Music and Graffiti.* New York: St. Martin's.

Hale-Benson, J. E. 1986. *Black Children: Their Roots, Culture and Learning Styles.* Rev. ed. Baltimore: Johns Hopkins University Press.

Hazzard-Gordon, K. 1990. *Jookin': The Rise of Social Dance Formations in Afro-American Culture.* Philadelphia: Temple University Press.

Hebdige, D. 1979. *Subculture: The Meaning of Style.* London: Methuen.

Jones, B., and B. Lomax Hawes. 1972. *Step It Down: Games, Plays, Songs, and Stories from Afro-American Heritage.* New York: Harper & Row.

Keil, C. 1966. *Urban Blues.* Chicago: University of Chicago Press.

————. 1979. *Tiv Song: The Sociology of Art in a Classless Society.* Chicago: University of Chicago.

Keyes, C. L. 1990. Rappin' to the beat: Rap music as expressive culture among African Americans. Ph.D. dissertation, Indiana University.

Kochman, T., ed. 1972. *Rappin' and Stylin' Out: Communication in Black America.* Urbana, Ill.: University of Illinois Press.

Nathan, H. 1962. *Dan Emmett and the Rise of Early Negro Minstrelsy.* Norman, Okla.: University of Oklahoma Press.

No Maps on My Taps. 1979. G. T. Nierenberg, producer. GTN Productions (film).

Purple Rain. 1984. R. Cavallo, J. Ruffalo, and S. Fargnoli, producers. Warner Brothers (film).

Romanowski, P., and S. Flinker. 1985. Graffiti. In N. George, S. Banes, S. Flinker, and P. Romanowski, *Fresh—Hip Hop Don't Stop.* New York: Random House, Sarah Lazin.

Rose, D. 1987. *Black American Street Life: South Philadelphia, 1969–71.* Philadelphia: University of Pennsylvania Press.

School Daze. 1988. S. Lee, producer. Columbia Pictures, Forty Acres and a Mule Filmworks (film).

Shuman, Amy. 1986. *Storytelling Rights: The Uses of Oral and Written Texts by Urban Adolescents.* Cambridge: Cambridge University Press.

Stack, C. B. 1974. *All Our Kin: Strategies for Survival in a Black Community.* New York: Harper & Row.

Stearns, M., and J. Stearns. 1964. *Jazz Dance: The Story of American Vernacular Dance.* New York: Schirmer.

Style Wars! 1985. T. Silver and H. Chalfant, producers. New Day Films (film).

Szwed, J. F. 1966. Musical style and racial conflict. *Phylon* 27:358–366.

Thompson, R. Farris. 1974. *African Art in Motion.* Berkeley, Calif.: University of California Press.

———. 1983. *Flash of the Spirit: African and Afro-American Art and Philosophy.* New York: Random House.

Toll, R. C. 1974. *Blacking Up: The Minstrel Show in Nineteenth Century America.* Oxford, UK: Oxford University Press.

Chapter 7 THINKING WITH MOVEMENT: IMPROVISING VERSUS COMPOSING?

Rajika Puri and Diana Hart-Johnson

In this chapter we address some common misconceptions about the acts of improvisation and composition in dance, because we believe such misconceptions lead to funda-mental misunderstandings about the very processes in-volved in thinking with movement. We want to illustrate that far from representing a dichotomy, improvising and composing are closely related. Whether a dance is consid-ered to be improvised or composed depends on culturally specific distinctions that reflect the values of a given society. The application of culture-bound assumptions to an investigation of "the dance"[1] or of human movement in general can lead to conclusions that are not only inappli-cable with reference to the body languages of other peo-ples but also indicative of a lack of comprehension of the movement idioms within one's own society.

COMMON MISCONCEPTIONS

During a lecture demonstration on anthropology and art conducted by Drid Williams, each of us was asked to perform a short stretch of danced movement without any explanation to accompany it. One of the excerpts was from an idiom of dance from southern India, the other a

This chapter was first published in the Journal for the Anthropological Study of Human Movement 1982, Volume 2(2). Reprinted with permission.

sequence of American modern dance. Following our short performances, Williams then demonstrated how a semasiologist might question us in order to elicit information about the sequences we had performed, their context, and their structure as a preliminary step towards gaining anthropological understanding of the idioms of body language to which they belonged. Members of the audience (consisting of students, teachers, choreographers, and dance performers) were also invited to give their impressions of what they had seen, to describe how they might initially classify the sequences, and to ask any questions they might have.

Some interesting points arose. Many in the audience thought that whereas the movements in the southern India excerpt[2] were prescribed by tradition and therefore "set," the modern dance sequence must surely have been improvised. Several audience members ventured that the former was *obviously* rule-bound, and that the latter was not.[3] The misconception lay in the fact that the southern India excerpt *had been improvised* and the modern dance sequence had been taken from a composition of Hart-Johnson's that had been choreographed a year prior to the occasion. The teaching experiment that Williams had set up was instructive; where we had expected a lack of proper understanding of an idiom we knew was unfamiliar to nearly all of those present (the southern India form), we were surprised at the misapprehension of their own body language and idioms by American dancers and practitioners themselves.

ADDITIONAL PROBLEMS

A second impetus for writing this chapter was provided by two articles written by well-known philosophers—Maxine Sheets-Johnstone and Joseph Margolis—in which they make certain statements about dance improvisation and about "thinking *in* [not with] movement" that we, both as professional dancers and as anthropologists of human movement, cannot accept.

Sheets-Johnstone says, for example, that improvisation is "unrehearsed and spontaneous . . . a form which lives and breathes only in the momentary flow of its creation" (1981:400). She argues that "to create a dance improvisation is thus not to create an artistic product, that is, to bring into being a form which might be rendered in future performances by different dancers. It is to create an ongoing present from the world of possibilities at any given moment." In a dance improvisation, "the process of creating is not the means of realising *a* dance, it is *the* dance itself" (1981:400).

One of the main assumptions that Sheets-Johnstone seems to make is that in an improvisation the only reference to "rules" consists of the rules of the improvisation itself, meaning, to do anything that one wishes, or, as she puts it, "to dance the dance as it comes into being at this particular moment at this particular place," with some additional constraints such as decisions to do a "contact improvisation"[4] or to alternate between group and individually performed movements. Composing, on the other hand, is apparently different because it allows one to edit, to ponder over any movement, and to change or even delete it. This leads her to the statement: "Thinking in movement as the process of creating the dance is thus different from thinking in movement as part of the process of choreography" (1981:401).

It is difficult to grasp the distinction Sheets-Johnstone wishes to make until one learns that "thinking in movement is obviously a bodily phenomenon" in which spontaneity is the result of a "kinetic declaration of animate existence"—clearly not a characteristic one can attribute to the process that someone like Balanchine goes through when he choreographs and so produces a dance. Sheets-Johnstone therefore not only sets up a dichotomy between improvising and composing but suggests that whereas in the composing process there is a "product" that somehow comes between the dancer and the dancing, in the former process of improvising there is no such "product" in the dancer's mind, so that thinking and doing are indistinguishable. Improvising in dance is thus not only a bodily phenomenon, but also "*the* dance."

In an article published in the same issue of the same journal, Margolis assumes a similar position. He says that dance movements are generated "in terms of the dynamics of motor activity controlled proprioceptively," and believes that a written score cannot "exhibit formal properties" without the assistance of actually seeing the movement performed (1981:419). We wonder whether Margolis can read any of the extant movement scripts and to which of these he refers.[5] Margolis declares that what is notated in a written score emphasizes "visual recognition *tout court*," and so he concludes that "the dance may be less accommodating notationally than music or drama because it is more autographic in spite of being a performing art" (1981:424). We were somewhat puzzled by these statements until we realized that these writers managed to confuse aspects of dance that performers and analysts of movement manage to keep distinct.[6]

At the same time, certain other distinctions are made that seem to demonstrate a lack of understanding of how dancers, choreographers and dance teachers think about dance; many of the aforementioned statements refer to dan*cing,* regarded by both writers as simply a "motor activity." No distinction is made between dan*cing, the* dance, *a* dance, and danced movements (see note 1). Propositions that refer to aspects of dan*cing* are then assumed to hold for "the dance" and "danced movements" in general as well. Since a dance score is expected by them to refer only to the motor activity, *the* dance is consequently found to be less accommodating notationally than is either music or spoken language.[7]

We believe that these writers do not take into account the fact that dan*cing* also includes the notion of the performance of *a* dance: it is not simply motor activity. Danced movements are not "just" bodily phenomena; they are concepts that can be written down without reference to the mechanics of movement. In fact, a dance score represents a notation of these movement concepts separated from any particular performance of them, just as a musical score refers to musical notes, or a written language text represents words, sentences, paragraphs, and thoughts that are unconnected with any *particular* performance of them.

A musical score does not contain any information as to the mechanics of performing[8] a piece of music, nor does a spoken language text (such as this book) give any clues as to how to use one's vocal chords. A written script of a dance need not capture the individuality of any one performance, although it is possible to write a score of an individual's performance. Rather, a script usually references the formal characteristics of a medium of expression. A musical score exhibits formal properties through its conventions such as key signatures, bars, staff, and differently shaded notes, all of which are connected with the principles of harmony and the rhythmic structure of Western music. As we shall show later, the same is true of a written dance score.

The kinds of structures that underlie a play are connected with the grammar and syntax of a particular language and, for example, with the principles of blank verse. They do not concern the physical structures of the throat and larynx. Why, then, should one consider a dance score any more of a guide to mov*ing* or any more of an aid to picturing how a movement should look than is appropriate to other types of script? Could we not look, instead, for formal properties that refer to the structure of a particular dance or idiom of dance? Why must one call the motor aspects of the act of danc*ing* "*the* dance," paying little atttention to dances themselves just because their structures are not directly visible in performance?

A USEFUL ANALOGY

Many people are much more naive (and they are often extremely vague) about dance and human movement than they are about spoken language and music. This is reflected in the fact that the very word "dance" in English is used to refer to several different levels of generality, which are often confused in everyday discourse. In order to gain more clarity, it is useful to make a linguistic analogy[9] that compares danc*ing, a* dance, and the written version of a dance to similar aspects of a spoken language. If one thinks about danc*ing* as the use of body language similarly to the ways in which we think about speak*ing* as the use of spoken language, then it is possible to make certain crucial distinctions.

The combined term "the dance" is a generic term, as is the term "language." One does not say, "I speak language"; one says "I speak Japanese, Dutch, French or English," that is, *a* language, yet we often hear people speak of dancing "the dance"—although professional dancers are usually clear as to the style or technique they mean. They are aware that they do not dance "the dance," but a specific idiom or idioms of dance (kabuki, Graham, bharata natyam, ballet, or tap). Just as in poetry reading we assume that a poet does not recite poems in general but *a* poem or *some* poetry in *a* language, so a dancer dances *a* dance in a particular idiom of dance.

In the written version of a poem, a conventional script (e.g., Roman or Cyrillic script) is used to write *a* poem in *a* language. In a dance score too, a conventional script such as the Laban script may be used to notate *a* dance ("Swan Lake") in *an* idiom such as ballet. In order to notate properly, or to a lesser extent to read, that dance, the writer or reader needs to be familiar with the idiom to which it belongs, just as one needs to know the grammar, syntax and phonological structure of a language in order to read or to write a poem, speech, or drama in that language. The resident notator of Paul Taylor's company, Jan Moekle, says that as she comes to understand Taylor's choreography, it becomes much easier to notate his work. Clearly the reason for this is that she is learning his body language and is beginning to recognize the structures that underlie his use of the diverse body languages of which American modern dance is comprised.

Knowing a language or idiom of dance means that one is familiar with the conventions, assumptions, and structures that inform it. This is what is meant by knowing the *rules* of a language. Thinking in terms of a body language enables us not only to understand the difference between danc*ing*, an idiom of dance, and *a* dance, but also to differentiate between the anatomical structure of the human body and the structures that underlie a dance or an idiom of dance.

Danc*ing* refers to the performance of *a* dance; a dance consists of movements that are generated by the structures of an idiom of dance. One can compare this to speak*ing*, which refers to the vocal articulation of words, phrases, and sentences that are generated by a person's use of the grammatical structure of a language. In both cases, the mechanics of moving body parts, whether to produce action or to produce sound, are not part of the investigation. No amount of understanding of the anatomy and kinesiology of the body in motion can help one to perform a jazz or tap sequence, unless one is familiar with that movement idiom, that is, unless one is acquainted with the rule structure of jazz or tap dancing.

The question can then be raised, Just what is the difference between the process of choreography or composition in a body language and the process involved in improvisation? Before we address that question, we will establish what we mean by improvisation.

WHAT IS IMPROVISATION?

Some commonly held notions are that improvisation consists of (1) creating on the spot, (2) performing free-form or without form, winging it, (3) trying to provide a reasonable substitute for what (it) was *supposed* to be (as in fudging it); or (4) doing something different each time. In our investigations of the notion of improvisation, we also found it useful to compare it to improvisation in other mediums of expression, as well as to try to discover what is meant by improvisation in different cultures, because what improvisation means to a Graham dancer is different from what is understood as improvisation by a *bharata natyam* dancer of southern India. Similarly, what to Jennifer Muller[10] is a process *toward* an end product might be regarded as the end product itself by a sand dancer or a tap dancer.

Questions also arose about what is regarded as "being the same" in two separate performances of the same dance. If a choreographed stretch of movement is performed in "the same way" on two separate nights, how does one account for the different "message or "feeling" that one gets each time? What part is "the same"? If one had seen Martha Graham's "Primitive Mysteries" performed originally in 1931, then seen the first reconstruction of the dance, made in 1964, in how far could one consider it the "same" dance? McDonagh notes that upon reconstruction of this work, parts were "choreographed . . . in the original spirit of the dance" by Sophie Maslow and that Martha Graham, while watching a rehearsal, referred to "the one in white as the Sabbath Queen" instead of "the Virgin Mary" (1973:275).

But first we examine the activity of dancing itself. As we have tried to show, many people regard improvisation *not* as a rule-based activity, but rather as a "free-flowing" "stream-of -consciousness" succession of movements selected in a totally random manner from all possible movements. Perhaps that viewpoint is based on the assumption that choreographed dances also consist of nothing more than a random selection of movements.

We believe that that viewpoint equates a dancer with a prelingual child producing its first "nonsense" sounds— the articulation of sounds that in later years he or she will no longer be able to produce. Although we imagine that in theory it is possible to continue making all the sounds that might emerge during this developmental process of experimentation with the vocal apparatus, we know that in practice, the child discards all sounds but those that achieve the goal of communication with the world, namely, the sounds of the spoken language of his or her society.

Similarly, during the process of dance training, dancers acquire a vocabulary of movements from instructors who have themselves been influenced by the idioms of dance to which they were exposed. Those idioms are marked by a certain exclusivity. That is to say, they make use of some movements but not others. This selectivity of movement vocabulary is itself a major factor that distinguishes dance idioms and styles of dancing from one another at a purely visual level if nothing else. Dancers, like spoken-language users, have made choices along the way that are incorporated into their modes of expression, thereby enhancing the probability of producing others. While engaged in the act of dancing (whether improvised or composed), the dancer makes choices *not* from an unlimited range of movement possibilities, but from those that belong to an acquired movement vocabulary.

The particular choices that are made are influenced by previously learned, performed, or as yet only imagined arrangements and rearrangements of that acquired vocabulary.[11] That vocabulary is governed by rules, as is the vocabulary of any spoken language. Even when speaking extemporaneously, a speaker can use language in new ways without fundamentally ignoring or changing its rules, meaning, its grammar. Knowledge of those rules is a prerequisite to the quick and facile manipulation of sound and meaning expressed in speeches, lectures, or conversation, as well as in papers, novels, or other written compositions.

Imagine for a moment a person who tried to utter extemporaneously a stream of English words in a syntactically incorrect order, for example, "Moon cow over the jumped the" or "Green is made is cheese of." The result is a very halting attempt that cannot be sustained for long before giving way to a completely tongue-tied state. The point is this: it is *more difficult* to produce a string of *un*grammatically ordered words than it is to produce a string of grammatically ordered words. We suggest that the same is true of stretches of movements. It is highly unlikely that a dancer will produce a series of ungrammatical movement sequences, and even when such is attempted, the dancer is aware of the rules that are being broken.

Grammaticality with Movement

In order to create a sentence and then call it *un*grammatical, one must necessarily know that a rule has been broken. Consider for example, this ungrammatical English sentence: "The lion killed the buffalo, wasn't she?" It is not necessary to know the exact name of the rule given to this transformation by linguists in order to be aware that one cannot use a form of the infinitive "to be" in a tag question that follows a sentence using a form of the infinitive "to kill." Correct usage requires a form of the infinitive "to do." In order to construct a grammatical sentence, one does not usually go through this thought process, but the rule can be said to exist in our implicit knowledge of English, or else we could not point to the sentence and say, "That's ungrammatical."[12]

Equally, in order to demonstrate an example of the kinds of grammatical rules that govern the Graham idiom of dancing, one could execute the ungrammatical movement phrase shown in Figure 1.[13] This sequence violates the rule whereby the contraction of the pelvis is meant to take place prior to a contraction of the rest of the torso, the arms or the hands. To a Graham dancer, this stretch of

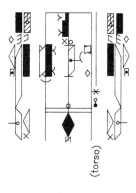   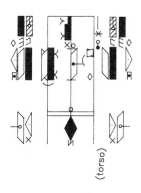

grammatical   * ungrammatical

Figure 1.

movement *looks* as funny as the sentence about the lion and the buffalo *sounds* to an English speaker. Even if the dancer may not be able to articulate which rule has been broken, the dancer finds the sequence unacceptable as a Graham movement. Another way of putting this is that the dancer "knows" a mistake has been made. Analysis of Graham technique allows one to note many fundamental rules that govern the idiom, some of which are presented in the section entitled Rules of Graham Technique.

Improvising, like choreographing, is a rule-based activity and although it might be argued that, theoretically, the entire range of possible movements is at the disposal of a person moving at any given moment, the actions chosen usually reflect the individual's exposure to certain specific sets of actions that are the result of training—formal or informal—whether as a dancer, acrobat, martial artist, or musician. One clear example of rule-based dancing that is improvised is that of the original American tap and sand dancers, whose movements were created in the context of matching and/or complementing jazz music—itself often characterized by improvisation within the structures of selected key and measured time boundaries. One could say that the jazz musician is theoretically able to choose from all available sounds and combinations thereof that are possible within the well-tempered clavier scale and the particular instrument that is played. However, jazz musicians confine themselves not only to the structure of, say, the blues, but also to a specific semantic intention during the course of any given piece.

It is highly unlikely that a blues saxophonist will, during a solo stretch, break into the strains of the "Blue Danube Waltz." If that *were* to happen, then one would be aware that a statement was being made *other than* all that is included in the general sense that is conveyed by "the Blues." If a tap dancer were suddenly to break into an *enchainement:* such as chassé, pas de bourrée, glissade, jeté (a sequence of steps from the vocabulary of ballet), the audience would similarly assume that some additional statement was being made.

Specific adaptations of the rules of a symbolic system by an individual are in themselves subject to rules that allow us to recognize and distinguish the work of a Beethoven, a Picasso, a Stevie Wonder, a José Limón, a Guy de Maupassant or a Shakespeare. When Bach sat down and "improvised" "A Musical Offering," based on a five-note sequence suggested to him, what did he do? Was it totally free-form, or did he adhere to the basic rule-structures of Western harmonics? What is the "same" and what is "different" about two completely improvised renditions of "The Tiger Rag," one by Art Tatum and the other by Stephane Grappelli and David Grisman?

In a dance improvisation there may be a prescribed set of rules, as for example, a structure that governs a particular stretch of movement, and another that governs an entire dance event. These improvisations are often rehearsed as frequently as any "set" dance. Also, there are various usages to which improvisations are put. American modern dance choreographers Jennifer Muller, Twyla Tharp and Alwin Nikolais constantly use improvisation, both as a means to find movement patterns for a dance that is later "set" and as a final product that is considered worthy of presentation on the stage.

The difference between *bharata natyam* and Graham's idiom of body language is interesting: a recital of the former is a highly structured improvisation. A recital of the latter consists of completely "set" pieces of choreography. Yet, a goal connected with the performance of a Graham piece is to appear to be dancing extemporaneously, whereas the *bharata natyam* dancer attempts to convey the ease that comes after constant rehearsal, even when the movement combinations are improvised.

IMPROVISATION IN *BHARATA NATYAM*

In describing a *bharata natyam* recital, the term "improvisation" is useful because no two performances of a dance necessarily use the same sequences of movement. The dancer normally varies the patterns of movement, the steps chosen, and the *hasta mudra* (hand positions) used, and except for the novice dancer, each performer's version of a particular dance is, in movement terms, different. For example, Figures 2 and 3 show two different versions, that is, two possible ways of performing "the same" passage.

In movement or visual terms alone, the stretches in Figures 2 and 3 look completely different. The notated texts, too, illustrate the differences in the rhythmic patterns beaten by the dancer's feet, the *hasta mudra* used,

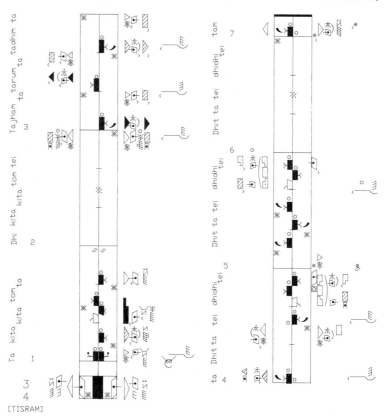

Figure 2.

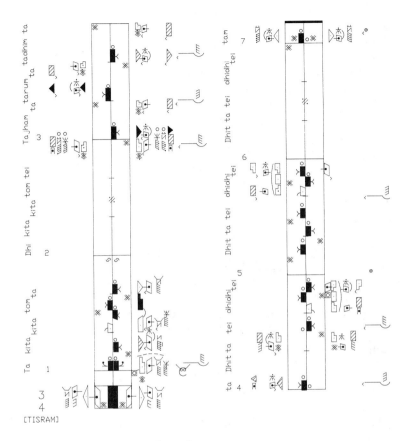

Figure 3.

and the sequential differences of movements of the arms, head, and eyes. Yet, in terms of what those stretches are intended to convey, they are the same. To the *bharata natyam* dancer, they represent *the same idea,* just as the following two sentences in English convey the same idea: "She unlocked the door and walked in." "She entered with a key." Although the two sentences use different words, they are loosely synonymous given a cultural context in which we know that locks are placed on doors and that keys are used to unlock doors.

The context that makes the two sequences of movement the same is the rhythmic combination that the two sequences express. The spoken syllables that express this rhythm have been placed along the left margin of the written texts, and the two stretches of movement are two different ways of expressing this rhythmic sound pattern, which is what confers similar identity on the two sets of movement. In an important sense, this rhythmic pattern can be seen as the "meaning" of the two sequences, each of which is an alternative way of "saying" that pattern in *bharata natyam.*

Like the ballet, ballroom dancing, flamenco and many of the dance idioms of Africa and the Caribbean, *bharata natyam* is an externally motivated idiom of dance. One of the general rules of such idioms is that they follow a certain set metric cycle. More specifically, *bharata natyam* follows the rules of the time measures of southern Indian music. The examples in Figures 2 and 3 are in a cycle of three beats (*tisram*) and follow the rule that each stretch of movement must end on the first beat of a metric cycle, which is why the written versions have the beginnings of an uncompleted seventh bar. If the reader looks carefully at the two versions, a similarity can be seen in the foot patterns, particularly in the rhythms that are produced by a performance of these steps. Beyond the rules concerning the musical structure are the rules that relate to the movements that the dancer chooses.

In *bharata natyam,* there is a set of steps that could be called the "vocabulary" of the idiom in the same way that one can speak of a vocabulary of balletic steps, positions, and moves. From that vocabulary, the dancer chooses steps that when performed cause certain patterns of sounds to be heard. That pattern conforms with the pattern of spoken syllables enunciated by the singer and the rhythms played by the drum. The choice of "steps" is dependent on the *sounds* a dancer wishes to make, and the sounds made in the execution of each step pattern are different.

There are numerous alternative ways of performing these rhythmic syllables; therefore, when one performs, one makes a split-second decision from among a set of choices, some of which may never have been performed before. Because this is not the same as performing a prescribed sequence, the term "improvisation" is more applicable to describe what happens in a *bharata natyam* performance than the word "choreography."

What was explained earlier is equally true of dramatic sequences in which the dancer is also externally motivated by the lyrics of a song. In these sections of the performance, the dancer has many alternative gestures to choose from in the interpretation of a single word, a phrase or a whole sentence. There are so many possibilities that no two performances are exactly the same, although the dancer might begin with a "standard" set of gestures, just as a jazz musician might start with the basic theme of the melody he or she is about to interpret. The dancer's skill lies in the ability to perform different variations to the repetitions of a single line of verse.

These possibilities are still governed by rules. For example, the legs and feet will always be in one of the basic *bharata natyam* positions, as shown in Figure 4. The hands will always form one of the thirty-one major hand positions such as   ᵢ or ᵢ , or else will be placed behind the back at the waist. The feet always mark rhythms in consonance with the metric cycle of the music. The eyes normally address (or follow) the direction of movement of the hand that is moving, or else they address a character imagined to be on the stage. Otherwise, the eyes are directed straight ahead. The importance of the eye movements is indicated in the written examples (Figs.

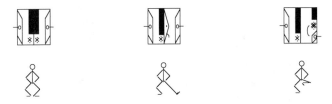

Figure 4.

2 and 3) in which a special column has been assigned to the eyes (👁), since these movements are constituent to *bharata natyam*. They are rarely, if ever, found in notated scores of the ballet or modern dance.

The rules described are those that make *bharata natyam* distinctive and they can all be elicited by analysis of a written score. They make it possible for dancers to communicate the meanings they intend and they do not constrain dancers any more than the rules of English constrain English speakers. If one decided to make ungrammatical statements, that is, to break too many rules, one would simply not be understood. The resulting movements would be nonsense—literally "non-sense." The rules are what make it possible for the dancer to convey meanings and, indeed, to move with fluency and ease.

Indian dancers are guided by the grammars, or structures, of their chosen idioms as they compose each single dance. In fact, only an extremely accomplished dancer can improvise on stage. The novice first learns set pieces, composed by well-known teachers or by other, well-known, dancers. Later on, the young performer begins to compose short sequences in rehearsal or to make slight changes in the composition, until finally becoming adept enough to compose large sections of a dance in performance. There is little difference between the processes of composition at a rehearsal and composition on stage. One does not think with movement any differently; one just thinks much faster and cannot afford to make mistakes. The editing process associated with choreography, during which one judges whether a movement would be appropriate, or when sequential substitutions are made, is also involved in improvisation—even if there is less time to think. In fact, the less time there is to think, the more one depends on implicit rules.

Many *bharata natyam* dancers set the basic structure and decide on the general framework of a dance before they actually improvise. It is this basic structure that is referred to in the identification of a composition or a dance, and the structure pertains more to the music, lyrics, and patterns of rhythmic syllables that are used than to the movement sequences that are performed to express that music. Even when credit is given to a particular guru (maestro) or dancer for the composition of a piece, this does not mean that the choreography as such has not been changed. At any given moment during performance, a dancer may create new combinations or even new gestures, so that one could say that a dancer choreographs *during* performance, which, in a sense is the same as saying that the dancer "improvises."

Thinking with movement during a *bharata natyam* improvisation is therefore no different from thinking with movement as part of the choreographic process. Whether one decided on a particular sequence of movements six months beforehand, or a millisecond before performing it, what one creates in both cases is a dance—a piece of choreography—something that has been composed.

IMPROVISATION, COMPOSITION AND GRAHAM'S BODY LANGUAGE

In Western modern dance, improvisation is often used as a process during which new movement ideas for dances or choreography are explored. Sometimes, the choreographer improvises, relying on dancers to remember what was done. Dancers are also meant to reproduce it, rather like human instant replay. Other composers who themselves no longer perform might ask their dancers to improvise in a certain way and then ask them to repeat a particular movement or work it into a phrase.[14] In either case, the improvisation serves the same function as do the many drafts of a formal academic paper in which the objective is to obtain a product that has been refined during the versions prior to the final one.

When she herself could no longer dance, Martha Graham depended on the improvisations of her dancers to create the body of her new work. While she provided the basic scenario for the piece, it was fleshed out when her dancers moved in front of her and she molded, changed and directed what they did. The dancers operated not only under their impressions of what Graham wanted and the ideas described by her but also under the distinct set of rules that underlay her standardized vocabulary of movements such as cave turns, contractions, standing back falls, darts, sparkles, bell jumps, knee vibrations, knee crawls, and triplets. Not just "any movement" turned up in a Graham dance. This does not mean that Graham did not sometimes include new movements that were outside her formal vocabulary. Occasionally, a dancer offered a movement that was "new" which might also have been acceptable to Graham as appropriate to the style and dramatic content of a particular work.

To most people who are familiar with Graham's body language, it is fairly well-known that entire sections of certain dances were created by her company members and that some parts of dances that she did choreograph were actually set to music by Louis Horst and other company members. Although the same process of communal input into choreography occurs in many other American dance companies, there is a fiercely protective attitude toward attributing the choreography to a particular individual. The application of copyright laws to choreographic works is testimony to the prevalence of that attitude.

CULTURAL VALUES AND TWO BODY LANGUAGES

In the United States and throughout much of the English-speaking world, there is a choreographer-performer distinction made that in other countries such as India and West Africa is not usual. In India, more stress is placed on the guru-*shishya* (teacher-pupil) relationship, and the "choreography" of an idiom is attributed to a guru, who is also regarded as the bearer of a danced tradition. There is less interest in assigning credit to an individual than there is in identifying the dance and the musical tradition within which a particular composition was created.

During a *bharata natyam* performance, the dancer creates the dance artifact extemporaneously (within the boundaries described earlier) and so determines what is seen and heard on a particular occasion. The question of origin of an actual sequence of steps is of less importance than it is in Western modern dance idioms. In fact, as we have seen, Indian dancers clearly confine themselves to an established vocabulary: they are not interested in creating "new" movement elements; rather, their concern is with creating new combinations of those elements.

In the Graham case, even if a sequence were actually choreographed by a member of Graham's company, the "credit" for the sequence goes to Graham. To illustrate: when the "daughters of the night" in "Night Journey" execute steps that were put together many years ago by a member of the chorus, or the character of the "victim" in "Cave of the Heart" performs a solo that was built as much *by* as upon Yuriko Kikuchi, the choreography was then, and is today, attributed to Graham. Perhaps this is because whether Graham herself created those particular combinations or not, the governing principles of these compositions consist of that set of rules that comprise the idiom of Graham's modern dance technique. It is interesting to note that although in modern dance, one thinks in terms of "choreographies," what is usually identified is the *idiom* of body language itself—the "technique"—and that is attributed to an individual.

RULES OF GRAHAM TECHNIQUE

Some of the rules that underlie Graham's idiom of body language are the following:[15]

1. Movement occurs slightly *before* the downbeat of a measure, so that by the time the downbeat occurs, the movement is aleady in progress. In the classroom, the length of the preliminary upbeat has been formalized in many exercises to equal either one, or one-half, beat. Underlying this convention is the idea that the dancer is meant to appear to "cause the music to happen."[16]

2. Movement of the pelvis, whether a contraction, release, tilt, or shift, is the beginning of any larger movement

and occurs before all other movements. It is unusual for the pelvis to move as an isolated body part, and although there can be movements of other isolated body parts in certain choreographed phrases, in general these do not occur in an ordinary technique class. An example of this

American Document Step

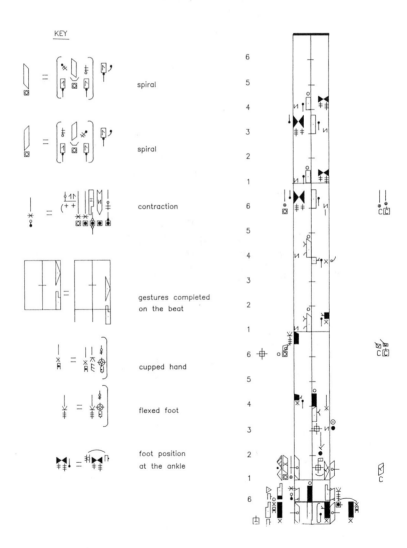

KEY

spiral

spiral

contraction

gestures completed
on the beat

cupped hand

flexed foot

foot position
at the ankle

rule can be seen in the written passages from *American Document* (Figure 5).

3. Movement through space that involves weight transfer (from one supporting leg to the other, from two legs to two legs or one leg, and from one leg to two legs) is initiated by a shift of weight at the center of gravity in the pelvis. This can be seen in the contrast between the simple Graham "walk" and the ballet dancer's "walk," in which the main feature in the latter case is a leg gesture that precedes the transference of weight.

If one had been asked to improvise for Martha Graham, one would have operated within the framework of these kinds of rules. To have done otherwise would have been to offer a non-sense, and the resulting combinations would certainly have been unacceptable to Graham.

As stated earlier, everyone's individual improvisations are a result of the various idioms in which one has been formally trained. In addition, they are governed by the rules for the body language of one's culture. A modern dancer is unlikely to include in any sequence that is performed, the hand gestures or eye movements found in *bharata natyam,* unless, perhaps, the intention were, say, to be satirical. The choice of movements one makes is based on the meanings one wishes to convey, and those meanings can be communicated only on the basis of shared understandings. Consequently, one always adheres to the set of rules that underlie the body language of one's idiom, and these in turn are connected with the body language of the wider society.[17]

CONCLUSION

We find that both the idioms of *bharata natyam* and Graham's "idiolect" of modern dance are largely identified in terms of their underlying rules, whether it is the case that one watches an improvisation or a composition at any specific time and place. Analytically speaking, the difference between composing and improvising seems to us, at any rate, to be very slight. The thought processes involved are not different, although, while improvising one does think much faster.

Whereas one *can* speak of composing without anyone's having to move, the term "improvisation" does seem to include an actual performance of the movements. Nevertheless, the artifact produced is as accommodating to notation as is a composition. One could imagine a dancer or choreographer "improvising" with pen and paper directly onto a Laban staff, which would be the same as to say that they were "composing," as when a musician "composes" directly onto score paper without playing the notes on any instrument.

When one speaks of "composition," attention seems generally to be focused on an end product;—an artifact to be treated as a commodity that can be bought and sold. Different societies place different values on these terms, and this is reflected in the ways that the terms are used. In southern Indian society, there is less emphasis on the creation of a product than on the skills with which a performer manipulates a dance idiom, which in turn is dependent on the dancer's fluency in the idiom.

On the whole, in Western modern dance idioms, there is greater emphasis placed on the end product: even improvisation is seen as a means to an end. When a professional dancer improvises in performance, credit for the improvisation usually goes to the leader of the company, whether it was Nikolais, Graham, Tharp, Cunningham or another. More often than not, the improvisation ends up in a set piece; yet the term "improvisation" is retained in order to emphasize the notion of spontaneity, novelty, and individuality—all important values in American society.

As one might expect from Indian society, there is less emphasis on the individual contribution over time;[18] a dance is regarded as public property and is identified by the idiom of movement to which it belongs rather than by the name of the individual performer or choreographer. The idiom itself is not attributed to any particular individual but regarded as a public, social fact. This is in strong contrast to Western modern dance idioms in which the choreographer often attempts not only to compose new dances but also to create a new ideolect of body language, which is then identified by the name of an individual. Because of this, there is an emphasis, in the American case, on breaking the rules of existing idioms[19] and on creating what are generally regarded as "new" movements. Great value is placed on the notion of improvisation as an *exploratory* process, as compared with the Indian case, in which, even though new movements are often created, the performer is not interested in their novelty value *per se,* nor is the dancer's social persona so strongly identified with them.

We have come to some tentative conclusions from this preliminary attempt to compare two widely different idioms or human body languages: the distinction between improvisation and composition that is generally assumed in the United States (including the writers we mentioned earlier) is based on the cultural difference of perceiving the individual as a more important entity than the whole, in contrast to the Indian view, in which the individual is seen as intimately bound up in the whole society and, indeed, is a kind of expression of the whole.

The two terms "improvisation" and "composition" have different meanings to members of different societies, although they can be useful to distinguish between dances that include prearranged movements and dances that are composed, as it were, in performance. We are convinced that the distinction between the terms by no means marks a difference in the end products or in the processes whereby the dance artifacts are created. Improvising and composing with reference to dancing are complex ideas and complex acts. They want handling with great care. In any case, discussion of them should be guided by the data that one seeks to understand.

Thinking in terms of a body language (not "thinking in movement") *does* assist one to uncover the rules that govern an idiom of movement, and these rules are referred to whether one improvises *or* composes. This leads to a better understanding of what human beings are actually doing and "be-ing" when they move.

NOTES

1. See Williams 1979:42 for the important distinction between *the* dance, *a* dance, and danc*ing*. "The dance," used as a term of referral, simply means the sum of the world's dances, not an internal process or an experience of moving.

2. The excerpt was from *Dasavataramulu* in the idiom of Kuchipudi from Andhra Pradesh, in which the ten incarnations of Vishnu (*Dasavatara*) are described. The dance is accompanied by lyrics that are interpreted with *hasta-abhinaya* (hand gestures), and the performer may vary those gestures in an attempt to convey the narrative meaning of the lyrics. The music is set to *misra chapu* (a metrical cycle of seven beats), and in the non-narrative sequences, the dancer improvises steps that fit into this rhythmic cycle.

3. Often, people seem to see more of their own associations and ideas about something that they see—or are even curious about—than what is actually there. Associations between age and rule-boundedness were the common ones made here, i.e. "ancient culture" = traditions and rules; "new culture" = freedom and nonrules.

4. Contact improvisation is a post-modern dance form that originated in the 1960s and is attributed to the efforts of Steve Paxton. It involves improvised movement of two or more bodies that remain in physical contact with each other throughout. Motivation for the movement lies in the effect of gravity and other natural forces on the momentum of the body. Ideally one has minimal consciously directed input into the movements. For a historical and ethnographical study of contact improvisation see Novack 1990.

5. For example, Benesh and Benesh 1977 and Eshkol and Wachmann 1958 and Sutton Movement Shorthand. These systems differ widely from Laban's script in important ways, and, were Margolis speaking of them, instead of Laban's script, some of his assessments would be more accurate.

6. See also Youngerman 1984 for a critique of Margolis's position.

7. "An intentional action is not the same as a physical movement since the latter can be described in various ways according to one's point of view and one's beliefs about the person performing it. One cannot specify an action, as

opposed to a purely physical movement, without taking into account what the agent intended" (Best 1974:193).

8. We would ask the reader to exercise great care here: musical scores bear terms such as "diminuendo," "ritardando," and "allegro con brio," but these are not references to the anatomy of the hands or arms or vocal chords; they are relevant to *how* the music may be played but not to the "mechanics" of playing.

9. For the difference between the usage of linguistic *analogies* and linguistic *models* with reference to the dance and human movement, see Kaeppler 1982.

10. Jennifer Muller danced for many years in the José Limón dance company, after which she joined Louis Falco (another Limón dancer) as partner in his dance company. Eventually, Muller and Falco split, each retaining about half of the dancers of his company and filling out their individual companies with younger dancers. Today Muller is best known outside of the United States—in France and the Netherlands primarily. Her style makes use of some of the principles on which Limón built his style and is pervaded by heightened sensuality and an extremely high level of energy. Muller is choreographically influenced by one of her earlier teachers, Antony Tudor, as far as her sense of phrasing and concatenation are concerned.

11. Levi-Strauss's notion of bricolage could be applied to this process. We would agree with him that, for the "bricoleur" and mythmaker, as for the dancer, "His universe of instruments is closed and the rules of his game are always to make do with 'whatever is at hand', that is to say with a set of tools and materials that is always finite" (1966:17).

12. See Myers 1981 for a more detailed discussion of the notion of ungrammaticality in spoken and body languages.

13. Notation for Figures 1 and 5 was executed by Jane Marriett of the Dance Notation Bureau in New York.

14. Indeed, the very word "dancer," on the whole appears to share the general fluid nature of "categories." When one thinks of a dancer (in Western terms), one thinks first of a lithe young woman between the ages of, say, fifteen and thirty. But the category in fact can be said to include men, those who no longer dance, those who may never have danced professionally but who choreograph, those who both perform and choreograph, and those who have never taken a "formal dance class." Along the same lines, but

speaking of the category of "emotional gestures" in choreography, Humphrey states that "there are feelings which
can be expressed in so many ways that there is really no one
pattern for them" (1959:118).

15. It is important to note here that this is only a fractional
listing of rules that can be found in Graham technique. As
with the rules of spoken languages, these are also subject to
change over time, and those presented here represent those
learned by Hart-Johnson during the first nine years of her
exposure to Graham: 1969–78. There are "archaic," as well
as new and updated versions of these concepts.

16. The two notated versions of the same stretch of movement
presented in Figure 5 demonstrate that, in general, underlying rules and structures can indeed be shown in a Labanotation score. Rather than go to the trouble of writing symbols
in an overlapping fashion so as to demonstrate that they
have already begun before the musical beat, one can provide a key explaining this concept and then write symbols
within the beat marks, which is easier to read. This is
similar to a musical key signature, which informs readers
about the mandatory flats or sharps to be played for the
duration of a piece of music. Other compound symbols for
danced movements may be abbreviated into one concise
symbol, such as can be seen in Figure 5 for the pelvic
contraction, cupped hand, and spiral. This is extremely
useful, for it distinguishes clearly between these specific
Graham movements and those of other idioms that may
loosely resemble them.

17. American modern dance arose primarily as a rebellion to
the strictures of ballet, such as the outward rotation of the
femur, the pointed foot, resistance to gravity, and "graceful-
ness" in general. At first, those principles were simply
reversed: where the foot was before pointed, it was now
flexed, etc. This revolution in dance technique was accompanied by the suffragette and other turn-of-the-century
movements that challenged the established roles and rules
of Western societies.

18. We refer here to the absence in traditional Indian society of
the notion of individualism as it developed in the West (cf.
Dumont 1970:4–20).

19. One notes that the breaking of rules presupposes the existence of rules and that those rules are known to persons
who break them. In addition, the resultant idiom (dialect or

idiolect) depends on which set of rules of which idiom are broken. Each "new" idiom of American modern dance comes about from the breaking of various rules, which explains why there is a lack of homogeneity among the various idioms subsumed under the general rubric of "modern dance."

REFERENCES

Benesh, R., and J. Benesh. 1977. *An Introduction to Benesh Dance Notation.* London: Adams and Charles Black.

Best, D. 1974. *Expression in Movement and the Arts.* London: Lepus.

Dumont, L. 1970. *Homo Hierarchicus.* Chicago: University of Chicago Press.

Eshkol, N., and A. Wachmann. 1958. *Movement Notation.* London: Weidenfeld and Nicolson.

Humphrey, D. 1959. *The Art of Making Dances.* New York: Grove.

Kaeppler, A. 1986. Cultural analysis, linguistic analogies and the study of dance in anthropological perspective. In C. J. Frisbie, ed., *Explorations in Ethnomusicology: Essays in Honour of David P. McAllester.* Detroit Monographs in Musicology 9. Detroit: Information Coordinators.

Lévi-Strauss, C. 1966. *The Savage Mind.* Chicago: University of Chicago Press.

Margolis, J. 1981. The autographic nature of the dance. *Journal Aesthetics and Art Criticism* 39(4):419–427.

McDonagh, D. 1973. *Martha Graham: A Biography.* New York: Praeger.

Myers, E. 1981. A phrase structural analysis of the fox-trot, with transformational rules. *Journal for the Anthropological Study of Human Movement* 1(4);246–268.

Novack, C. 1990. *Sharing the Dance: Contact Improvisation and American Culture.* Madison, Wisc.: University of Wisconsin Press.

Sheets-Johnstone, M. 1981. Thinking in movement. *Journal of Aesthetics and Art Criticism* 39(4):339–407.

Williams, D. 1979. The human action sign and semasiology. *Dance Research Journal* Annual X. CORD, New York.

Youngerman, S. 1984. Movement notation systems as conceptual frameworks. In M. Sheets-Johnstone ed., *Philosophical Explorations.* London and Toronto: Associated Press.

PART II
COMMENTARIES

Chapter 8 THE INDEXICAL STRUCTURE OF VISIBILITY

Bonnie Urciuoli

THE INDEXICAL STRUCTURE OF SIGN SYSTEMS

The chapters in the first part of this volume demonstrate in abundant ethnographic detail how much structural continuity there is among all action sign systems (to use Williams's term), a category that must include language itself. The continuity lies in the principles that organize meaningful action, rather than in the units that package meaning. In that regard, language is one system among many. Indeed, while its grammatical-semantic organization makes language structurally distinct, language is not thereby a model by which to measure the meaning-making properties of all action sign systems.

The term "action sign system" is very apt. As the previous chapters variously demonstrate, signification *is* an action and so must be located in time and space. The defining properties of meaningful action are precisely those not visible in a grammatical-semantic model, the units and rules of which are essentially timeless (cf. Bourdieu 1977). The creation of meaning is above all embedded in human relationships: people enact their selves to each other in words, movements, and other modes of action. All selves are culturally defined, as time and space themselves are culturally defined. Time and space are never simply there; they are continually cut to fit the agenda of the moment.

The property that language shares with all sign systems is its indexical nature: its maintenance and creation of social connections, anchored in experience and the sense of the real. Linguistic indexes may be grammaticalized or lexicalized as shifters—devices that locate actions in time and space: personal pronouns, verb tenses, demonstratives, and time and space adverbs. These are deictic in that they point outward from the actor's location. The structure of action fans out from the center, the locus of *I* and *you,* to delineate where and when everything happens relative to the central actors: *he* and *she* versus *I* and *you, there* versus *here, then* versus *now,* present versus nonpresent (past or future). This is the structure of parole in language, the structure of each situation of speaking and the key to the ongoing evolution of linguistic categories (Jakobson 1960, 1971; Benveniste 1971 [1956], 1971 [1958]; Kurylowicz 1972; Silverstein 1977). Discourse by its very nature is socially embodied. The indexes that embody discourse extend beyond pronouns, adverbs, and verbal categories both to the sounds and shapes of speech that identify the actor with a particular group and to the speech acts marking the actor's intent as others recognize it. In short, indexes make the social person.

The indexical creation of the social person (and the terms of action) is the performative nature of action. A considerable literature has grown up around performatives since Austin (1962) introduced the term. Most relevant to the present discussion is Silverstein's (1976, 1977) argument that performatives are a mode of indexing: indexicality, a sine qua non of language, may be more or less creative; the more an index creates the who, what, when, and where of the action, the more performative it is; the more an index maintains the status quo of action, the more presupposed (and less performative) it is. Performativity may be thought of as a process that sometimes surfaces as an explicit formula (commands, promises, etc.) but is more often implicit. Any index can be performative, depending on the dynamics of the context.

Let me now summarize, in the light of these remarks, what I will argue throughout my discussion. First, imagine a continuum (or set of continua) of possible action signs, ranging from most to least embodied. Any subset within this can make up a system: body actions (dance), hand actions (signs), vocal actions (sound), or inscribed actions (writing). We tend to see only one such subset as a single system (dance as opposed to writing, or sign as opposed to speech); nevertheless, systems do "mix and match." Indexicality is anchored in the central embodiment: however it is expressed in writing or talk, hand signs (as Farnell and Kendon show), dance (as Kaeppler, Friedland, and Williams show), or even fights (as Macdonald shows), its sense derives from that anchoring. That anchoring is never simply physical. People always operate from cultural ideas about what the body is, what interaction is, and what time and space are.

Each of these subsets has (as the chapters in this volume show) a different potential for enacting a self. Certainly we all know from our own experience that speech facilitates ways of being social, or of understanding, that writing does not, and vice versa; similarly, hand signs and dance facilitate ways to be social or show understanding that speech does not allow. To put it another way, each system allows a different possible way to "be yourself." Not all systems are equally valid in all societies: some societies do not recognize certain types of signs as legitimate systems of meaning or may recognize them as systems but with less status than other systems. Euro-American societies, for example, privilege speech and text (and text over speech)—the systems most displaced from the body—so that the public self that counts most is the self that can be spoken or written (preferably written). Politically, this becomes dangerous when a society is in a position to dictate what is or is not a valid system. Thus, Euro-American epistemologies have long been reproduced by institutions that can privilege speech and text as universally valid and *natural*. Especially privileged are the most textlike aspects of speech—the referential—in which context (which is embodiment) counts least in the creation of meaning. The flip side of this, of course, is that any sign system that cannot be reduced to reference falls outside the charmed circle, and entire populations are robbed of valid ways of being in the eyes of the elite. The chapters in this volume make this very clear.

PERFORMING THE PERSON IN CULTURAL TIME AND SPACE

No indexical systems can be reduced to the merely physical, however "trivial" or "natural" an action may appear: the problem is to address embodied action without essentializing the body as natural (Abu-Lughod and Lutz 1990). All physical embodiment is cultural embodiment, because it always involves a theory of the body.[1] If all sign systems have in common that they are indexically structured, then all meaningful action is concerned with the interactive contruction of a person. Each time an index occurs, its terms depend on who the actor is being; that in turn depends on the relationship between everyone involved and what they are doing together there at that moment. The point that marks where and when *I* stand consists of an intersection of the social frame and cultural definition of a relationship and the particular events of the moment. The terms of *here* and *now* can expand or contract to take in *this* room or *this* planet, *this* minute or *this* millennium, depending on what action *I* am engaged in, who with and why, and how it all defines *me.* This is social action in Weber's (1978) sense: motivated, oriented toward others, and continually subject to interpretation. Defining *here* and *now* at any given moment is a social action, always dependent on the *I-you* relation. At every moment, the person is a cultural creation, which means in turn that indexicality is at every moment symbolically mediated.

Each sign system in this collection generates and defines a person. Some do so through a grammaticalized sign language system, as Kendon and Farnell describe. Some do so through formalized dance or ritual, as Williams and Kaeppler describe. Friedland's city dancers and Macdonald's fighters appear to cross a line from formalized movement to routine social interaction but that line is a construct, because no "lines" exist prior to action. As Farnell and Williams suggest, these systems are continuous in their principles of structure: they can create and align and locate selves among other selves, and they can make cultural sense with those selves. In language, this is framed by speech acts; in our broader concept of sign system, it is framed in what we may call the signifying act. (This makes a speech act a signifying act done with language, as opposed to signifying acts done with dance or martial art.)

All signifying acts should be referable to a shared frame (cf. Williams, this volume). A speech act is how we classify what we say—how we mean it to be taken: "that's not a statement, that's a question." This is not mere classification of words; this is a judgment about the nature of the action. Similarly, a signifying act is not simply a bit of behavior but the way that the actors perceive its cultural intent. Again, this is not to take language as a model for social action, but to find points where principles of social action specifically emerge as language. A signifying act can no more be reduced to its physical terms than a speech act can be reduced to words or grammar. The best gauge for the existence of a signifying act is the fact that the people involved have some concept of how to do it right. If people share a sense that there is something there to be judged, then the bits of behavior cohere into an act. And if the act is done wrong, it will not work: nothing is created or localized.

This is where the play of visibility becomes an issue: how does an analyst know when and how signifying acts work? No outsider can reduce this aspect of the system to rules. The play of visibility and invisibility—what is or is not or cannot be seen, who sees it and who does not, and why—turns very sharply on the operation of indexicality from the actor's perspective; otherwise, the systematicity never becomes clear. Farnell and Williams address this theme most precisely.

In her discussion of time and directions in Plains sign, Farnell asks why the signer moved her hands differently on two occasions of signed deixis when nothing differed in the spoken translation. The signer signed her deixis as a body system, making distinctions that are not coded in speech. Sign clarifies the way in which a deictic system is constituted on its own terms, and it turns out to be more, rather than less, analytic than speech if we know where to look.

In her exegesis of three bows, Williams explicates emergent performativity. The basic question is the identity of a physical action. There is no more reason to assume that the three bows are equivalent than there is to assume that three homonyms have the same meaning. There are three different sets of constitutive relations and so three semasiologically different acts emerge. This point is likely to be missed if the analyst makes a falsely iconic equation. The three bows are not only parts of different systems but are performatively very different. Each bow unfolds a different reality, a universe peculiar to its own system.

In each case, a body is no simple physical object, but a person acting from a particular point, creating signs that define a self with respect to other selves. Farnell's signer operates from a body ideally located in a circle of social space suffused with moral and ethical space, however sadly elusive that circle may be in current life. Deixis and directions make full sense only when the self's *here* has a social locus because a speaker or signer carries that space with him or her: the physical space is part of the social space. The directions mapped from deictic reference in that space have a bodily immediacy that the verbal systems of English do not code. A different world unfolds from the deictic act. The alignment of space becomes a creative social alignment and so is performative.

Williams directly links the unfolding of space and time to an unfolding of person. There is no such thing as space or time in a simple sense. Time and space are conceptual, moral, and ethical before they are physical. If the selection of time and space indexes is reduced to the utilitarian (as it usually is), the actor is essentially disembodied, at best one-dimensional, with no real motive, in Weber's sense of motive. The social dimensions that could come into being remain invisible, like the ten or eleven dimensions curled up inside molecule-sized universes in some recent cosmological theories. Williams makes it clear that cosmological space or metaphysical space or dramatic space all emerge performatively from the enactment of self, just as a promise or threat unfolds from the words, nuances, and intonations of the self in the moment of utterance, enclosing a world of action. The meaning of all subsequent action—the Mass, the tai chi, the ballet—flows from that moment.

While Williams describes formalized systems, Macdonald shows that formalization is not a necessary aspect of embodied performativity. Words and fighting are performative with respect to each other. The complementarity only makes sense in the light of the Koori theory of person: an autonomous, predictable being who is never alone and who is touched on all sides by nets of relations. Words threaten to break the pattern and reveal unpredictable social volcanoes, dangerous because they could isolate one. Fights restore a person to the unspoken and therefore predictable social landscape by hiding the rifts. Fights relocate and redefine the self. Like the gestures, words, and signs of the Assiniboine, Koori fights and words are continuous as a system, and in each case the indexical continuity turns on a theory of person: the Assiniboine person within the social circle and the Koori person balanced in ambiguity.

Congruent theories of self inform both Australian papers, although the ethnographic focus varies considerably. Kendon, like Farnell and Macdonald, proposes a continuity of word and sign whose complementarity turns on a local theory of person. He hypothesizes that signing has spread as far as it has among Central Desert people because it embodies (pun intended) a low-key, unintrusive respect for personal boundaries. Not only is signing an alternative channel for saying what one has to say, but also it allows one to enact the values for right being, and of course signing re-creates those values at the same time. Macdonald's Koori fighters and Kendon's Central Desert signers have in common a sense of the absolute, all-encompassing social web in which autonomy is delicately respected by respecting boundaries and where that is accomplished, either by not saying what cannot be said or by knitting up the holes when it was said. Macdonald's fighters operate from a theory of predictable person, in which the enactment is the becoming: one becomes what one already is, but with the knowledge now made public. Boundaries of selves are respected where they are predictable.

Like Williams, Kaeppler and Friedland deal with performative aspects of dance, though from quite different perspectives. In each case, the dance is a mode of becoming. Kaeppler's and Friedland's dancers embody powerful social icons in the human order of reality. Kaeppler's dancers quite literally embody a historical moment whereas Friedland's embody a social moment. To paraphrase Williams, the dancer's *I* becomes the performance role, a self within the special space of the dance. The dimensions of that space are exactly what an outsider (stereotypically white, Euro-American, middle-class, adult) would be least likely to catch. The performative dimension would become invisible to the outsider but is very visible to those within: an intense re-creation of a very localized moment from somewhere else in time and space.

THE POLITICS OF VISIBILITY

Needless to say, visibility depends heavily on what the observer looks for. As Kaeppler notes about the hula, there is no one correct text. There is a characteristically Euro-American "museum collector" attitude to non-Western dance (as Friedland also notes), an attitude congruent with an ideology of the single (primal, invariant, pure) text or object. But there cannot be a single (pure, correct) text if the meaning of the performance turns on the mutual involvement of performer and audience (cf. Bauman 1977). The visible and the hidden but known flow like the folds of an elegant garment or building, in which the delicacy and purity of what can be seen depend in part on the audience's knowing what cannot. In the process, the performer and audience come together as only coparticipants can. Friedland's inner-city dancing children engage in the same process. The social iconography works insofar as the audience knows how to read the social originals, so that the portrayal evokes and reaffirms everyone's sense of who they really are. The order of representation runs directly counter to the Euro-American standard. In Kaeppler's and Friedland's cases, what is hinted at is necessarily part of what counts as meaning. In the Euro-American ideology of knowledge, what counts is what is on the table, semantically speaking.

Local knowledge of what can and cannot be visible is part and parcel of local theories of person encoded in signifying acts.[2] Rosaldo (1982) raised this connection when she argued that "the things we do with words" ("we" being the Ilongot of the Philippines and the things done with words being Ilongot speech acts) cannot be derived from a reference-centered (Euro-American) theory of speech acts. Ilongot speech acts make sense only in terms of Ilongot theories of social person, just as Euro-American speech acts make sense in terms of Euro-American theories of social person, privileging the primary of reference and meaning based on truth value, and, above all, the atomistic individual. Terms like "speaker's intent," for example, downplay the degree to which "intent" is a multivalent construction. Ilongot speech act theory is based on the egalitarian interdependence of social relations so that the rightness of acts, including words, is judged by their place in social relations.

The complementarity of words and actions (what can be said, what must be seen, what must not be said) are the rules of visibility that link signifying acts to person in native Australian performativity. Kendon shows that Central Desert signing works by making highly visible what is socially proper. Signing allows a person to *obviously not say* that which, if it were said, would damage the persona. The physically visible becomes socially invisible so that the person can become properly social.[3] Macdonald shows that what is not said about people's fights must be as widely understood as what *is* said about fights. The complementarity of fighting and talking (how a person's story is told and who tells it) lets a person put his or her "real" Koori self forward. This complementarity is not additive; meaning lies in the tension.

This brings us to the heart of why grammatical-semantic language is not a good model for other sign systems. Sign systems, language included, happen as speech events in Hymes's (1974) sense (after Jakobson 1960). Grammatical-semantic properties of language are not sufficient for a full theory of linguistic meaning because meaning at every turn emerges from an interplay of functions, stylistic and interactive, as well as referential. There is always an interplay, as much in a physics text as in a poetic recital or the gossip that takes place over the coffee machine. This functional interplay can be highly performative. How the interplay works and how it involves a complementarity of word and gesture depend (like pronouns and deictics) on the local theory of person. Kendon's point about the social ideology of signing versus speaking recalls Bakhtin's (1981) argument against divorcing the word from its ideology because both are inherent in the sign's social production. As Kendon notes, there are times when ambiguity is more appropriate than otherwise. A theory of action that gives ambiguity a central place in the construction of meaning is clearly not operating under the same terms as a Euro-American semantic theory. Moreover, Kendon's discussion of gesture as icon of properly social person, like Williams's discussion of actions embedded in performed worlds, demonstrates the semiotic impossibility of formally categorizing physical gestures without a theory of enacted person.

Macdonald also shows the importance of the onlooker in the performative process. Koori fights happen in carefully defined spaces. Once fights are verbally initiated in those spaces, they must be visibly concluded. Fights do not create conflicts so much as they bring conflicts to light. Fighting allows one to be what one was already known to be. Like the place of ambiguity in sign language, knowing the known runs counter to Euro-American "intuitions" about language meaning. Until poetic/performance perspectives allowed new frames of meaning, the repetition of form or of previously known material was considered simply redundant (and implicitly inefficient) information. But as the chapters in this volume show, knowing what is known is highly defining. One has to be *able* to say, "I see," and then carry on; when this is not possible, something is wrong with the social order.

We cannot assess the social act without knowing the theory of person and indeed a theory of reality itself, a theme running through all these chapters. In the Australian worlds presented by Kendon and Macdonald, underlying realities are not neutral; they are dangerous and one has to choose what one represents via language. In Euro-American semantic theory, reference is fundamentally neutral. Anything that is "really there" in the world can simply be referred to; any other mode of signification is categorized as "not in the real world" and therefore as "not really meaning anything." The dynamics of native Australian signifying acts operate under a different set of assumptions about reality. They keep reality controlled and safe through careful selections of the visible. Anything posited is observable, so anything posited had better be controllable. Control is exercised by both performers and audience.

As Kaeppler shows, a bias toward mechanical representation also keeps us from seeing what goes on in the hula, the skillful manipulation of what is and is not hidden. The process of performance is as important as the product, or, rather, the process and product cannot be analytically divorced. Kaeppler places indirection directly in the heart of the cultural picture. Western ideas of indirection, such as redundancy and ambiguity, are basically utilitarian: when they occur, they must be alternative means to an end. But, as Kaeppler shows, and as we saw from another angle in the Australian material, indirection is not a substitute for communication, which ideally would be direct, but directness is not feasible just at the moment. In Hawaiian dance, indirection is itself a basic and essential value, and its enhancement is as elemental in cultural performance as is the poetic manipulation of form in spoken discourse.

If the process of signifying is emphasized over the product, the disembodied act, it is much harder to sidestep the sociality of enacted discourse and much easier to see how political the act of representation can become. This theme touches each chapter insofar as each describes a system in which word and movement are continuous. Outside observers are far more likely to perceive the isolated bits that might fit into their own classification systems than they are likely to recognize a continuous system. This presents a fundamental problem of crosscultural understanding. But what happens when the observer is more privileged than the observed? Representation is always political, mediated by those in a position to do so. In the worlds touched by Euro-American history, the mediators, often academics, are trained in normative modes of representation; investigation and publication are subject to approval by legitimating public institutions and private agencies. None of this is exactly news to anthropologists, sociologists, or historians, but the resultant intellectual and social baggage are very hard to sort out. We can see only what we see. The "facts" that fit the hegemonic scheme of representation become officially visible; everything else fades.

The politics of public representation is especially dangerous for the colonized because the process of colonization has already robbed them of so much of their public personhood. In the United States, the people most strongly affected are those who had least to say about becoming part of the U.S. polity: Native Americans and African-Americans. Each group becomes typified by activities segmented from context by Euro-American collectors: sign language and tapdancing. Each activity is connected to another typifying stereotype: stoic, silent Indians and black people who "sho' got rhythm." Throughout U.S. history, these collected representations have been perniciously performative.

Friedland clearly details the class and race politics of representation. Folkloric dance collectors look for fast-stepping movement clearly bounded from other activities. If the dancers are young, poor, and not white, their own classification of what they are doing is unlikely to affect the collector's judgments. The irony of course is that, by local standards, the collectors are the least educated (and educable) audience and the audience most likely to miss the iconography of the social commentary that is the source of much of the performativity. What the collector accredits as visible and declares to be a dance will not be what the local performers and audience see and will not include whatever gives the dance its performative quality. It will, however, be the basis for further caricature of the Exotic Other on the streets of Philadelphia (performativity by fiat) and the basis for further estrangement and colonization. The social iconography will be classified as "play" (and probably as "childish play"). The category "dance" will be reserved for performances that, like tapdancing, function as product and art commodities—salable in nightclubs, theatres and ethnic museums.

The stereotype of "Indian sign language" is, as Farnell suggests, rooted in a popular Euro-American sense of the iconic as primitive (discussed in some detail later). The iconicity of the primitive is a very romanticized image in Euro-American thinking. It also provides a productive focus for constructing an Other, and the process of colonizing is heavily interwoven with the construction of Others who are subject to different laws and mores. The historical motives for this process probably require little exegesis. Typifying representations of native Australians must have quite similar political dynamics.

This mode of representation is consistent with an epistemology based on *facts:* knowledge as product. Facts become performative by obscuring their histories of social production (Latour and Woolgar 1979). Successful facts are context-free, invariant, and eternally true, like the pure semantics of linguistic reference. The most visible, objectlike, and important bits are those most divorced from obvious connections to ordinary action.[4] This privileging of thing-ness rests on the assumptions that experience is not a mode of signification and that the indexical is not "really" part of meaning. The same ahistorical dynamic holds for the creation of grammars and dictionaries. This is exactly Bakhtin's criticism of static linguistics: when words are stripped of the worlds that produced them, the voices that speak through the words are lost.

Not only are the original voices lost in the process of collection, but they are also replaced by the synthesized, ahistorical voice of the typifying Pure Other. The collected words and actions become a standard by which the collecting society can define itself. This is certainly not a new process; it has been documented back to Herodotus.[5] The danger lies in the political imbalance, in the fact that the original voices are in no position to answer back, their public performativity completely co-opted.

KNOWLEDGE AND THE PLAY OF FORM

A discussion of the performative qualities of moving and dancing and fighting surely must consider the importance of form and play. A person's sense of self, the particular knowledge of who "I" am, within a general cultural framework, is re-created from moment to moment in all the signifying acts of all the relations in all the events that make up a person's life. There are moments in relationships that are especially performative in this respect, moments of intense creation or realization of self. Some moments divide one self from others; some moments dissolve points of opposition between selves. Oppositions dissolve most readily when people share a common perspective, which can emerge from an appreciation of form, a sense of play, and a sense of shared knowledge in order to build a bridge of spirit across the biological packaging that separates people. Any activity that coordinates action to create a unity from many selves—dance, ritual, religion, sport, even military actions—can generate performative moments.

We tend to equate a sense of form with aestheticism, play with recreation, knowledge with pure cognition.

These categories are misleading. Art is one (not the only) way to typify the experience of form. Recreation is one (not the only) way to typify the experience of play. Cognition is one (not the only) way to typify the experience of knowledge. Sharing a sense of form or play or knowledge is a mode of coexperience, each closely related to the other. There is (to use our own categories) an artfulness to play, a form that fits, as fitting form has charm. The discourses of theoretical math and physics are heavily laced with metaphors of play and form and sensation: an elegant theory, a sweet solution, a fun problem. The performative effect of artful, playful knowledge on the texture of human relations and cultural identity has been abundantly detailed by Basso (1979).[6] Friedrich (1986a,b) persuasively argues that cognitive, aesthetic, and social knowledge intersect in the acts of the human imagination and are never inherently separable. Indeed, the very terms "cognitive" and "aesthetic" are categorical distinctions imposed after the fact. I would take this argument further. We learn to know, and to play, and to appreciate form all at the same time as we learn our relations with each other. Each can be intensely locative, creating a profound sense of being as together as people can be at that moment; they can make time seem to stand still or to stand eternal. They generate moments of cultural birth echoed in what we call folktales and songs and dances.

A thing-making epistemological ideology obscures this fundamental performativity. The same logic that separates speech, sign language and movement, or formal action (dance) from nonformal (fighting) also falsely dichotomizes referential and nonreferential, particularly instrumental and poetic. The same "rage for order" (Friedrich 1986b:138) privileges the linear, the rationalistic, the monofunctionally referential, the orientation toward a single goal. But in a deep sense, language and action are not "for" anything, not vehicles or instruments toward a goal. All systems of action are ways of being. Referential, stylistic, and interactive functions of language—of action—cannot be reduced to "information," which is then classified as ambiguous, redundant, or indirect. These modes of meaning are angles in the unfurling of a small social universe splayed out from the momentarily anchored configuration of *I-you* and everyone else. Human signification is a never-finished process of creation in ever-shifting locations.

The more multifunctional that signification is, the more socially dense it becomes. The representations signaled by movement systems ("reference," so to speak) and the deictic arrangement of social space are necessary but insufficient elements of performativity. It is play and form and knowledge—or the knowledgeable play of form—that light the fire: in a ritual, in a dance, in a fight, in a basketball game. The same holds true for language. But since what is theoretically privileged about language is its grammatical-semantic segmentability, that very privileging obscures what is in fact most performative about language—the way in which it creates a space for people to become less separate than their biological packaging suggests.[7]

ICONS, SYMBOLS, BODIES, AND FALSE CLINES

Farnell introduces, as a key issue in this collection, the Cartesian tendency for Euro-American thought to reduce the physical and the iconic to "raw sensate experience." The closer a sign system is to a moving human body, or to an explicit or "natural" representation, the less semiotic it appears to Euro-American observers. Conversely (and ironically), signs become more visibly semiotic to Western eyes as they grow closer to what Westerners perceive as abstract or symbolic. There is a cline in Euro-American thinking in which so-called "abstract symbols" (where human agency is hidden from view) are typified as sophisticated, while signs based on pictures or experiential connections (where human agency seems obvious) are typified as primitive. This cline exists in popular ideologies of self and other (see later) but it also weaves in and out of academic circles, including anthropology, sociology, and linguistics. The more visible and explicit the human agency in the signifying act, the less the act looks like a stereotypic Western sign.

In practical experience, there is no such thing as a simple sign. As Peirce (1956) noted, icons (representational signs), indexes (signs of coexistence) and symbols (arbitrary signs) are ways of knowing that do not operate independently of each other. Icons are symbolically mediated: we even have to learn to see.[8] Symbols need some kind of motivation (Friedrich 1979). And, above all, all signs are indexical in that they must be experienced and made socially real or they cannot enter our consciousness. At the same time, all experience has to be symbolically mediated. As Douglas (1966) and Leach (1964) have argued, we cannot experience what we have no category for. There are no pure icons and there is no basis for seeing, say, a sign language as not symbolic and therefore primitive.

Popular ideologies, however, create oppositions. If "we" are sophisticated, abstract, and symbolic, then the people who are historically and/or geographically (and/or developmentally, see later) distant from us are perceived as relatively simple, concrete, and iconic. The stereotyping is subtle and can be pernicious: the iconic has come to signify the launching point of human consciousness— naive and primitive: the archetypal drawings in the cave (for which there is no evidence that they are either naive or primitive). Children's language is stereotyped as iconic, for example, baby talk as onomatopoeic. Sign languages are popularly perceived as *merely* iconic, as when a counselor for the hearing impaired once typified American Sign Language deictics for tense or distance (hand gestures moving away from the body) as "just gestures that show something is far away or long ago," prefaced with "all they do is . . .". The sense that iconicity is mystically preserved in children and "primitives" strongly suggests a cultural attitude of ontogeny recapitulating phylogeny.

Gesturing in conversation, when associated with ethnic stereotypes (the voluble Greek or Italian), is similarly devalued. The reprimand "don't talk with your hands" carries an underlying message about the declassé, unsophisticated manner of demonstrating what one means instead of simply saying it. The more sophisticated a sign system is assumed to be, the less iconic, or for that matter, indexical, it is assumed to be. Linguistics suffered for a long time from the "merely context" syndrome. Context is politically trivialized by Bernstein's (1975) typification of (1) restricted code (depending far more heavily on indexing than on explicit reference) as working-class, and (2) elaborated code (grammatically and semantically explicit) as middle-class.

This cline of value has another twist. The more distance that the means of sign production puts between the sign and the body (thus extending the sphere of human agency), the more Euro-Americans are likely to value the sign. Westerners have usually classified non-Westerners who have obvious, elaborate technologies as more evolved or sophisticated than non-Westerners who do not have such technologies. Tangible art, writing systems, and mechanical gadgets, however alien in form, seem familiar in concept and are easier to value than are intangible social products. It was a very long time before Western observers were able to see how artful and elaborated were the ways in which Aboriginal South Americans or Australians sang or danced or talked about social relations or cosmologies or any other construct. The technology they had did not extend the sphere of human agency over large distances in the same ways that Westerners habitually associate with "civilization." Such people were long regarded as primitive and still are in many white Euro-American imaginations.

The same cline operates in language channels. The Western imagination has valued written over spoken language, and spoken over signed. Sign language is most embedded in the physical: it is visual; it makes much use of the iconic *and* involves the body. Spoken language is more distanced and disembodied: heard rather than seen, and arbitrary in its semantic structure. Written language is even more distanced and disembodied, in space and in time, and it involves learning elaborate physical inscriptions, a process that is generally quite institutionalized. Furthermore, the cline of value has been extended to the *kinds* of writing systems that exist. For example, Gelb (1963 [1952]) places the pictographic at the least evolved level (since it is most obviously "iconic"), syllabic at an intermediate (dealing with sounds and therefore more abstract but still representing syllables and so partly iconic of the human voice), and the phonemic/alphabetic at the most efficient top level (since it is most analytic, breaking down sounds in the most steps, and less obviously represents syllables, and is therefore least iconic, most displaced, and most valued). Signs become more valued (and so politically visible) to Euro-Americans as the human agency responsible for the signs becomes less visible. This ironic visibility inversion becomes a real problem when the signifying systems lie beyond the purview of Euro-American intellectual institutions.[9]

Finally, the ideology of sign carries an implicit ideology of person. The value of signs decreases in direct proportion to increasing race, ethnicity, and class distance from the Western middle-class, white point of departure. This distance is temporal as well as spatial. Fabian (1983:118-135), discussing the Western ideology of the visual, argues that the exoticism of the iconic is cut from the same cloth as the removal of the Exotic Other from the ethnographer's time into a sphere of timelessness. Timeless truths could be simply (and linearly—again the rage for order!) represented by striking images (quaint Indians? fighting Aborigines? black kids playing in the street?) that told the truth of the Other once and for all. The visual becomes the "natural" reduction of knowledge. The passage of time and the complex creations of knowledge that emerge from action over time can be left out of account.

In the shadow of such closure, the chapters in this volume open the way for local representation. They make visible the local principles by which persons emerge from their acts and indeed make clear why people's acts are significant and systemic.

CONCLUSION

The oppositions by which people make meaning are not static. The essence of systematicity lies in the fact that oppositions are constantly renewed. Invariance (the idea that the forms and meanings of language exist in some abstract sense, free of contextual variation) is a caricature of systematicity that slips easily into an epistemological tradition of timelessness.

There are several implications to the idea that oppositions are processually dynamic, constantly renewed in social process through signifying acts, rather than invariant, a priori givens. One implication is that individual languages (Spanish, Chinese, etc.) are not firmly bounded, integrated monoliths but that grammatical and lexical levels may be differentially integrated into human relations: grammar may index the structure of day-to-day interaction while the lexicon may index a person's long-term group identity (Gumperz and Wilson 1971). Another implication is that language boundaries are fundamentally social categories—ways of typifying actors by the language forms that they use (cf. Hudson 1980:34–36). This principle applies across different kinds of action systems. The distinctions of category between dance and sign and gestures say more about the classifiers' ideology of meaning and person than about the systems themselves.

The way in which grammatical-semantic language has been held as the model of meaning recalls Desmond's argument that many ape language experiments seem designed less to find out what apes do with symbols than to show how close or far apes are from being human (Desmond 1979:54). In effect, the concept of invariant signification—the Platonic form of language—is a way to measure our status against that of the Other, wherever the

Other is found, however the Other is defined. The assumption that language comes in a monolithic package, existing apart from other systems of action, is precisely the same kind of assumption that, as Schneider (1984) argues, has habitually been made about kinship. Our assumptions about what institutions like kinship are made of, or what they do, say a lot about our own cultural symbols but should not be taken for universal truth. The same is true of language: Euro-American ideologies of form and meaning, in codifications since Aristotle, have been themselves highly performative, using grammars and dictionaries and theories of grammars and dictionaries and separating invariant systems from, and raising them above, all other modes of signification to re-create our own symbols of knowledge. The image of language that emerges is an article of faith, but, as with kinship, faith in the existence of a concept does not ensure its universal validity.

The problem is much like that contained in the metaphor that Gould (1977) poses vis-à-vis human evolution. Just as human beings are not the top of the ladder or the apex of evolution but one branch on a bush, so language is not the apex of communication systems but one (albeit one structurally particular) development among many. In fact, to further complicate the picture, it is most unlikely that human language is a monolithic entity with a single defining criterion either in its evolution or in its current state (see also Fouts 1983; Bickerton 1981:217–218). Perhaps the deictic aspects of language developed in directions consonant with evolving social structures at the same time as (to take the Chomskian line) grammaticalizing and symbolizing aspects developed in the course of neurological evolution. Perhaps these semidistinct aspects came to coevolve early in human evolution, implying a coevolution of all manner of signifying processes *as cultural processes,* in which the key dynamic would be the ongoing re-creation of oppositions defining social location and in which the signifying act would be the linchpin, a role very much like the one Habermas (1979) proposes for the speech act in the evolution of society. It cannot be forgotten that social evolution has a cultural dimension: forms of social relations do not exist independent of the cultural sense made of them, and cultural sense is made through signifying acts. Just as words and syntax may express various aspects of identity and social life, so body signs may express what words do not. The dimensions for making meaning, which become available by using the body, may complement the dimensions available by using the voice.

There is a considerable, and growing, literature on the problem of invariant form and meaning. The discipline of sociolinguistics developed as a critique of invariance; I have cited a small portion of it here. Most of what I have said in this chapter is not news in the study of language in culture or language in society. But invariance is a subtle and pernicious attitude, with a long history and a powerful influence on the very terms and objects of semiotic study. I have explored here the critique of invariance that flows from an indexical perspective on systems of movement. The chapters in this volume draw us ever farther away from a view of language that selectively illuminates the fixed elements of structure and obfuscates the dynamics that keep the process of signification alive. Instead, they give us a refreshing sense of signification as continuous creation, of actors stepping in and out of an ongoing stream, taking positions, engaging, disengaging, and reengaging, with never a point where the process stops. The results of this exploration should be as healthy for linguistics as for the anthropology of movement.

NOTES

1. Apropos of essentializing the physical as semiotically primitive, Jakobson (1978:5ff.) makes much the same point in his discussion of the transition from a reductionist phonetic to a truly structural-phonological theory of sound. In most early work on phonetics, the study of sound started with physical creation and articulatory movements, accumulating these into a system. A phonology, argues Jakobson, starts with the structure of the system and works inward. Thus a sound is not a *thing*. A sound is an aspect of the system.

2. Kaeppler argues that such knowledge involves competence in the sense that language does. While I absolutely agree that dance and language involve the same kind of symbolic/ indexical systemic understanding, I do not believe that "competence" is the appropriate term for it. Chomsky's definition of competence is static, the property of an idealized individual independent of interactive knowledge. But as Kaeppler herself demonstrates, systemic knowledge is essentially interactive, and the term "competence," in linguistics, dance, or any other action system, carries baggage that masks this dynamism.

3. In the light of these remarks, Kendon's assertion that "the voice, issuing as it does from inside the body, has a more intimate connection with the person" could be reinterpreted. As Fabian (1983:119-120) argues, Euro-American concepts of time and process with respect to "exotic peoples" have led to an equation of the aural with the personal and the visual with the depersonalized, a concept that has worked its way into much of the writing on oral traditions. In other words, the intimacy-distance contrast is not a natural given. Rather, the signers may be contrasting the unmarked (taken-for-granted) spoken communicative mode with the sign as the marked mode, so that it is the markedness that allows for, say, the depoliticization of varying viewpoints in the process of coming to a consensus. It would be useful to know what the indigenous theory is.

4. The same logic that informs pure semanticity also informs the search for the perfect timeless fact by which a person or a society can be saved: Democracy, True Love, Free Silver, the One Holy and Apostolic Church, the Transcendent Archetypes of early Victorian anthropological theory, New-

tonian space and time, and, of course, Truth itself. It also reinforces analytic schemes based on archetypal "objects" that are easily labeled and categorized: language traits, culture traits, and museum artifacts.

5. Herzfeld (1987) sees this as anthropology's classic dilemma, refracted through the history of Greek-European relations.

6. The classic treatment of play is by Bateson (1972), who sees play as a formal imitation of a defined activity but with different goals and with a distinct metacommunicative frame. He never quite explains why play is fun. Basso (1979) shows both why the Apache find joking fun and what joking does to Apache relations.

7. An architectural metaphor quite suitably suggests itself here: the structure of meaning turns on the creation of social space. In fact, architecture is highly indexical. Alexander et al. (1977) describe architecture as a pattern language built from multiply linked structures embodying modes of experience and ways of being. Alexander's concept of architecture not only is based on a highly performative sense of form and play but also exploits a dense multifunctionality very reminiscent of a Jakobsonian speech event.

8. The National Public Radio program "Soundprint" ran an interview on January 15, 1989, with a blind woman who explained how, after losing her sight at age ten and regaining it past age forty, she had to relearn the interpretation of visual images in three-dimensional space, as when she describes the moment when she realized that the white or light gray long conical "pole" next to the house across the street was actually the driveway.

9. When these chapters were first given as papers, American Sign Language translations were given simultaneously by two signspeakers who alternated between papers. Even those of us who could not read ASL were caught up in their performance, which markedly broadened the physical focus of attention. The effect was especially marked when the interpreters represented elements of other movement systems (such as Plains sign) in ASL. Several observers commented afterward that so kinetic a channel changed their perspective on what the whole session was about, even if the observers could not read the actual signs.

REFERENCES

Abu-Lughod, L., and C. Lutz. 1990. Introduction: Emotion, discourse and the politics of everyday life. In C. Lutz and L. Abu-Lughod, eds., *Language and the Politics of Emotion.* New York: Cambridge University Press, 1–23.

Alexander, C., S. Ishikawa, and M. Silverstein. 1977. *A Pattern Language.* New York: Oxford University Press.

Austin, J. 1962. *How to Do Things with Words.* Cambridge, Mass.: Harvard University Press.

Bakhtin, M. 1981. Discourse in the novel. In *The Dialogic Imagination.* Austin, Tex.: University of Texas Press, 259–422.

Basso, K. 1979. *Portraits of the Whiteman.* New York: Cambridge University Press.

Bateson, G. 1972. A theory of play and fantasy. In *Steps to an Ecology of Mind.* New York: Ballantine, 177–193.

Bauman, R. 1977. *Verbal Art as Performance.* Rowley, Mass.: Newbury.

Benveniste, E. 1971 [1956]. The nature of prounouns. In *Problems in General Linguistics.* Coral Gables, Fla.: University of Miami Press, 217–222.

————. 1971 [1958]. Subjectivity in Language. In *Problems in General Linguistics.* Coral Gables, Fla.: University of Miami Press, 223–230.

Bernstein, B. 1975. *Class, Codes and Control: Theoretical Studies Towards a Sociology of Language.* New York: Schocken.

Bickerton, D. 1981. *Roots of Language.* Ann Arbor, Mich.: Karoma Press.

Bourdieu, P. 1977. *Outline of a Theory of Practice.* Cambridge, UK: Cambridge University Press.

Desmond, A. 1979. *The Ape's Reflexion.* New York: Dial.

Douglas, M. 1966. *Purity and Danger.* London: Routledge and Kegan Paul.

Fabian, J. 1983. *Time and the Other: How Anthropology Makes Its Object.* New York: Columbia University Press.

Fouts, R. 1983. Chimpanzee language and elephant tails. In J. DeLuce and H. Wilder, eds., *Language in Primates.* New York: Springer-Verlag, 63–75.

Friedrich, P. 1979. The symbol and its relative non-arbitrariness. In A. Dil, ed., *Language, Context and the Imagination.* Stanford, Calif.: Stanford University Press, 1–61.

————. 1986a. Linguistic relativism and poetic indeterminacy: A reformulation of Sapir's position. In *The Language Parallax.* Austin, Tex.: University of Texas Press, 16–53.

————. 1986b. Linguistic relativity and the order-to-chaos continuum. In *The Language Parallax.* Austin, Tex.: University of Texas Press, 117–152.

Gelb, I. 1963 [1952]. *A Study of Writing.* Chicago: University of Chicago Press.

Gould, S. J. 1977. Bushes and ladders in human evolution. In *Ever Since Darwin.* New York: W. W. Norton, 56–62.

Gumperz, J., and R. Wilson. 1971. Convergence and creolization. In D. Hymes, ed., *Pidginization and Creolization of Languages.* New York: Cambridge University Press, 151–167.

Habermas, J. 1979. *Communication and the Evolution of Society.* Boston: Beacon.

Herzfeld, M. 1987. *Anthropology through the Looking-Glass.* New York: Cambridge University Press.

Hudson, R. A. 1980. *Sociolinguistics.* New York: Cambridge University Press.

Hymes, D. 1974. *Foundations in Sociolinguistics.* Philadelphia: University of Pennsylvania Press.

Jakobson, R. 1960. Linguistics and poetics. In T. Sebeok, ed., *Style in Language.* Cambridge, Mass.: Massachusetts Institute of Technology Press, 350–377.

————. 1971. Shifters, verbal categories and the Russian verb. In *Selected Writings of Roman Jakobson Volume II.* The Hague, Netherlands: Mouton, 130–147.

————. 1978. *Six Lectures on Sound and Meaning.* Cambridge: Mass.: Massachusetts Institute of Technology Press.

Kurylowicz, J. 1972. The role of deictic elements in linguistic evolution. *Semiotica* V:174–183.

Latour, B. and S. Woolgar. 1979. *Laboratory Life: The Social Construction of Scientific Facts.* Beverly Hills, Calif.: Sage.

Leach, E. 1964. Anthropological aspects of language: Animal categories and verbal abuse. In E. Lenneberg, ed., *New Directions in the Study of Language.* Cambridge, Mass.: Massachusetts Institute of Technology Press, 23–64.

Peirce, C. S. 1956. Logic as semiotic: The theory of signs. In J. Buchler, ed., *The Philosophy of Peirce.* London: Routledge and Kegan Paul, 98–119.

Rosaldo, M. 1982. The things we do with words: Ilongot speech acts and speech act theory in philosophy. *Language in Society* 11:203–237.

Schneider, D. 1984. *A Critique of the Study of Kinship.* Ann Arbor, Mich.: University of Michigan Press.

Silverstein, M. 1976. Shifters, linguistic categories and cultural description. In K. Basso and H. Selby, eds., *Meaning in Anthropology.* Albuquerque: University of New Mexico Press, 11–55.

———. 1977. Cultural Prerequisites to Grammatical Analysis. In M. Saville-Troike ed., *Linguistics and Anthropology.* Washington, D.C.: Georgetown University Press, 139–151.

Weber, M. 1978. Basic sociological terms. In G. Roth and C. Wittich, eds., *Economy and Society.* Berkeley, Calif.: University of California Press, 3–63.

Chapter 9 CARTESIANISM REVISITED: THE GHOST IN THE MOVING MACHINE OR THE LIVED BODY

Charles R. Varela

BODY-DEAD/BRAIN-DEAD AXIOM

In the introduction to this collection of ethnographic studies of action-sign systems, Farnell alludes to the intersection of anthropology and philosophy on the issue of Cartesianism and its relationship to human movement. Of concern is the fact that Cartesian dualism is a constituent component of social theories in the behavioral sciences. The human being is thereby presumed to be a veritable ghost in the social machinery of cultural life. In other words, the behavioral sciences endemically presume a disembodied actor. This means that neither gestures nor bodily movements are subsumed under the description of action but are seen only as behavior. At issue is not only the failure to include the body in references to the actor but also the failure to regard body-movement as genuine action, a phenomenon I refer to as the body-dead/brain-dead axiom.

The body-dead/brain-dead axiom is to be distinguished from Bryan Turner's (1984) discussion of the neglect of the body in social theory in which he identifies an absence and a furtive history. While Turner talks of the absence of embodiment, he does not include movement and therefore the genuine agency of the body. This does not mean that he rejects the agentic nature of body movement; on the contrary, his three prescriptions for an "adequate sociology of the body" are consistent with such an inclu-

sion. This chapter offers a conceptual clarification of
Turner's call for "embodiment [as the] exercise of ... some
form of corporeal government" (1984:245).

It is my contention that until this axiom is understood,
successfully challenged, and dismissed, the disembodied
actor is likely to remain ensconced as a category in our
interpretive endeavors. On the other hand, however, if
attempts to include the disembodied actor fail to engage in
a justified dismissal of the axiom, then such inclusion,
however well intentioned, is likely to be ad hoc and
unsystematic. The consequence of this professional good-
heartedness and alertness to the fashions of the day will be
that the rest of the discipline may not be convinced to take
it seriously. In this chapter I address the problem that the
behavioral sciences are dead to the moving body—they do
not *see* movement as action—because they are brain-dead
to the concept of the moving body—they do not have the
philosophical perspective that would allow them to *understand* movement as action. I present a way to understand and challenge this so that a dismissal is both
justified and sufficiently convincing to engage our professional seriousness. I dedicate this effort to the scholars
whose work is represented in this collection—their seriousness has inspired my effort and informed its realization.

The aim of this paper is to address the body-dead
brain-dead axiom by critically confronting the conception
of the "lived body." To realize this difficult aim I will look
at this notion itself in the context of Merleau-Ponty's
existential phenomenology and his Saussurean-inspired
philosophy of history. I will also examine the notion as it
has been used by the philosopher and dancer Maxine
Sheets-Johnstone in her conceptualization of improvisational dancing and as it has been accepted and promoted
by the anthropologist and poet Michael Jackson for an
anthropology of the body. My central contention is that
the notion of the lived body or bodily intentionality is a
sensitizing but not a definitive conceptual solution to the
problem of the disembodied actor in the behavioral sci-

ences. Thus phenomenological existentialism is viewed as a transitional position, not a final one. A similar view regarding the contributions of Merleau-Ponty has also been advocated recently by Marjorie Grene (1985) in her discussion of the new biology and the new philosophy of science. For example, she contends that Merleau-Ponty's *Structure of Behaviour* (1967) and *Phenomenology of Perception* (1989 [1945]) are now scientifically out of date, and the theory of perception developed in the latter has been updated by the perceptual theory of J. J. Gibson.

For an understanding of the cogency of this judgment two integrally connected strategies will be pursued. First, I will show that there are certain internal conceptual difficulties in Merleau-Ponty's notion of the lived body within his existential phenomenology and that he was in the process of transcending those difficulties in his ventures into the philosophy of history via Saussure. The second strategy is the analytical means with which to carry forth the first: the ethogenic standpoint of Rom Harré and especially the new realist philosophy of science that is its ground.

Harré's specific service to us in reference to the internal conceptual difficulties of the notion of the lived body is the idea that, contrary to the Humean tradition that prevails in philosophy and the behavioral sciences, the ideas of substance, causation, and agency are internally connected and compatible with each other. In this light, human agency entails both that the person is a real entity—a substance—and that the exercise of agency is a real event—a causal force. The notion of the lived body does not entail an entitative concept (substance) of the individual, the subject, and so lacks a genuine concept of the person. On the other hand, however, it represents an ambiguous location of agency. We shall see that a concept of person is genuine only insofar as it is grounded in the ideas of substance, causation, and agency. The surrogate concept of subject involves only the idea of agency; it carries no genuine conception of power or force. The subject is thus a free-floating quality; it is not grounded in substance. The notion of lived body was a rejection of the Cartesian trick of privileging the mind as agentic to the exclusion of the body, but, without a concept of person, the body itself is ambiguously granted agency. To be sure, Merleau-Ponty suggested that mind and body are both centered in, and mediated by, the subject's being-in-the-world, but this does not resolve the ambiguity regarding the location of agency.

What is crucial here is that two issues are in danger of being conflated: one is the issue of agency and the body, and the other is the issue of the theoretical status of being-in-the-world and its relationship to person and agency. As might be expected, Merleau-Ponty believed that bodily intentionality accounts for agency and the body: the agency of the body is claimed as an "ultimate fact," that is, a fact of which he knows only *that* it is so and not *how* it is so (Russow 1988:41–42). Reversing the center of privilege in Cartesian dualism from mind to body is ultimately rooted in the tacit acceptance of the conceptual incompatibility of causation, substance, and agency presumed by the Humean tradition. If mind is a ghost in the machinery of the body, moving or not, then the body is the only reality left for the location of agency. If the body as machine—the objective body—is rejected as such because of its deterministic status, then the body as lived—the subjective body—must be accepted as the only remaining alternative to determinism. Somehow, as a Jamesian act of faith, the body is not viewed as deterministic as long as it is lived, and therefore, it is assumed, the subjective body must be the only proper location for agency.

The difficulty with this notion is that the agency of the body—its intentionality—is acausal because Merleau Ponty tacitly associates causation with determinism. This means that the intentionality of the body cannot be genuinely agentic; that is, the force of bodily intention is as ghostly as the force of the Cartesian mind! Clearly then, the notion of lived body as an anti-Cartesian basis for a conception of the embodied actor does not work, and it does not because it cannot. The status of intentionality, mental or bodily, remains problematic for the precise reason that the actuality of the body cannot establish the reality of intentionality. As long as the agentic status of intentionality is implicitly taken to be acausal, neither the facticity of the body—the objective body—nor the experientiality of the body—the subjective body—can grant intentionality the status of reality. The reality of the agency of intentionality is the power of causation, and that power belongs to a person not an intention. People intend, not bodies; minds don't intend, people do. And, as I intend to show, people are causal in their agency because as persons they are social.

A Harréan turn in our philosophical understanding of causation and agency, the person and the social, and mind and body will permit us to regard people in a different way. People are necessarily social and so are socially interacting persons employing their discretionary causal powers of authorship in the use of mental and bodily predicates in the deployment of various lingual and gestural systems. This is my reading of the significance of Urciuoli's correction of traditional linguistic theory in its neglect of both the social constructional activity of language-in-use and of action-sign systems, and her correction of Habermasian communicative theory with its focus on the speech-act and its omission of action-sign systems (Urciuoli, this volume, chap. 8). Utilizing Drid Williams's fruitful conception of the signifying act—the human action-sign—Urciuoli has transcended the limitations of these two theories by including both action-sign systems and social constructional activity in linguistic anthropology.

Indeed, it is in reference to the conception of the signifying act that Merleau-Ponty's venture into the philosophy of history will be revealing. In the course of his intellectual development, he shadowed the ambiguous notion of being-in-the-world onto a sociolingual and gestural construal of Heidegger's notoriously persistent notion (Descombs, 1980, pp.73–74). But that is where Merleau-Ponty left it. It will be my contention that Sheets-Johnstone's and Jackson's resort to the notion of the lived body tends to restrict them to Merleau-Ponty's existential phenomenology, thus depriving them of the liberating perspective of Merleau-Ponty's expansion into the philosophy of history via Saussure. As a consequence, both scholars have missed the fact that the idea of bodily intentionality was sensitizing but not definitive, and thus they have overlooked its transitional status. The import of this is the recognition that Merleau-Ponty's promising position stands as an invitation for us to realize what he could not: the systematic connection between language and gesture, and from this point, especially, to get to the moving body as genuine action.

I will show that such a connection can be made through the concept of the signifying act, but not through the concept of the lived body and its gestural expressiveness, nor its refinement into the idea of the body as flesh. Resort to the latter in the work of Sheets-Johnstone and Jackson thus constitutes a degenerate form of Merleau-Ponty's conception, because they merely restate the concept and ignore his invitation to tackle the problem of language and gesture. They are thereby blocked from developing a conception of the signifying act. This means that while they may be able to avoid the intellectualist fallacy of talking *about* the body—the observed body—they can do so only by committing the phenomenalist fallacy of talking *of* the body—the experienced (or felt) body. They are never able to get to talk *from* the body—the enacted body.

The concept of the signifying act allows us to deal systematically with the enacted body, that is, the person agentically deploying a semiotic system for body movement in the cultural space of social action. And in that systematic treatment, ethnographic description can make the profound shift from accounts of movement in word glosses to accounts in movement scores, which is to say, to descriptive accounts backed up by rigorous textual methodologies. Ultimately, "talking from the body" means that the movement itself is transcribed and the movement itself is read. This is exactly what one does not find and will never be able to find in any work produced by either

Sheets-Johnstone or Jackson, the point being that their philosophical commitment is responsible. As we shall see, it must be concluded that their significant contribution to the problem of the embodied but unmoving actor in social theory is a clear demonstration that a Merleau-Pontian behavioral science of the body is a dead end.

AXIOM OF THE DISEMBODIED ACTOR AND MODERN INDIVIDUALISM

It is important to remind ourselves that the problem of the body is itself subsumed under the broader and preexisting problem of Western individualism in modern society. (The point of the reminder is that people or persons together—not minds or bodies —have worked out a new language with which to define and understand themselves.) With the rise of modernity, the organic-realist conception of the individual and the mechanistic-nominalist conception of the individual come into conflict. The organic-realist view formally represents the Judeo-Greco-Christian tradition in which the individual is conceived as a differentiation from within an organically and spiritually defined living whole. Formally speaking, the one and the many (unity and diversity, God and man, man and woman, group and member, constant and variable, essence and accident) are connected in a special whole-part relationship. The one as a unified whole is a transcendent supernatural or superempirical reality. This idea is variously manifest, of course, in the hegemony of the Hebraic community, the Greek polis, and the Roman Catholic Church. The Gregorian chant is musically expressive of that transcendentalist idea: many individual voices sing, but only the voice of one is heard. In this worldview, the individual is ontologically derivative. The whole is real, the part is a fiction; thus the part is dependent primarily on the whole for its being and so is primarily a part of the whole. The fictional status of the individual in this paradigm refers to the principle that an original separability of the individual is impossible.

The rise of modernity was the occasion for an ontologically conflicting conception of the individual. The concept of individualism summarily captures that complex idea. In my judgment, a major clue to the cultural theory crystallizing this ontology into a collective representation was the scientific revolution, in particular, its new conception of method and its new conception of the nature of Nature. Science shifted the ideal of epistemological authority from the mystery of authority (faith, belief, revelation, intuition) to the mastery of authorship (the rationality of theory and research). In the surrounding revolutions of Protestantism, social contract theory, and industrialization, the same basic idea of the primacy of the individual was becoming established (Stark 1963, Berman 1970, Zijderfeld 1970, Morris 1972, Lukes 1973:45–122, Baumer 1977, Kumar 1978, Berger 1979:1–29, and Dumont 1986:23–112). Here, because of space limitations, I must restrict my focus to the epistemological and ontological revolutions in science.

The change in ontology from supernaturalism (the supernatural explains Nature) to naturalism (Nature explains Nature) was profoundly important. By the early nineteenth century when LaPlace informed Napoleon that astronomical theory had no need of the hypothesis of God, the secularization of science was effectively in place and its sovereign notion of reality was naturalism. More and more, that sovereignty began to take hold in the everyday world of commonsense. Mary Shelley's Frankenstein— the modern Prometheus—is telling testimony to the monumental import of the sovereignty of science and its principle of naturalism.

With the ideas of system, machine, and determinism, science was demonstrating the principle that nature explains itself. Descartes's resort to mind-body dualism, with the correlative co-ordinates of inside-outside, and Kant's resort to the transcendental ego and its grounding in the noumenal realm of creation and construction were, above all else, cultural-ideological reponses to the newly emerging issue of freedom versus determinism. To see clearly how their response bears directly on the problem of embodiment, the sociological import of the scientific revolution for the rise of individualism must be examined briefly.

The mechanistic-nominalist conception of the individual is the bedrock of individualism. Now that nature is conceived predominantly as a deterministic system of causal laws, the formal understanding of whole-part relations changes radically. The one is now dissolved in the many: the part is real, the whole a fiction. The fictionality of the whole refers to the principle that structures are reduced to aggregates of parts. The part is primarily independent of the whole and thus is primarily apart from the whole. The direct consequence of this is a new ontology for the idea of the individual: from the previous principles of organic derivation and differentiation we move to the principles of mechanical origination and separation. In other words, the individual is by nature originally separate from other individuals, and its nature is originally individual and as such a natural given. The formation of various natural wholes now conceived as aggregates is a mechanical event, as is the fundamental nature of the interaction of the naturally given individual's defining any such aggregates. The everyday importance of all this is poignantly revealed in Albert Camus's *The Stranger,* in which Meursault rails against the pure abstract nature of society and proceeds to reduce its reference to ordinary individual human beings. The sociological import of these new principles of origination and separation is manifest in the idea of the mastery of authorship.

What was crystalizing here was the principle and the policy that the authority of God and the collective in matters of truth, reality, and meaning was being transposed in toto to the authority of the individual and mind; and finally to depersonalized observation and theory. The mastery of authorship confers upon that authorship the virtual authority of God. Mary Shelley understood exactly that. In becoming a doctor of science, Frankenstein became the creator of a human creature; however, his moral irresponsibility to his creature in partnership with the creature transformed it into a human monster. With this understanding we can suggest that modern individualism is a possessive individualism. It entails the absolute right of possession and dispossession regarding the agency and authorship of oneself, mind, and body under the auspices of individualistic advantage.

Cartesian dualism and Kantian transcendentalism must now be seen in the context of the modernity of possessive individualism. To legitimate ideologically the absolute authority of the individual qua individual, Descartes formulated a philosophical theory of that authority in its phenomenological form, "I think, therefore I am." He was contributing to the creation of the reality of individualism by using the rational and charismatically legitimated device of definitional fiat, establishing the principle that the mind is a separate reality, a mental substance, and its separateness is manifest in its location internal to the individual and internal to itself apart from the body. This principle expresses an emerging modernist obsession with incorrigibility.

Hume precipitated a crisis when he used a puritanical reading of empiricism apparently to destroy the reality of the new individualism of the self (the "I") as the ground for the mind ("think"). That is, if introspectional perception does not identify the self, then it does not exist (after all, as the new slogan in the making was to declare, seeing is believing). Kant responded to Hume's empiricist dogma that only the visible is real (observation as both inspection and introspection), with the rationalist dogma that the apparent reality of the visible is strictly due to the genuine reality of the invisible. This dogma is based on a theory of interaction between the individual as subject and the world as object and the partnership of individual and world in the construction of that world by the individual.

In all of this philosophical activity, the theoretical foundations for the cultural ideology of possessive individualism were being thrashed out. It is particularly clear that the mind and its ground in the self is the exclusive and prepotent ontological concern. The implication is that the body and its movement are taken to be ontological givens, considered unproblematic, and regarded as being defined strictly within the phenomenal realm of mechanism and determinism. The self and mind are exclusively identified within the noumenal realm of spirit and freedom. Henceforth, everything of value that is human, for instance, personhood, authorship, and agency, has essentially nothing to do with the phenomenal world of visible physical objects.

The positivistic construal of Darwinian evolutionary theory enriched this picture by complicating the deterministic system of the human body. Determinism is extended to include the dynamics of evolutionary time and the dynamics of an organic energy-drive system (Freudianism is the paradigm example). As a consequence, a fundamental conflict is established with regard to mind and body at the very core of the idea of modern individualism. While the mind of the individual is exclusively the real location of the agency and authorship of the self, the body of the individual is exclusively the real location of causation and movement.

This conflict is of great importance. Because the mind is the natural site of agency and authorship and the body is the natural site of causation and movement, to assign causation to the mind and agency to the body would be to commit a category mistake of foundational proportions. Freud and Merleau-Ponty of course do just that. In Freud's case, the idea is something like this: there must be meaning to an individual's behavior because there is more to mind than the conscious. Thus there must be an unconscious causal process generating the meaning of conscious acts of apparent agency: determinism explains (away) freedom. In Merleau-Ponty's case a parallel and challenging idea emerges: there must be meaning to an individual's act since there is more to generating meaning than the mind. Therefore, there must be an amental bodily process that is the agency and not the causation of meaning: freedom triumphs over determinism.

It is clear why Merleau-Ponty rejected Freud's concept of the unconscious and translated it instead into the concept of the ambiguity of perception (Merleau-Ponty

1964b:224–243). He hoped the sting of determinism would be neutralized thereby. However, in the decade of Merleau-Ponty's death (1960s), his translation failed to convince psychoanalysts and was duly dismissed (Descombes 1980:69–70). This correctly revealed the inadequacy, if not superficiality, of Merleau-Ponty's notion of the ambiguity of perception. The point being that the deeper issue of the failure concerned determinism and the problem of the relationship between causation and agency in reference to freedom. Neither Merleau-Ponty nor the psychoanalysts dealt with that issue because they could not. They lacked the appropriate new realist philosophy of science that was in the making in the very same decade.

This, then, is the legacy of Cartesian dualism that is the inheritance of the behavioral sciences. A metaphysical conflict between our categories of mind and body exists. Human traits are assigned to mind and natural traits to body, thereby creating deep metaphysical confusion. Our acceptance of these categories as performative resources for the social construction of our mutual identities and value creates the reality of being disembodied in our individuality and being disembodied actors as we live our social lives. When psychoanalysis attempts to resolve our confusion and to reconstruct our reality, it does so by committing the category mistake of dissolving the human in the natural: determinism is the reality behind the appearance of freedom. Ultimately, for Freud, biology is the psychological reality behind culture. This is the deep error of a positivistically informed depth psychology of the individual (Varela, forthcoming). Classical behaviorism merely renders Freud's mistake with puritanic efficiency by translating mind into the strict complement of biological structure, the function of physical behavior. It is in this regard that we can appreciate the wit who, in noticing the connected achievements of both of these psychologies, remarked that psychoanalysis or behaviorism is such a perversion that only a very brilliant fellow could have thought it up.

The perversion consists in the absurdity of believing that the mind unconsciously generates meaning that appears in consciousness apart from the agency of the person whose consciousness it is. Behaviorism, on the other hand, would have us believe that the mindless body moves by being caused itself to do so apart from the person whose body it is. In this combined psychoanalytic and behaviorist misadventure, we have the disinheritance of the mind (the person doesn't think, the mind does) and the disinheritance of the body (the person doesn't move, the body does). If one prefers psychoanalysis, the mind thinks and moves the body by doing both behind the person. If one prefers behaviorism, the body moves and thinks for the person by doing both independently of the person (underneath?).

It is quite clear that neither Cartesian dualism nor psychoanalytic and behavioristic responses to it are acceptable. When we eventually understood that positivism is a misconception of science and that neither of the two psychologies are, or could be, natural sciences, even apart from their positivist commitments, then the unacceptability became decisive. In having eliminated these responses to Cartesian dualism, however, we are still left with its legacy. Although Freud-free and Skinner-free zones for social-psychological analyses of cultural life have been erected, sociology and anthropology continue to honor that legacy, ensuring that embodied but static being and action are the order of the day via the endemic body-dead/brain-dead axiom discussed earlier.

But let us return to the Merleau-Pontian philosophical response to Cartesian dualism in the wake of psychoanalysis and behaviorism. Earlier I indicated that the response is essentially a reversal of the center of privilege in Cartesian dualism, although that reversal is conceptually unstable because of the resort to a Heideggerian construal that mind and body are centered in being-in-the-world. In that understandable but unsatisfactory response, Merleau-Ponty's contribution has to be seen as sensitizing, not definitive, and therefore a position that is transitional and not final. Bodily intentionality, the agency of the lived body, in being taken by Merleau-Ponty to be an ultimate fact indicates the infertility of his resort to the idea of being-in-the-world.

The import of this situation is that we should pursue the contrary understanding that people intend, not bodies; and minds don't intend, people do. "People" here refers to the concept of the individual not merely as a subject but as a person and therefore an agent. It also and must refer to "person" as a social actor causally empowered to engage in social and reflexive commentary with the resources of vocal and gestural (i.e., movement-based) semiotic systems. The crux of the matter is that Merleau-Pontian existential phenomenology constitutively lacks a genuine concept of person and agency, and lacks any clear concept of the social nature of the person as agent (Turner,1984:54). My firm thesis is that Harré's work allows us to clarify this dual failing without sacrificing Merleau-Ponty's brilliant venture into the philosophy of history via Saussure in which he invites us to somehow connect language and gesture. Indeed the clarification explains why the concept of the signifying act provides the connecting link between language and gesture.

SHEETS-JOHNSTONE AND THE MANIFESTATION OF BODILY LOGOS IN IMPROVISATIONAL DANCING

Almost three decades ago Maxine Sheets-Johnstone published what was probably the first philosophical study of the dance (Sheets 1966). From that ground-breaking work she eventually published an article, "Thinking in Movement," which was devoted to the philosophical investigation of improvisational dancing (Sheets-Johnstone 1981). A former dancer turned professional philosopher, her stance is existential and phenomenological, Sartre and Merleau-Ponty being the principal sources that inform her approach to the dance. The ideas of freedom and the lived body are the central categories with which she launches her investigations. The discussion on improvisational dancing shall be the major focus of my examination here, but it is important to note that Sheets-Johnstone has developed her position in a new but related direction since then, by moving into biology and evolutionary theory en route to formulating her conception of a philosophical anthropology. The culmination of this is her new book, *The Roots of Thinking* (1990).

The focus of this new direction is a concern "with evolutionary continuities and existential realities" (Sheets-Johnstone 1983:132). The theme Sheets-Johnstone is pursuing is "the possible conjunction of human evolution and human freedom through the body" read as "animated text" (Ibid.,130–131). This reading is to afford her "a grasping of the primordial strata of meaning in the body of human knowledge about the human body" (Ibid., 132). The key idea throughout is that of "viewing the [human body] as a locus of meanings and continuities" (Ibid., 130) and seeking phenomenologically to achieve "an illumination of what is there in experience [of the body] . . . an illumination of the invariant principles engendered in the experience [of the body]" (Ibid., 132). It is clear that Sheets-Johnstone is searching for the roots of human freedom through the body in the evolutionary continuity with other animal species. It is important to bear this theme in mind as I now proceed with the examination of "Thinking in Movement."

"Thinking in Movement" is rooted in mixed purposes. The central purpose is to present an account of improvisational dancing—not *an* improvised dance but *the* improvised dance. The intent is to differentiate between choreographed and improvised dancing. That distinction identifies her focus: to give an account of one type of dancing—improvisational—and in that account to deal with that genre of the dance itself. The specific intent is to get at the nature of the improvisational process,a process considered to be both creative and generative. Sheets-Johnstone wishes to identify the core of that creative process generating the dance. This task is set as follows: to get at (1) the essential character (generative core) of (2) the spontaneous creation of (3) dancing (4) as experienced by a single dancer.

The second point, spontaneous creation, advances toward a precise differentiation between choreographed and improvisational dancing. The creation of improvised dance is deemed to be pure spontaneity: no future, no past, only the instant of birth and thus only here and now. As such an absolute spontaneity, a dance is independent of any relationship to time or to any other form of dancing. Improvised dancing is meant to be an ongoing or prolonged present of pure instants of spontaneous creation. Although the dance itself is consequently in process without rules, according to Sheets-Johnstone, there does appear to be at least one rule: the rule *of* the dance is that there are no rules *for* the dance.

This feature is not to be taken to mean that we have here a mindless body, a machine in motion without a ghost. Quite the contrary, what we have is a *mindful body*. A body that is mindful is a lived body. It is exactly this thesis that propels Sheets-Johnstone into the consideration of certain traditional philosophical assumptions she is in fact challenging with this investigation into improvisational dancing. These assumptions stem from Cartesian dualism.

What may well be the major thesis of her article is the idea of the mindful body, or what Sheets-Johnstone calls "bodily logos." What we have here is

> that fundamental creativity founded upon the bodily logos, that is, upon a mindful body, a thinking body, a body which opens up into movement, a body, which, in improvisational dance, breaks forth continuously into dance and into *this* dance, a body which moment by moment fulfills a kinetic destiny and invests the world with meaning. (Ibid., 406)

Thinking in movement is the dynamic logic of fundamental creativity, of which improvisational dancing is allegedly representative. The mindful body in movement is mind literally inhabiting its natural mode of being: mind actually living *in* movement. This mode of natural being is a declaration of animate existence. In each moment of spontaneous creation of declared animate existence, there is the instantaneous unification of sense and motion. An instance of sense and motion is an interfusion such that sense or perception and motion or movement are a homogeneous whole. Thus we have thinking in movement, not thinking *with* movement, as pure spontaneity and as pure motion (Puri and Hart-Johnson, this volume, chap. 7).

The critical feature of thinking in movement as pure motion, especially a purity of motion that is a pure spontaneous creation, is its rationality. Its rational character is, of course, kinetic, not intellectual, but nevertheless an action of directly "wondering the world." In this action, the world is explored and systematically ordered. We have here a form of lived movement, generated moment by moment, and thus, a meaningfully lived movement.

The notion of mindful body or bodily logos as pure spontaneity, pure motion, and the creation of a pure form of lived meaning is admitted by Sheets-Johnstone to be conceptually ambiguous. Her own position is that the cognitive character of bodily logos is rational, though she clearly understands that it would be seen by some scholars to be prerational, a primitive, not a sophisticated mode of being. This is precisely where the traditional assumptions of Cartesian dualism are implicated. Sheets-Johnstone asserts not only that two of these assumptions determine that the notion of bodily logos will be construed as prerational being but also that it is just those assumptions that the notion of bodily logos directly challenges.

The first assumption entailed by Cartesian dualism is what may be called the human distinction: human thinking is simultaneously rational and linguistic. Our thinking is rational, and that is because it is always conducted within a symbol-system with rules. Thus language is the agency for symbol-making and meaning-making. In that role, it mediates thought and determines that movement is the vehicle for thought. This assumption of the human distinction reifies thinking and in so doing, Sheets-Johnstone believes, humankind is being exalted, denying both that mind may be nonlinguistic and still rational and that this form of rationality may be in evidence throughout other animal species.

This last point about our shared animal character and non-linguistic rationality is Sheets-Johnstone's peripheral purpose. The account of improvisational dance itself as a creative-generative process, and the notion of bodily logos as the essence of that process, ultimately have implications beyond aesthetics. If mind is a fundamental dynamic of kinetic rationality that is nonlinguistic (not simply prelinguistic), we can begin to tie aesthetics, epistemology, and evolution together into a meaningful picture of humankind: we are most human when we are free, and we are most free when we are our fundamental animal self. Apparently, neither communion nor community puts us in more intimate touch with our humanity than our continuity with the animal kingdom.

The second assumption relates to Ryle's version of Cartesianism, the ghost in the machine model of mind: it is *in* the body but not *of* the body. Thinking therefore is what a mind does; what a body does is behaving, not thinking. Mind and body relate such that thought is a covert process; that is, it is prior to overt behavior into which it must be transformed. The notion of bodily logos is a direct challenge to this mind-thinking and body-behaving model: thinking in movement refutes the belief that mind is necessarily prior to its overt expression. Thinking *of* movement and so thinking *then* movement is one possibility, but only a possibility, not a necessity. Thinking in movement is movement as thought itself, "significations in the flesh" (1981:400). Movement is therefore mind wondering the world directly and directly making one's way in the world. However, in the light of Sheets-Johnstone's assumption that evolutionary continuity is unproblematic, the basis for our shared animal character, the question can still be raised, Is thinking in movement a moving machine without a ghost, or a ghost in a moving machine?

There is no doubt that Sheets-Johnstone's paper is rooted in the conviction that Cartesian dualism is ultimately overcome by seeing mind as a commonality among species, so that our human distinction is an afterthought, so to speak: linguistic rationality comes after nonlinguistic rationality. With this conviction, we are neither machines nor ghosts, but simply Darwinian animals in movement and so, on occasion, in thought. In time some of us begin to think about the movement in which we have been wondering and making our way. But the question only persists: even if we are Darwinian animals in movement and sometimes in thought, are we at least ghosts in moving machines? How does shifting mind to the body as bodily logos avoid the problems of Cartesianism and mechanism?

MODERNITY AND THE PARADIGMS OF SUPERNATURALISM, POSITIVISM, AND NEW REALISM

If we consider the paradigmatic developments in modern intellectual attempts to know who we are in the world in which we find ourselves, three can be identified: supernaturalism, positivistic naturalism, and, quite recently, the twin anti-positivist revolts of new realism and neo-Wittgensteinian naturalism (Keat 1973). For the purposes of this chapter I will suspend consideration of the neo-Wittgensteinian revolt. Generally, the rise of science meant a shift from supernaturalism to naturalism: nature was to be assumed to include both the effects and the causes of all phenomena found in nature. (Fig.1)

Supernaturalism in its perspective of western man/woman is based on the assumptions of speciality (divine selection), discontinuity (spiritual status), and voluntarism (free will). Cartesian dualism was the modern version of this tradition, which was to be bypassed by the new paradigm in the making, positivistic naturalism. In fact, what was happening in this development was the inversion of the three former assumptions. From speciality to commonality (natural selection), from discontinuity to continuity (material status), and from voluntarism to determinism (mechanistic lawfulness). In honor of

Darwin I will refer to this paradigm as the "descent-of-man perspective." The birth, establishment, and identity of the behavioral sciences were and are in part still grounded in that perspective. The gradual demise of the positivist conception of science by the 1960s was a consequence of the anti-positivist revolt of the new-Wittgensteinians and the new realists. Thus by the 1970s we found ourselves in a postpositivist age, and as a result, with an emerging new paradigm.[1] In honor of both Jacob Bronowski and Rom Harré I will refer to this paradigm as the "ascent-of-man perspective."

Although naturalism has been accepted, some substantive refinements have been made. The original idea of continuity as a revolt against supernaturalism is still in force. However, we must now distinguish a metaphysical (ontological) discontinuity between man and nature from a functional discontinuity *within* nature between species. As Bronowski has pointed out, evolutionary theory is incomplete if it cannot account for the evolution of complexity, and not simply for the survival of species.[2] This fundamental change in focus, from the survival of species to complexification, signals the ascent of species. This is an ascent to a higher level of a certain kind of complexity and it is of great moment here, for now it can be said that new assumptions are indeed crystallizing. If humankind is not special in virtue of our commonality (because natural selection is the reality of our earlier becoming), then at least humankind is unique. After Bronowski's suggestion concerning our uniqueness, we have, in addition to commonality, the new assumption of specificity, that is, the unique evolutionary ascent of a species. There is a deep change here, because the selective natural process now begins to include both the environment *and* the species as the theoretical site of the selective process. In our case this is the particular entry point for an agentic perspective, that is, if the species is an agent of evolutionary ascent, then agency, especially, is a natural predicate of the activity of individuals. In fact this is itself confirmed by Harré's concept of the power of causal production as the power of agency. Consequently, natural selection within the human realm of evolution becomes a natural and social (interactional) electivity.

Quite clearly, then, two other assumptions are emerging here and I propose to call them "speciation" and "determinationism." The evolution of complexity means that functional discontinuity within nature and between species is a required concept and thus a new fact. This is speciation. Because specificity refers to the evolution of complexity and because the natural selective process, in being (at times) a process of ascent, now entails the contribution of the agency of a species, therefore determinism must be complemented by the principle of determinationism. Now, when the human species is considered under the auspices of this new paradigm, the assumptions of specificity—our natural electivity, speciation—our cultural status, and determinationism—our human agency, permit us to differentiate between the *human animal* and the *human being.* The descent-of-man perspective tells us about an animal that happens to be human, and the ascent-of man perspective tells us about a human being that happens to be an animal. If our natural mode of be-ing is *human,* and that is functionally—not metaphysically—discontinuous with respect to other species, then the major clue to who we are is grounded in the *unique* status of our species *self-determination.* And a status, particularly, whose unique evolutionary complexity is in variegated sign-system.

I now wish to examine briefly one feature of our unique status in order to clarify the new paradigm called "new realism" (Warner 1990:133). In common with all species we have the requirement of survival, and this, to be sure, certifies our undeniable and most significant continuity with all species. However, we must declare that what is unique to our way of human be-ing is that we do not simply live in order to live (survival); we live in order to live meaningfully (existence). We can formulate this thus: human being is cultural, and being human is social and is therefore psychological. The conceptual point is that we live from meaning, through meaning, and for meaning. When we socially construct the performative practices of social commentary and reflexivity, especially in the critical mode, we explicitly, and at times ecstatically, are discovering that we *exist.* To exist is to stand out as a significant difference and so to be above chance. To transcend chance is to function in a critical reflexive mode: to think about, talk, and talk about, and therefore to live self-consciously and meaningfully. Existence differs from survival and profoundly so when the critical mode assumes the role function of Weberian charismatic leadership, the agency of revolutionary change. Whether it be a Mohammed, a Jesus, or a Socrates from the very distant past, or a Gandhi, a King, or a Sadat from our very recent past, the critical vision of a new meaning places the charismatic leader in a foundational conflict of mutual exclusivity with the power structrue of the culture. Thus, to choose existence is to affirm the new, renounce the old, and risk extinction; to choose survival is to affirm the old, renounce the new, and risk nonexistence. Such leadership is often conducted with full and poignant knowledge that, beyond a certain point, extinction is inevitable.

Through such historical examples we can note the species specificity that marks the ascent of the cultural being of human animals and the gradual self-definitional process by which nature and culture are effectively differentiated. At the heart of that difference is the functional and not the metaphysical discontinuity between survival and existence: human beings live, but in order to do so, they have to mean it or die an ontological death. The ascent of culture is a social transubstantiation into human being.

The intellectual context in which we work today is not transitional: we have been in a postpositivist age for at least two to three decades (Hassan 1985; Lash 1989). I contend that our main business with respect to the philosophy of the behavioral sciences concerns the formulation, utilization, and development of what Marjorie Grene (1966) and Rom Harré (1990) separately call the conceptual reformation of our understanding of the human practice of being and knowing. I submit that today the new realist paradigm represents our best rational choice and commitment. The assumptions of specificity, our natural (social) electivity, speciation, our cultural status, and determinationism, our human (social person) agency—all indicate the natural form of being human.

It is with respect to the postpositivist age in which we live and the new realist paradigm that is being articulated with some success that I can critically engage Sheets-Johnstone's position. It can be clarified by situating it in paradigmatic perspective. It is my contention that the author's use of the conception of bodily logos is strictly informed by her commitment to functional continuity and not to functional discontinuity. She defines human being by identifying the unique status of that being with a feature that we apparently share in common with other species: thinking in movement, of which improvisational dancing is supposed to be its cardinal instance. The implicit conception is this: to be human is to be free; to be free is an act of pure spontaneity; and to be spontaneous is to be our fundamental (continuity-commonality) animal self. The mixed purposes of Sheets-Johnstone's article place her in a mixture of paradigms in which the human animal and the human being are conflated.

In both the nineteenth century and the first half of the twentieth, it was new, it was exciting, and it was indeed fruitful, to attempt a conception of human being as a theoretical derivative of a conception of human animal. The first major phase of the Darwinian revolution rightfully obliged a commitment to that proposition. Specifically, this was a direct result of the continuity assumption and its reductionist program: the simple explains the complex, the earlier the later, the human animal explains the human being, and so on.

What we have learned since then is that the reductionist program of continuity in a special sense is unfruitful: it is easy to go back, but, once there, we can never in principle return to where we are now. This is directly due to the emergent character of evolution, the logical form of which Bronowski (1977) called an open and unbounded plan. In such a plan an evolutionary solution to the problem of survival is not given in advance but is created in the lived historicity of a species. The reductionist program calls for a conception of evolution as a mechanical process, the logical form of which Bronowski calls a closed and bounded plan. In such a plan a solution to a problem is given in advance. One can certainly achieve a definition of our species specificity from the assumption of continuity via a description given in terms of commonality, but that description will be pointless because the ascent of a species cannot be accounted for by its descent. The logical character of the descent version of the evolutionary process in principle rules out emergence. The ascent perspective means that the evolution of complexity cannot be predicted, and while there will be commonality between species there will perforce also be a functional discontinuity. We are led to ask, then, of what theoretical value is a description based on the assumption of commonality and prediction?

Furthermore, because prediction (description of event-regularity) and explanation (description of the causal production of events) are separate and different theoretical moments, we must say that there is a deeper point. The description of regularities prescribed by the descent perspective—the prediction of continuity and commonality—cannot include a description of the agentive power of particular species—the explanation of discontinuity and specificity—that comes from the ascent perspective. Explanation and prediction fruitfully coincide when both are on the same evolutionary level, in this case that of ascent. For, in the case of ascent, the regularity to be described will be that very agentic achievement that has emerged. The point is that, to offer a prediction based on the continuity-commonality assumptions is to describe something as it *was,* but not necessarily as it *is.* In our case, to offer a decisive description of human freedom in terms identical with animal freedom, whatever that may mean, would indeed be describing us not as we *are* but as we are *no longer.* This certainly would be a case of Being and Nothingness, but that is not exactly what Sartre had in mind. Sheets-Johnstone has in effect attempted to account for the early Sartrean notion of freedom as pure spontaneity in evolutionary terms that in fact reduce the notion to spontaneous motion and not improvisational dancing.

Now, admittedly, this may be the fault of both Sartre and Sheets-Johnstone, although I doubt it in the former case. Sartre later set freedom within the cultural context of socal life: "It is . . . men who make . . . history on the basis of real, prior conditions . . . otherwise men would be the vehicles of inhuman forces which through them would govern the social world" (Sartre, 1968:87). Nevertheless, to conceive of the freedom of human being as identical with the freedom of animals to move spontaneously is not of interest descriptively because it is not suitable to our theoretical interest in a different order of natural kinds, human beings. And this is true even if it is what Sartre had in mind, but, of course, his classic battle against Freud's conception of the unconscious was exactly the revolt against positivism—in particular, the principle of determinism—of which the unconscious was so notoriously representative. Indeed Freud too was conflating the different orders of natural human kinds. Sheets-Johnstone's reading of Sartre here was not in his best theoretical interest, nor ours. For we and Sartre are interested in the existence of human being and the freedom expressive of that elective act. Less than that is what some animals do, human or not, and that is of interest only if one is interested in nonhuman animals. It may well be that whatever fruitfulness remains in the use of continuity-commonality assumptions is the clarification of the lower from the vantage point of the higher. We may and can clarify animal performance at its best relative to our species in reference to a select biological criterion of interest (a neurological-cognitive criterion in this case). However, *we* are simply no longer interested in what *we* can do at *their* best. Sheets-Johnstone's conception of body logos is insensitive to that distinction, but the insensitivity is paradigmatic, not descriptive. Insofar as she works from the perspective of positivist naturalism, however uncritically and unintentionally, her descriptive achievement cannot accomplish her descriptive intent to tell us about the freedom of human being. And this is not to say that she commits herself to this paradigm, some of whose assumptions, I contend, she is working from.

An obvious objection can be raised regarding theory and description. Sheets-Johnstone explicity asserts that she intends to give a description of *the* (improvisational) dance and not a theory of *a* dance (improvisational). Granted her precision in attempting to distinguish her task, there is a problem nevertheless. To work from the classic phenomenological claim of the descriptions of things as they are is a claim no longer taken seriously. Such a claim issues from the positivist assumption of the separation of theory and description (or, more generally, the separation of conception and perception). The assumptions of continuity-commonality direct Sheets-Johnstone's descriptive treatment of the dance and lead to two devastating consequences. Her description of human freedom as pure spontaneity in the form of improvised dancing is irrelevant as a description of the freedom of human being. In reference to other animal species it tells us only about what we can do at *their* best and what they can do at *our* poorest. Second, the theoretical intent of her description is irrelevant. If she intends to achieve a conception of human freedom by way of this resort to improvisational dance and evolution, such a conception is impossible, because she cannot arrive at a concept of what we do at our best.

This last point raises a fundamental question about her thesis. It implicates her in the assumption that improvisational dancing is not what we human beings do at our best. And what is meant by "at our best" consists of two things: what we can do from our unique human powers and capacities, and what we do when those powers and capacities are realized in reference to standards of excellence (in a given local culture). The suspicion is that Sheets-Johnstone made the choice of improvisational dance because in Western idioms of dance, improvisation is (frequently) not dancing at our best (see Puri and Hart-Johnson, this volume). My point here is that her paradigmatic assumptions define a theoretical interest that is embedded in her descriptive focus. As long as she retains the classic phenomenological posture of the theory-description distinction, she will not recognize that her descriptive focus betrays an embedded theoretical interest. The issue is this: her assumptions compel her toward a theoretical conception of the freedom of the *human animal* that contradicts her implied theoretical interest in the freedom of the *human being*. This is my reading of Sheets-Johnstone's relationship to Sartre's work: I am conjecturing that her thesis is rooted in the desire to ground his conception of human freedom in human action, on the one hand, and in biological evolution, on the other. Improvisational dance was meant to mediate the two poles of interest.

The absolutely crucial issue, however, consists in her assumptions about improvisational dancing. Why would anybody assume improvisational dancing is not what we do at our best but what we do at the best of other species? Why would anybody assume thinking in movement is thinking in dancing? And why would anyone assume that spontaneous creation of movement is the spontaneous creation of dancing? Puri and Hart-Johnson clearly demonstrate that unless one knows the rules for structuring a dance idiom, itself imbedded in a local culture, one *cannot* distinguish between a *choreographed* and an *improvisational* dance (this volume, chap. 7)! And finally, when a dancer uses the word "movement," why would anybody assume that the dancer means movement at our poorest and at the best of other species? And, to be sure, if they do, why would anybody assume that that should be taken seriously?

The crux of the matter comes to this: Sheets-Johnstone assumes uncritically that improvisational dancing is not what we do at our best but is the best of other species and therefore is the poorest of our own. Now, either one is talking about dancing or one is talking about moving, but not both, and in the human realm, neither can be removed from the sociolinguistic sphere of human meaning-making. Spontaneous movement play does indeed occur, as do spontanteous practical and symbolic actions of all kinds, but improvisational dancing is a dance-act expressive of our best, and disciplined by excellence, and it is of a different order, as Puri and Hart-Johnson illustrate. It may be an emergent sort of danced version of a Jackson Pollock action painting (a painter's vision of improvisation?), but if so, in that case what we have is "the sophistication of extreme simplicity." To create an improvisational dance is to create the appearance of that extreme simplicity given the sophistication of an artist. There is spontaneity and there is spontaneity: a rose is a rose is a rose is not necessarily the same rose—it may be a role enacted by Nureyev and Fonteyn.

If indeed it were the case that spontaneous, improvisational dancing solely referred to us at our best when committed to excellence, and art were our intent, then it would seem absurd to claim that such art is rational but prelinguistic or nonlinguistic, and so entirely removed from other semiotic systems such as spoken language meaning. Even if one were talking about human movement and not dancing, if its spontaneous generation is claimed to be prelinguistic, its rationality would be problematic. It would be like calling the body rational because it is ordered, and intelligent because it is intelligible. Dancing, improvised or not, compels us to insist that it is necessarily languagelike, in the sense that it is part of a semiotic of some kind. The point here is that human word-talking, sign-talking, or enactments of any action-signs are systematically connected semiotic forms. What is now required is the theoretical imagination to envision the verbal but nonvocal languages of the arts. In my judgment, denying this problem of an artistic semiotic is a theoretical failure of nerve. This is exactly what Langer heroically understood and attacked when she developed her thesis about the nondiscursive nature of artistic language. Even if her philosophical theory is a failure—and, alas, I believe it is—a failed solution does not entail a failed theoretical problem.

From my remarks thus far I have to declare that Sheets-Johnstone is in fact talking about improvised human movement play while her intent is to talk about improvised dancing. Even if we grant that spontaneous, improvised movement is created, the status of her category remains in force. It is neither the cognitive status nor the creativity of the activity in question that determines its descriptive status but rather the order of creativity. Movement as she defines it, spontaneous or not, is activity at their best and our poorest and so represents the failure of ascent.

In addition, when discussion concerns a species already ascendent, something new is involved. To be at our best is to exist, but to be at our excellent best is to transcend. To remain at the level of movement may be creative, but to ascend to a complex dance act is transcendence. Sheets-Johnstone's argument would lead her to deny this and to claim that we are merely exalting ourselves with such talk, as if in doing so we can only have the identity of spiritual beings within the old supernaturalistic paradigm (Ibid.,400–401). But this misses the paradigmatic point. To exalt ourselves at the expense of acknowledging the Darwinian revolution is one thing, but to do so from within that revolutionary framework in specific reference to the biologically legitimate distinction between the descent and the ascent perspectives, is quite another, for the act of transcendence in ascending to art, or science, or any one of Cassirer's cultural symbolic forms of knowledge, is exaltation. Human being is existence, human excellence is exaltation, and the process is transcendence.

But *who* is transcending? Descartes was wrong in his insistence on the mind and not the body. Sheets-Johnstone is wrong in suggesting the mind in the body (notice she does not say thinking *with* movement as Puri and Hart-Johnson do). Her thesis is Cartesianism revisited—Descartes with a twist. A phenomenal act of faith is required to escape Cartesianism by burying mind in the body and declaring that a bodily logos is the phenomenological essence of human being. However unintentional, there is an involvement and a consequent responsibility implicated in the positivistic naturalism that residually informs her work. As we have seen, evolutionary theory in the modern synthesis requires an enlargement of its premises if the evolution of complexity is to be accounted for. For, without the kinds of enlargement that Bronowski (1977), Gould (1977:63–69, 251–259;1985:55–73), Margolis (1984:64–82, especially 72–75), Delbruck (1986), Mayr (1988:8–23) have attempted, neither culture, action, nor the social person can be understood as the human natural phenomena that they are. A deterministic model of evolution cannot do it—the logic of the plan is wrong. In addition, Popper has shown that indeterminism is not enough: animals could still be envisioned as computers. And that would make each of us, if in motion, a ghost in a moving machine. Thus, the concept of bodily logos is a case of a ghost—rational agency—in a moving machine— improvisational dancing.

No, it is not the *mind* that moves the body, nor the *body* that minds itself in moving, but the *person* acting. It is the person who thinks, moves, and dances, but the person is missing in Sheets-Johnstone's movement, thinking or not. And the person is not simply lost, it is unavailable in any nonhuman animal's "thinking in movement." Descriptions made from the positivistic assumptions of continuity-commonality dictate a conception of animals as moving machines and of the human animal as a ghost in the moving machine. The person is lost, and only a person dances or improvises, choreographs or theorizes.

A person who dances and/or theorizes does so in terms of a semiotic of some kind from a local culture. The ultimate and devastating failure of this phenomenological approach to movement, especially when compounded by being residually embedded in a reductionist program, is that the historical and cultural ontology of the human being is lost to the evolutionary and species ontology of the human animal. This means that the primary social reality of personal agency—the signifying act and the construction of meaning—is lost. Sheets-Johnstone's focus on improvisational dancing and her paradigmatic commitments, intentional and unintentional, place her in the classic modernist stance of individualism and the solo act of being and meaning. This is not only no longer "the way we think now" (Geertz, 1983), but also no longer the way anyone should think about being human anymore.

CARTESIANISM AND LOSS OF THE PERSON

Sheets-Johnstone's "Thinking in Movement" has taught us that the problem of Cartesianism has not been properly confronted and dealt with. The problem of mind and body and their relationship is not the deep issue. The problem, rather, is that of the missing person in the Cartesian perspective. In this regard Cartesianism constitutes two kinds of errors. One of them is the notorious misreading of the quite proper *inwardness* of mental life as the fantasy of *interiority*—the theater of the mind (Toulmin 1979). Thus in reference to the error of interiority, we have the foundational inside/outside dualism, the nonmaterial world of an inner mind versus the outside material world, including other people. The derivative of this is the mind/body dualism—the separation of the interior mind of the individual from his or her own material body. The theater-of-the-mind metaphor generates a root absurdity: the individual speaks what the mind is thinking. This separation of language and mind implicitly privileges the individual without the crucial notion of person. The focus now is the *mind,* not language, and the individual as the *subject,* not the *person as a social being.* And it is clear why: Cartesianism is an intellectual formulation of the new ideology of modern individualism. The theme of the ideology is the conceptual legitimation of the absolutism of the individual in matters of meaning, reality, and truth. The transference of such authoritative matters from the collective to the individual (subject) meant the denial of the "other" (object), generalized or singular. The human being is now to be identified with the location of epistemological authority, and that is the mind and the individual, not language and the person (necessarily entailing other persons). This intellectual method of legitimating individualism is, viewed from the way we think now, to be seen as a performative procedure for the political control of the other, favoring the self against other in matters of the construction of meaning. Modern individualism is the political declaration of the hegemony of the self against the other in social action.

The other error implicated in mind-body dualism is an equally pernicious but as yet a far less emphasized mistake, namely, that of confusing the *body* with the *organism*. The human organism is an asocial, complex, biological entity, and the human body is a social, complex, cultural entity. The human organism can be regarded as the natural individual and the human body as the cultural person (the rationale for this will be presented later). The mistake of confusing body with organism generates a special kind of root absurdity. This can be seen in the way the two errors are linked.

By disconnecting mind and language, the Cartesian fallacy of interiorization has in fact led some thinkers to fashion a peculiar dissolution of mind-body dualism. The notion of thinking "behind" speaking ultimately turns "mind" into a mentalized organism. Freud gave us one version of this: the structural unconscious (superego, ego, id) is a veritable semanticolingual biological engine. Lévi-Stauss gave us another version, stressing the logical category as against the Freudian stressing of the affective category (Rossi 1974:19). The result of the linkage of these Cartesian errors is another indication of the loss of the person: an individual speaking his or her mind (inwardness: person) is lost to the individual speaking for his or her mind (interiority: subject). The human being is now the "individual" and not the "person": interiorization shifts the focus from a person-to-person relation to a mind-and-self relation (the mind and itself). The mind is now the subject within the body, and the other is an object. The absolute priority and centrality of epistemological authority in its transference to individualized location required this separation from the other and this conversion of the other into an object (the objectivist stance). These were the new phenomenological details that represented the fulfillment of the prescription of the hegemony of the self over against the other.

It is important to emphasize again that the subject is now the subject of predication (i.e., of experience, of mentality, etc.,) and is not the person engaged with other persons in the moral space of a local culture. Ideally, the subject of predication is an open category admitting n-number of construals. But since Cartesianism is the theoretical fulfillment of the ideology of individualism, those construals are exclusively restricted to the predicates of mind, body, and their cognates. Merleau-Ponty's rejection of mind-body dualism avoided both the Freudian and the Lévi-Straussian versions of an unconscious mentalized organism by centering mind and body in the Heideggerian concept of being-in-the-world (Spurling 1977:14–16, 21–22; Descombes 1980:74). But Merleau-Ponty never came to, although he came *up* to, *who* that being-in-the-world *is,* other than the subject of experience (phenomenology) and embodiment (phenomenological existentialism). From the Husserlian consciousness *of* the world (intentionality) he shifted to a consciousness *in* the world (bodily intentionality):

> The relationship of subject and object is no longer the cognitive relationship in which the object always appears as constructed by the subject, but a relationship through which . . . the subject is his body, his world, his situation, and in a certain sense enters into interaction with it. (Merleau-Ponty 1964a:72)

The last sentence, with its string of possessives beginning with the body and ending with the situation and its implied world of others, is certainly an apparent relief from the where-on-earth-is-it land of Heidegger's being-in-the-world! Merleau-Ponty's concept of the ambiguity of perception, which accompanied his Heideggerian move, was the means by which he avoided a Freudian unconscious. But, frankly, the relief from Freud's Cartesian darkness—the hidden subject—to the open side of the subject—its body—constitutes only a subtle shift to another part of the region of the ambiguity of perception. Merleau-Ponty's move from Husserl's privileging of perception, through Freud's work, and onto Heidegger, was a fruitful move from the interiority of mental life to its inwardness. This characterization is one way to define Hamlyn's suggestion that Merleau-Ponty's notion of the individual is "solipsism with a body" (1989, p.328). And this is not an inconsiderable achievement. Nevertheless, that "situation" and "world" now include an ambiguous implication of "other(s)" are not much more than an unpacking of being-in-the-world. But in this category set there is no genuine conception of culture, social interaction, and person as summarized in Geertz's article "The Way We Think Now" (1983:147–163) and noted in Turner's discusion of their absence in the work of Marcel, Sartre, and Merleau-Ponty (1984:54).

Geertz's article captures a Kuhnian shift from the individualist model to the culturalist model of human nature. This allows me to locate further the character of the Merleau-Pontian "terrain of the '*entre deux*,'" that conceptual space, as Merleau-Ponty himself says, where the Hegelian freedom of "the synthesis of *in itself* [thing] and *for itself* [consciousness]" can be found (Descombes 1980:56). Descombes has described this sense of Merleau-Ponty's project as "an unfinished and precarious one" in which subject and object are neither reconciled nor dissolved but resolved "between-the-two," a "finite synthesis" of "product/producer, active/passive, instituted/ instituting" (Ibid., 56–57).

In the individualist model, human nature is biological (as actual or virtual), it is lived psychologically (as interiority or inwardness), and it is therefore social and may be experienced as such. In short: if P(psychological), then S(sociological) because of B(biological). At the core of this model is the predisposition to the related ideas of internalized mental structures, the unconscious, and its cognates. Freudian and Lévi-Straussian theories are the old-fashioned determinist versions (hard and soft, respectively), while Jungian theory is a degenerate type, regressing to the mysticoromantic creationism of the old charismatic in modernist dress. In the culturalist model, the nature of being human is cultural (nonspecific biological form requiring specific adaptation), it is lived socially (constructed, reproduced, reconstructed), and it is therefore psychological and may be experienced as such. In short, if S (social), then P (psychological) because of C (culture) (Bruner 1990:1–32).

Until their cogency is persuasive, any of the forms of individualist models—for example, the old-fashioned biological determinism of instinct doctrines or the new-fashioned biological determinisms of either sociobiology or cognitive psychology—are to be regarded as variations on the fallacy of internalization. This fallacy is based on the twin positivist assumptions of metaphysical materialism and individualism. Its theme: the secret of the social is the psychological, ultimately to be materialized in the organism. As we shall see later, the identification of a fallacy of internalization is Warner's development of Harré's theory of causal powers, as the latter is embedded in the ethogenic standpoint. Harré's standpoint is a social psychological version of the culturalist model. It is a fruitful way to explore fully Urciuoli's suggestions that we move from the speech act to the signifying act and from the invariant structures of linguistic and other such social theories to the activity of socially constructing, person-empowered, signifying acts.

We can appreciate anew Merleau-Ponty's final position in which the lived body and its intentionality graduate into the concept of the gestural body as lived flesh. His position can, I contend, be understood as the stretching of the individualist model to its end point, thus taking it and Merleau-Ponty to the edges of the cultural domain. But in this construal, his thought does not, because it cannot, enter into the heart of "the way we think now." Culture, social construction, person and self, and semiotic systems with their various forms of signifying acts are central concepts unavailable to any version of the individualist model. Merleau-Ponty's variety was transitional, sensitizing, and it was deeply envisioned, but there it remained, "*entre deux*."

As I indicated earlier, Merleau-Ponty's interest in Saussure in reference to the philosophy of history meant that he saw the next philosophical frontier to be the nexus of the sociolingual and the sociogestural (Descombes 1980:71–74). This is the other way in which he came up to the cultural world of persons but no further. And it must be made quite clear in this regard, that identifying the nexus of language and gesture does not necessarily entail either the conceptual grasp of the body as a socially lived cultural entity, the socially lived body as a moving body, or this moving body as the person who is its social agent. This is not to condemn Merleau-Ponty but simply to indicate sharply how he was neither an anthropologist nor a sociologist in his philosophical thinking. It is also to admire how advanced he was as a philosopher in thinking toward the social. Wittgenstein just before him and Kuhn just after him indicate a watershed in the thinking of philosophers as they are discovering the person-centered sociocultural nature of being-in-the-world.

It is of more than historical importance to note that merely to identify the subject with the body and its flesh, and to capture this as an 'I can' rather than an 'I think', was hardly news, even in Merleau-Ponty's time. The Darwinian field of activity-centered and opportunistically situated animals became the grid presupposed by American pragmatism. Informed by the Emersonian vision of the socially grounded and agentically empowered individual, James, Dewey, and especially Mead biologized that vision with an emergentist-creativist reading of evolutionary theory. In Mead's first major paper in 1900, the individual qua individual was conceived as a causally empowered personal discoverer, problem centered and socially situated (Varela, forthcoming, chap.7). It is not *mind* or *behavior* that Mead chose as *the* defining term for his basic proposition that the "unit of existence is the act." It is *conduct.* And it has two primitive meanings: conduct is movement and conduct is moral (cultural). Thus for Mead the human individual is an embodied (biological) person (causally empowered agent) in social space, and the act *is* the conduct of movement(s). By 1913 he had completed his celebrated conception of the social nature of mind and self. With that completion, action as "conducted movement" was refined to "a person's conduct of gesture."

To be sure, Mead was preoccupied with vocal gesture, but it is absolutely clear that he was not restricted to that kind of gesture. First, he was particularly preoccupied with his project to defeat Cartesianism by showing that the solipsistic ghost was neither a ghost (because mind is conduct) nor solipsistic (because mind is social conduct). Second, Mead declared that human beings are "endlessly proliferating gestures" (Varela forthcoming, chap. 7 and 8). In 1913 Miguel de Unamuno nearly perfectly articulated the core of the Meadian achievement:

> To think is to talk to oneself, and each of us talks to himself because we have to talk to one another. . . . Thought is interior language, and interior language originates in outward language. So that reason is properly both social and communal. (Quoted in Toulmin 1979:7)

In the spirit of Mead's work then, it must be said that the idea *for* the signifying act is there. However, what is still missing is the idea *of* the signifying act as it has been articulated by Williams (1982). A Meadian construal of the signifying act would be that it is gesture, and of course it is a person's gesture. What is emerging here is a deep challenge to Merleau-Ponty's position (and thus contrary to Csordas's recent endorsement of it [1989:5–12, 34–39] for anthropology) concerning the best reading of "I can." Mead's work compels us to declare that it is the primacy of the person and gesture and not the primacy of perception and experience that is critical. Being-in-the-world is thus the being of a person in the social act of performing culturally grounded spoken language and other semiotic systems. From that standpoint one can bridge the apparent gap separating language and gesture. Language and other semiotic systems are centered in the conduct of gestures, structured by appropriate rules for their signifying uses. And it is precisely the person who is the missing link in the connection to be made between language (lingual gestures) and gesture (action-signs). For it is the person as the social actor in the local culture who has become knowledgeable and in some cases literate in its various semiotics and who has been enabled to display the cultural ways in which vocal (lingual) and nonvocal (action-sign) gestural acts can be and are significantly performed.

STRAWSON AND THE RESTORATION OF THE PERSON

Virtually on the eve of Merleau-Ponty's death, in 1959, Sir Peter Strawson published his important book *Individuals.* The fundamental importance of achieving a metaphysically rigorous conception of the person is that it enables him to demonstrate that the concept is a major solution to the problem of Cartesian dualism. The logic of the solution is this: the concept of person is logically primitive in the working of our language, and, in so being, dissolves the asocial features of interiority and individuality which have marked and marred Descartes's philosophy of mind and body. Strawson has shown that the person is lost in Cartesian dualism, and its restoration is realized by understanding that Cartesianism, against itself, in fact presupposes the person, and thus our primordial social being (1959:101–103). Thus, being-in-the-world *is* being a person in a linguistic world of other persons. As Langford has more recently said in his intricate refinement of Strawson's idea, persons are necessarily social (1978:280–282). And linguistic conduct is a person involved in the act of the ascription of mind and body predicates. But such an act is the ascription of predicates to self and other. Strawson remarks simply on the matter: ". . . 'in pain' means the same whether one says 'I am in pain' or 'he is in pain' . . . [it is the same for] first-person meaning, and second and third-person meaning" (Strawson 1959:99). And each lingual partner always presumes that the "other" is a self-ascriber (Strawson 1959:103–108). Person, not perception, is primary, and the person acting is the point of the act rather than bodily or mental intentionality. That one is intentional is given in the primacy of the person. People intend, not bodies. Minds don't intend, people do. Such people as persons—not as minds or as bodies—conduct linguistic and other semiotic practices of predicate-ascriptions. Merleau-Ponty referred to the lived body as "the sentinel standing silently at the command of my words and acts" (Hall 1983:344). Quite so: his linguistic predicative act commands both body and mind ascriptions. When one takes that linguistic act as a given, then attention to be-ing is now available, mental and physical, or whatever. The experience of the body can be electively attended to. Thus, talk *about* the body, that is, with the third-person pronoun and its objectivist rhetoric, shifts to talk *of* the body, that is, with the first-person pronoun and its subjectivist rhetoric. Merleau-Ponty's discourse on the lived body is elective talk of the body from the first-person subjectivist standpoint. But what the discourse cannot permit one to engage in is talk *from* the body in the terms of a non-vocal semiotic.

Thus the Merleau-Pontian standpoint permits us to hear people talk when they are speaking, but not to understand (not guess, suggest, or believe) that they may still be "talking" when they are not speaking. As one example only, a group of Plains Indian sign-talkers sitting around and not speaking for some time, but periodically laughing uproariously, is beyond the existential phenomenological position, in principle (see Farnell, 1994). And any degenerate form of existential phenomenology, either the strong version of Sheets-Johnstone or the mild version of Jackson, both repeat and demonstrate that conceptual impotence. Both may talk *of* the body and thus avoid the intellectualist limitation, but talking *of* the body and doing so in subjective-experientialist terms, is not talking *from* the body in the conduct of a nonvocal, semiotic, gestural system. And fatally, a rejection of literacy in principle as intellectualist (despite their own literate practices) means that movement literacy, being outside the common spoken or written variety, cannot even be imagined. Even when noted in the practices of others, it simply cannot be taken seriously. Becoming literate by learning Labanotation, for example, is an impossible because irrelevant prospect. Consequently, word glosses, the translation and reduction of actions into spoken language terms, will absolutely and automatically be provided instead of movement scores, as if by some mysterious necessity.

Now it is my contention that the key to this systematic failure, at least from a conceptual point of view, is the systematic loss of the person in the primacy of perception. The key to being able to graduate from talk of the *experienced* body to talk from the *enacted* body, warrants a grasp of the principle that the person must be primary in our conceptual understanding. Being-in-the-world consists in the being of a person in a cultural world of socially constituted linguistic and other semiotic conduct. In current discourse, Mead's "conduct" has become "practices."

PRIMACY OF PERSON AND PRIMACY OF CAUSATION

The next step in the argument is to connect the primacy of the person with the primacy of causation. The point here is that "person" presupposes the agency to author the linguistic practices of predicate ascriptions of all varieties. In order to have a genuine conception of person as possessing the agency to author, the conception must be connected to the ideas of substance and causal power, for without these, "agency" becomes a free-floating occult quality sustained only by an act of faith, that is, as feeling, experience, or simply getting on with living (not thinking philosophically). The deep problem of Cartesian dualism lies in the failure to ground agency ultimately in anything but an act of faith. To believe that intentionality indexes agency because it is mental has of course failed: this is the point of the ghost-in-the-machine metaphor. But to then believe that agency is saved because it is identified with the body (thus a bodily logos) is equally a failure. Without causation, the "force" of intention is a ghost, regardless of its mental or bodily identity.

As long as causation is associated only with deterministic causality, agency is contradicted by causation. In this case, causation cannot be conceptually available as the foundation of agency. And without "cause" there is no "force," and consequently there can be no agency. Thus the traditional Cartesian version of agency precisely is the ghost *and* the machine; the Merleau-Pontian version of Cartesianism is the ghost *in* the machine. In either case, agency as intentionality is a ghost. To believe that the body can be the house of freedom through the trick of calling it the lived body is merely chimerical. The actuality of the body as physical or experienced, by itself, does not and cannot establish the reality of agency. The Harréan view is that the reality of agency is the reality of natural kinds of particulars, that is, substances, having the power (potential, i.e., latent force) to produce consequences (force, i.e., actual power) (Harré and Madden 1975:82–100; Harré 1986b:281–316). The concept of person is one kind of substance naturally endowed with the power to produce consequences. It is in this exact sense that the next step in the argument is to connect the primacy of the person with the primacy of causation. In that connection agency is agentive because it is grounded in the reality of the causal powers of substantial things. The philosophy of science that has made this kind of critical understanding possible is new realism.

NATURALISM AND THE NEW REALIST REVOLT AGAINST POSITIVISM

During the 1960s, the decade of Merleau-Ponty's death, a conceptual reform was crystallizing in the philosophy of science. Its theme was a revolt against the positivist conception of science (Harré 1970, 1975, 1986; Keat 1971:3–16 and 1982:chap. 1 and 2, 228–240; Bhaskar 1978; Manicas 1987:chap. 12 and 13). In the following decade, the import of the achievement was clear: every

major assumption constituting that conception of science
was overturned (Manicas 1987:243–244). It is now necessary to draw a distinction between actual scientific practices and philosophers' (in this case, positivist) normative
speculations about those practices. A direct consequence
of this is that we are no longer to conflate naturalism and
positivism. On one hand, naturalism refers to the scientific revolt against supernaturalism, that is, nature explains itself. On the other hand, naturalism refers to the
practices of scientific rationality in its endeavor to explain
nature in its own terms. As Keat has shown (1971:6–9),
there are two complementary construals of scientific practice, namely, neo-Wittgensteinian (Kuhn, Hanson, Toulmin, etc.) and new realist (Bohm, Bunge, Harré, etc.). The
direct implication for the behavorial sciences is that there
is *The Possibility of Naturalism* (Bhaskar 1979; Margolis
1984). Thus the study of people can be scientific in the
same sense—naturalistic—but not in the same way—
experimental and deterministic—as in the natural sciences. Consequently, experimentation, with its strict demands of closed conditions, complete manipulatory
control, and a mechanistic conception of causation, is
impossible in principle and is a perversion of the condition of human being. This is so because, first, it is rooted in
the fallacy of individualism, which eliminates the cultural
reality of human being, and second, it is rooted in the
fallacy of determinism, the elimination of the agentic
reality of human action that reduces action to behavior.
The fruitful result of this breakthrough beyond individualism and determinism is the freedom to develop methods
of explanation and research suitable to the natural condition of being human, the theme of which is methods
defined within the natural history tradition in science.

Positivism, of course, has been the source of both of
these fallacies, which fact allows us to understand anew
the witticism referred to earlier concerning behaviorism
and psychoanalysis. The deeper point is the perversity of
a positivist reading of being human. And for some time
now it has been quite clear that only the very mediocre or

ambitious or both can keep up the positivist reading in the behavioral sciences.

However, there is another side to this issue of positivism and the antipositivist revolt. Some behavioral scientists remain ignorant (deliberately or otherwise) of the new realist version of the revolt, particularly. They thus still conflate naturalism with positivism. This is a mediocrity or ambitiousness of a different sort. For instance, it invites one to become antiscientific and thus to indulge in some sophomoronic form of mysticoromantic pschologism, sociologism, or anthropologism. It can be said that the flight into phenomenology and into existentialism in some cases has functioned as a cover and a cover story for those so engaged. Failure to discover and comprehend the fundamental fruitfulness of new realism risks the failure to solve the fundamental problems besetting the behavioral sciences, such as, among others, the body-dead/brain-dead axiom.

NEW REALISM AND THE FALLACIES OF DETERMINISM AND INDIVIDUALISM

Harré's unique contribution to the demise of positivist hegemony can be presented as a coordination of two insights: one concerning science, the other concerning behavioral science. Harré is rigorously impassioned to preserve the conceptual integrity of scientific rationality and the relevance of that rationality for the possibility of naturalism in the behavioral sciences (Harré 1986a:chap. 1). We must be very clear about this: the "possibility" refers to naturalism and not to natural science. For the sake of absolute clarity I will offer a formulation of a deep principle of Harré's on these matters. Insofar as the conceptual integrity of scientific rationality is preserved, the possibility of naturalism in studying people is a real possibility. A new realist science of people means the study of human beings qua human beings, that is, as people in their cultural life of person-to-person semiotic actions (Harré 1984:3–112). In this way, scientific study is appreciative and not depreciative of the humanity of being human. Positivist behavioral science is obviously depreciative of the humanity of being human. In the root reduction of culture to the individual, explanatory efforts entailed the reduction of action to behavior and some variation of unconscious mental/neural structures. Given the appreciative attitude of a new realist study of people, such a science is genuinely a social or cultural science or, more precisely, a social psychology.

Harré's ethogenic standpoint is one version of a new realist science set within the natural history tradition in the biological sciences (Harré 1983:68, and Mühlhäuser and Harré 1990:1–40, 87–130). Thus, ethogenics is rooted in the biological methodology of ethology, the study of animals in their natural setting and not in the artificial setting of the laboratory. Centered in the concept of discursive or conversational practices, persons are *positioned* in reference to each other for the sake of ongoing linguistic and semiotic actions (Davies and Harré 1990:43–63). Neither the sociologistic tradition of collectivist terms (e.g. role, group, social system etc.), nor the psychologistic tradition of individualist terms (e.g. personality, trait, drives, etc.), are metaphysically acceptable (Davies and Harré 1990:44). This is a direct consequence of the fact that the logic of causal powers leads to the rejection of transcendentalist forms of accounts in the behavioral sciences (the reasons will be given later). Thus, ethogenics is an immanentist form of account and must be distinguished from other varieties of new realism, namely, the theoretical realism of Keat and Ury, and the transcendental realism of Bhaskar (Keat 1982:240–243; Bhaskar 1978). At present, it can be represented most concisely in the form of three doctrines (Harré 1983:68; Mühlhäusler and Harré 1990:1–40, 87–130).

Sociological doctrine. Two orders of society are posited: the expressive and the practical. The expressive order refers to the dimensions of honor, reputation, worth, and so forth; the practical order refers to work with material things and resources of biological knowledge. The explanatory principle unifying these orders is what Harré has called Goffman's law: the expressive order tends to dominate the practical order. The expressive order can be understood as grounded in the existential realm of cultural life, that is, that of meaning, socially constructed for ordered/coordinated living. The practical order is simply the realm of survival, that is, the interface of culture and the natural world.

Psychological doctrine. Former notions of social structure are translated into structures of action. This strategy blocks traditional theoretical inclinations to reify social structure deterministically. The agency/authorship of the structures of action is identified with the actors, particularly their intentions and beliefs. The locations of actors' intentions and beliefs is collective, less so are they individually located. The explanatory idea is that access to these agentic features of persons is given in the study of the actors' accounts. The centrality of social action, personal agency, and collective localization indicate the social construction strategy that is constitutive of the ethogenic standpoint.

Social psychological doctrine. The social construction of mind is derived from the discursive practices of the local culture. The explanatory idea resides in a distinction between the twin identities of person and self. The local culture is lived by embodied and indexically located interactors arrayed throughout discursive vocal space (and, we would want to add, nonvocal space). These actors are the real entities (natural kinds: substance and powers) of social life to which the term "person" exclusively applies. Persons (interactors or social actors) are the source models for the cultural myths or beliefs that define a subject of predication for the agentic and authorial centering of experience. Ideally, centering functions to organize thinking, acting, and memory so that agency crystallizes into the responsible authorship of conduct. The subject of centering is the self. While the person is a real indexical entity, the self is a referential real resource that is used to construct personal identity. The constructional activity is conducted through the auspices of social discursive practices (Mühlhäusler and Harré 1990:88–104, 114–122).

That the power of the social constructional strategy is significantly exploited from the Harréan standpoint is indicated in two telling ways (at least to sociologists). Harré has made two fundamental contributions to the development of the Meadian theory of the social nature of mind and self. Uniting the contributions is the introduction of a discursive turn into Meadian theory. First, Mead's famous "taking the role of the other" is seen as the consequence of learning the linguistic practices of the local culture's pronominal usage—first, second, and third person. The second- and third-person standpoints refer to Mead's significant and generalized other, respectively (Harré 1986b:151–152). Second, Harré has completed the Meadian social theory of mind as an interplay of the components of the self, the "I" and the "Me." "I," or first person pronoun practices, systematically vary cross-culturally; thus the "I" as well as the "Me" must be socially constructed (Mühlhäusler and Harré 1990:97–104).

A logical next step in the development of Harré's discursively grounded social construction theory would be the consideration of verbal nonvocal semiotic practices, that is, movement systems and not only physical being (Harré 1991). This would permit Harré, for instance, to give an account not only of several people moving a piece of furniture together (his own image) but also of Graham dancers forging a new version of "Rite of Spring" or of a group of Plains Indian sign-talkers laughing uproariously between the silent telling of yarns. Without such a development Harré's discursive turn must be judged only half of one. Williams's semasiological approach has already taken that step, having been inspired by Harré's causal powers theory of human agency to develop the concept of signifying acts (1982:161–182).

Thus, signifying acts refer to the moving body in the production of action-signs and constitutes a systematic conception of the genuine agency of embodiment. In Harré's notion of physical being, reference is made to the

idea of "bodily enactments," but without any clear implication of the genuine agency of embodiment. The significant difference resides squarely in the fact that the action-
sign is a systematic derivation of the concept of the
semasiological body (Varela 1993).

The Fallacy of Determinism: Proper Restoration of the Person

The fallacy of determinism entails the loss of causality in
the natural sciences and thus the loss of agency in the
social sciences. The result is the fundamental loss of the
person in the social sciences: the subject as social knower
and cultural being disappears. Without causality, agency
is impossible. Without agency, authorship is impossible.
And without authorship, being human is impossible. The
proposal is that human living is the person-centered
authorship of knowing beings in social situations of cultural action. From this perspective we can reread
Durkheim's response to the Hume-Kant controversy.
Durkheim's fear was misplaced: Hume's conclusion that
there is succession and not necessity in the relationship of
cause and effect in the world undermined the Newtonian
view of order in nature. Durkheim construed this to mean
that the fundamental possibility of science and society is
threatened. However, the issue is not the necessity of
order but the necessity of causal production. Durkheim's
"social fact" was thus ill conceived: the fact of social life is
not its necessary order and constraint and then human
beings living deterministically within it. This feature was
residual postivism tucked away in the notion of the social
fact. This has been the lingering problem of the realism of
the social fact. The danger of the Humean subversion was
the loss of agency and production in the natural sciences
and thereby the loss of personhood and authorship in the
social sciences. Durkheim failed to understand this and so
his mission to rescue Kantianism, science, and sociology
for modernity is a misguided and failed attempt.

Briefly, the fallacy of Humean subversion involves the

reduction of causality to correlation. Consequently, causal production is dissolved in relationality (Dewey), function (Cassirer), experience (James), or events (positivism) (Dewey and Bentley 1949, Cassirer 1953, James 1943, Harré and Madden 1975). This is why strong and weak forms of empiricism cannot ultimately be genuinely scientific, as in the case of positivism wherein event-description and prediction are conflated with explanation. Certain kinds of empiricism can be ambiguously scientific, as in the case of pragmatism, wherein experience or relationality is emphasized without the coherent possibility of explanation. As a significant and relevant example for this chapter particularly (as we will see, in view of Jackson's resort to James's radical empiricism), insofar as William James unfortunately committed himself to a weak form of empiricism, causality and human agency were conceptually unavailable to his definitional efforts. In James's radical empiricism, his choice to abandon substance and causality (albeit inadvertently) for function and experience was aimed at saving agency by avoiding determinism (James 1943, pp.4–22). Since at the time, one of the themes of positivism was the assimilation of causality into determinism, James was correct in choosing function and experience, but the choice to do so was unfortunate in its philosophical consequences. The category of subject was a moral preference over the category of object embedded in the then supposed otiose net of laws, substances, and causes under the concept of determinism. In this context James's radical empiricism is best understood as a forced choice. James was forced into the absurd choice of affirming both the reality of the particular—in this case the person and the "stream of consciousness"— and the denial of its substantiality. What he was left with was a neutral category: the subject and its reality referenced only by its functioning in a situation of relationships, and its reality warranted only by the feltness of its agency. In short, the feeling of agency is the experience of agency. However, that 'feltness' or 'experience' somehow confers the status of reality onto human agency is nothing more than a Jamesian act of faith. It is fully understandable therefore why James could announce, "My first act of free will shall be to *believe* in free will [emphasis provided]." He believed in agency, and thus had the feel of and for agency, but he could not conceive of how to formulate it. This weak form of empiricism means, paradoxically, that what was radical about James's empiricism was the unintended loss of causality and hence agency.

Scientifically, causality and agency are conceivable only when they are grounded or embodied in substantiality. Without the category of substance there can be no conception of causality as agency, and therefore there can be no conception of the agency of a person. When person is grounded or embodied in substance, agency is ensured, because causality is then in its proper place. In view of this, I contend that Merleau-Ponty's resort to embodiment was not sufficient and is no longer relevant. His position is transitional at best, since his conceptualization, albeit sensitizing, is not scientifically correct. This is because the body alone cannot establish the agency of intentionality; causality does. Agency is the causal production of consequences, and substance is required to ground that productive agency. Thus, first, it is the substantive person and not the lived, felt, or experienced body that ensures agency. Second, the point of embodiment is not to save agency from the rationalism that stems from a conception of mind in which causality is the same as determinism. Rather, the point of embodiment must be, initially, to locate causality in its proper place, in the substantiality of our physical thinghood (particularity).

Now this allows us to see that substantiality entails two aspects of thinghood—the organism and the body, and not the mechanical and the lived body. What will properly differentiate organism and body is not any resort to "experience," "feeling," "lived-body," or, finally, "being-in-the-world." These are, ultimately in the light of new realism, weasel words. The issue of agency and authorship involves locating the agency of causality in the substantiality of a person. Thus it is not a question of locating agency and authorship in the mind or in the body. As long as naturalism is conflated with positivism and therefore causality and substance are conflated with determinism, we will have lost agency and authorship in "experience," "feeling," or the "lived body." Agency must be embodied in substance in order to have the causality that makes for the productive power of consequences. In this conceptual move, the concept of person can be properly restored. Strawson's idea that the concept of the person is logically primitive requires a grounding in a scientific concept of natural kinds of causally empowered substances (Strawson 1992:114–124). New realist philosophy of science satisfies that requirement.

Causal Powers, Substance, and the Body

In the social sciences, two of the most influential standard accounts of scientific thinking are Cassirer's *Substance and Function* (1953) and Dewey and Bentley's *Knowing and the Known* (1949). With regard to causality, however, both are seriously misleading. Dewey and Bentley's work can be regarded as a refinement of Cassirer's concepts of substance (philosophy: thing as primary, relation as secondary) and function (science: relation as primary, thing as secondary). These became their concepts of self-actionalism in the case of substance, inter-actionalism as a combination of both substance and function (interaction of pregiven substances), and transactionalism (a field of relationships purified of substances). In those authors' understanding of science, the concepts of function and transaction stress the distinctive shift from thing to relationship.

We have here an example of the persistent error of reducing causal relation to correlation and hence the disappearance of power (potential: latent force), force (actual: manifest power), necessity, production, *and* substance. Harré has made it eminently clear that this standard reading of science is simply wrong. The history of physics, for example, is in fact the triumph of a dynamical theory of matter over both the materialist and the phenomenalist theories (Harré and Madden 1975:161–175). With that achievement, causal powers theory has become the way in which causality is understood in physics (see Strawson's failure in this regard, 1992:116–117).

Central here is the subtle change in the conception of the body. In the commonsense materialist version, substance consists of an individual entity (substratum) *and* its complex of (empirical) qualities: bulk, figure, motion. The rejection of this traditional substance-quality model (Aristotelian: Cassirer's substance) for the phenomenalist alternative (Galileo: Cassirer's function) was radical and devastating. It meant that the idea of substance as a substratum (subject) independent of its qualities (predicates) was replaced with another error, a substanceless and free-floating set of qualities. In both the substance-quality and the substanceless-quality models, causality is unavailable. In the former, cause is an occult phenomenon because it is identified with a substratum mysteriously independent of its qualities. In the latter, it is obvious that without substance there is no ground for the embodiment of causality (Harré and Madden 1975:165–175). Harré and Madden's comment concerning this predicament is apt:

> Of course, "substance" was not an empirical concept, but that did not require one to reject the basis of the scientific account of nature as rooted in real things responsible for appearances. It required a better conception of what individual things must be. (Ibid.,173)

A "better conception" is the dynamical theory of matter in which various forms of matter are not derived "from matters as machines, that is, as mere tools of external moving forces, but from moving forces of attraction and repulsion originally belonging to these matters" (Ibid., 170). Note carefully that the dynamical theory conceives of matter as immaterial (nonmaterial: either quality model) and as substances responsible for appearances (the qualities). Thus we have, as Harré declares, matter as "fields of potential" constituted by "centres of mutual influence." A field of potential locates powers for effecting influence at centers defined as real and immaterial things (Ibid., 161, 175–183). This formulation is as provocative as it is exact. How can real individuals be immaterial and be responsible?

Traditional and radical empiricism, positivism and pragmatism, respectively, commit the fallacy of actualism, that is, the error of identifying reality with perception, experience, and materiality. Implicit in this error is another, that of separating theory and observation as if the latter were a case of immaculate perception. Thus, as Hume would have it, since we cannot "see" cause as power or force, causation is a subjective fantasy occasioned by the habit and expectation of regularity. But as Harré reminds us, our perceptual apparatus is a biological evolutionary accident. And, we may add, perception entails direct ordering procesess as well as all sorts of indirect interpretive sets. Kant of course was right: one cannot separate perception from conception, nor conception from perception without disastrous consequences. Hume was absolutely wrong. Harré correctly reminds us that the Michotte experiments on the perception of causality have demonstrated that we do directly perceive causality (Harré and Madden 1975:60–62). The question of how you interpret the perception of causality is a separate question, and, of course, Hume was also wrong in his interpretation. Harré suggests that since Hume was a historian and not a scientist, we should not be surprised.

So, the demand for materiality, I propose, is a covert plea for epistemological narcissism; that is, as modern possessive individualists, we demand that knowledge be *our* acts of *incorrigible* sensation, experience, and perception. Instead, the question of immateriality would suggest a sophisticated and fruitful new realist response to the failure of positivism and the empiricist fallacy of actualism. But, now, what of the question of things being responsible? This goes to the heart and soul of the matter of causation and agency and thus to that of person and authorship.

Harré is firm in his argument that the tradition of believing that the scientific conception of causality is the

projection of human volition is itself a consequence of
assuming that only human volition is the experiential
basis for the direct perception of causality. The projection
of human volition as the fact of causality can assume one
of two forms, individualistic (Whitehead's error of ani-
mism and pan-psychism) and collectivistic (the
Durkheimian error of the social fact as constraint and
coercion). The combined assumptions of volition as causation and the projection of volition represent what Harré
calls "the inferential predicament." In order to defini-
tively block the predicament, we must reject the assumptions, and four reasons are given for doing so, only two of
which I will single out here (Harré and Madden 1975:58–
62).

First, our best theory is that the idea of causation
originates in the observations and experiences of causal
actions among things themselves apart from human beings. As mentioned earlier, the Michotte experiments
demonstrate that pure mechanical causation is a direct
primary perception. Especially, Michotte has shown that
the Humean assumptions of the necessity of habit and
expectation for the perception of causality are unneces-
sary! Second, causal powers theory clearly regards the
case of human causation as a "subspecies of 'cause'
significantly different from the subspecies that includes
physical objects and events" (Harré and Madden
1975:59). In other words, although production is the
general form of causality, human agency is a special type.

Now this is certainly to be expected in the context of
biological evolution. The development of open and unbounded plans in which solutions to adaptive problems
creatively succeed those problems strongly suggests the
evolution of new kinds of agentic structures. Relevant to
human beings and in reference to neurological criteria,
the emergence of instinctive brains, social brains (higher
primates), and cultural brains (human beings) strongly
supports this special thesis of causal powers. The human
brain (organism) is the natural ground of our causal
powers, and is the occasion of enablement for their transubstantiation into personal powers through the cultural

grounding of them in the acts of social interaction. Social construction is the interactional mechanism that transforms our powers from organism to person, and with that, our substantiality from the organism to the body. There are thus two kinds of embodiment here: the natural embodiment of agency in the organism, which makes possible the social embodiment of authorship in the person. Thus, the principle of the primacy of the person, set within the understanding of the reality of causal powers and the immateriality of substance, leads to the conclusion that the body is the person. And the concept of person is that of a pure agent, that is a psycho-social entity unaffected by *any* neurophysiological discoveries.

Causal Powers: Logic and Principles

We can now ask, What is this special type of human causal power and what is the general form it exemplifies? Schematically, it can be characterized as, "y decided to do z (or does z) and then justified his action by reference to x." What is rejected by this scheme is, "x caused y to z." The absolutely crucial distinction is that in the former scheme, "y refers to a self that initiates causal sequences but is not causally activated itself" (Harré and Madden 1975:59). The rejection of the standard deterministic "x caused y" scheme does not mean that it does not obtain for us; after all, we are objects in the natural world as well. It does mean, however, that if human agency is construed only in that way, such a deterministic scheme is inappropriate and otiose—inappropriate because it is a wholesale substitution eliminating the human type, as if the latter is a fiction. That is simply wrong and arbitrary. My suspicion is that, in part, this uncharitable disposition is an endemic feature of the Cartesian construal of modern individualism. The principle of the hegemony of the self as subject over against the other as object is the point: objectifying "other" maximizes one's control. The standard deterministic schema is otiose because it is a subversion of the general form of causation given in causal powers theory. It either is, or threatens to be, the denial of the very idea that causation is the power of production. It is now necessary to consider two definitions of causal power from Harré and then Bhaskar:

> A Particular Being has a Tendency (disposition: tendencies, powers/forces, propensities) which, if released, in a certain type of situation, is manifested in some observable Action but when blocked has no observable effect. Adding the releasing and blocking condition introduces the basic element of agency into the causal story. Further advance (in the story) . . . involves the discovery of the mediating mechanism (of production) and the precise state of the particular being in which the tendency is grounded. (Beyond certain conditions for the ascription of tendencies) . . . Dispositions are ascribed to actual occurrent beings, but, in most contexts, they seem to refer to possible (powers) rather than actual (forces) manifestations of the typical behavior cited in the consequent of the leading conditional clause. (Harré 1986a:284)

> 1. X has the power (or liability) to do (or suffer) y.
> 2. X is predisposed towards doing y.
> 3. X will do y, given an appropriate set of circumstances, in virtue of its nature in the absence of intervening (or countervailing) causes.
> 4. X possesses powers in virtue of falling into a natural kind; tendencies in virtue of its being a type within that kind. (Bhaskar 1978:229–231).

It should be noted carefully that in causal powers theory we are systematically able to connect agent/patient, action/behavior, (pro)active/reactive, power/liability. Causal activity is a constituted disposition to realize power or liability under appropriate circumstances. We should also note the concepts of release and block. Their implication is that natural things are powerful particulars of various physical and biological kinds. Nature is naturally active, some of it alive. Thus, for instance, the concept of stimulus has been disastrously misunderstood generally in psychology and particularly in behaviorism. When, for example, Skinner switched his terminology from elicited (from Pavlov) to emitted behavior, the deterministic meaning of stimulus was retained. In other words, even after admitting the natural activeness of animals, environmental reinforcement took up the deterministic slack. In science, however, "stimulus" means the release or blockage of the power/liability of particulars to produce consequences in a field of other such particulars. This is a radically different metaphysical view of the empirical world, and thus it is a markedly different conception of empiricism. In being so, it surpasses empiricism in its various positivist, phenomenalist, and pragmatist forms. In this regard, for example, Harré can remark that "Science is empirical because we may fail to find what we want." He means, of course, the finding of evidence for the causality of powerful particulars, that is, "that a rider can throw up his spear and catch it again, while at a gallop" (1986a: 83).

Experience is possible precisely because of our causally empowered ordering devices in partnership with nature and with each other. The Kantian insight into this constructional nature of being human was certainly penetrating but Kant also pioneered the more profound idea of a dynamical philosophy of nature, which formulated the basic causal powers theory in science. But the constructional power of human being is emergent within and defined by a cultural, social, and semiotic world. The empiricisms cited earlier—the traditional, phenomenalist, and pragmatist—require a setting firmly within the framework of the new realist philosophy of science. In that setting, both the traditional and phenomenalist varieties of empiricism are dismissed when overhauled in terms of causal powers theory. In the case of Jamesian experientialism, James's recognition of the causal agency of things and his feel of and for human agency can be conceptually clarified and used to ground the emphasis on experience (Harré and Madden 1975:57–58).

To present two fundamental principles of causal powers theory implicit in the definitions provided, I will examine Harré and Madden's treatment of a concrete example of a powerful particular.

The executioner had a good eye, a strong arm, and a sharp axe, and he whacked off the king's head. Swinging the axe in just that way [necessarily] caused the king to lose his head. . . . [This example is one of countless others], the lava flow, the medicine, the light rays. . . . The agency is there, to be sure [in each case]. There is no other 'force', there is no other cause, than just these specific things. But these things are forceful: they operate: they produce. And they [do so] . . . in that specific way we call necessary. (Harré and Madden 1975:57)

Two fundamental principles of far-reaching significance can be identified from these considerations, namely, (1) *structural integrity* and the *fallacy of bifurcation,* and (2) *causal activity* and the *fallacy of activation.* Harré and Madden present them as follows:

We must avoid at the outset the reification of an abstract term. The notion of causal power should not be conceived as an undefined descriptive predicate that refers to an ontological tie that binds objects and events together. The exercise of causal power is not a force or power that has an existence of its own but refers to forceful particulars at work. There are not both things and causality in nature but causally active things. This [causal] necessity . . . was no ontological tie *behind* the events that bind them together. . . . It lay rather in the concrete situation, in the force used to swing the axe, in the sharpness of the axe, the angle of descent, and the contact with a yielding substance. And it always is. The efficacy of casual power is nothing general. . . . And it is with the concept of powerful things and integrated structures of things . . . the concept of generative mechanism . . . that we devise an ontological tie . . . for the connection of causes with their effects. (Harré and Madden 1975:57)

The principle of structural integrity is the idea that things, animals, and people are individuated natural kinds identified by their constituted systemic wholeness. Thus, the power of a particular resides in the natural constitution of its kind: in brief, its structural integrity. The fallacy of bifurcation refers to separating a particular *from* its causal power and locating it *outside* itself, or separating a particular *from* its causal power and locating it *inside* itself. In either case, causality is isolated as a reified, abstract term (an occult phenomenon), which as an undefined descriptive predicate functions as an onto-logical tie behind events, binding them together.

The principle of causal activity then simply follows from the foregoing principle. If causal power is the force *of* a particular and not a force *and* a particular, then causality is the "activity of forceful objects at work." The fallacy of causal activation is clear: there cannot be an outside or inside power of a particular (except of course other power-ful particulars) that forcefully activates the particular. The fallacy leads one seriously to ask absurd questions such as, "Where is the explosion before the dynamite is deto-nated?" Marx and Durkheim, Freud and Lévi-Strauss, in effect, asked and answered such a question according to their variations on the theme of collective or individual unconscious mental structures. If you believe that mind is located behind a speech act or behind a signifying act, you will look for an explosion before it happens, in and behind that happening. It is this understanding of the logic of causal powers, that is, the principle of structural integrity and the fallacy of bifurcation and the principle of causal activity and the fallacy of activation, that conceptually leads to a turn to discursive practices in the social sci-ences grounded in an immanentist metaphysic.

The Fallacy of Individualism

Warner's concept of the fallacy of internalization is a useful development of causal powers theory (Warner 1990). Internalization is the idea that the psychological is the secret behind the social, and ultimately some form of biologization of the psychological is to be realized. The strategy required is to read social life back into the indi-vidual people who live it. Thus the fallacy is rooted in the twin positivist assumptions of individualism (reality is individual) and metaphysical materialism (the reality of the individual is material). The strategy is realized by three procedures.

Desocialization. The action of social relationships becomes instead the action of psychobiological dynamics. For example, Freud took the interrelationships of the moral authority of the local culture, the mental features of its individual members, and an interest in their individuality and systematized them into the complex dynamic of superego (culture), ego (individual), and id (individuality).

Decontexualization. Situated meaning is identified and read back into individual mental/neural structure.

Depersonalizaton. The agentic production of action is relocated in an individual mental/neural process (Warner 1990:141–143).

The internalization fallacy, I would suggest, originates partly in the ideology of modern individualism and is generated within the auspices of the positivist conception of science. A positivist reading of individualism thus is a particular rendering of the individualist human nature model. The theme, strategy, and procedures that realize the verbal formula of the model if P (psychological) then S (social) because of B (biological) inverts Marx's sixth Feuerbachian thesis that "the essence of man is no abstraction inhering in each single individual."

The assumption of metaphysical materialism used in an individualist explanatory schema involves the mistake of conflating body and organism. In the reduction of body to organism, the organism becomes an asocial and complex mentalized system/engine (Warner 1990:138–140). The substance of human physical thinghood is displaced and identified with the organism. Embodiment in this context is the body as organism. As a result, the powers of the natural individual organism are conflated with powers of the social individual person. This is the final consequence of the dogma of empiricism and its assumption of metaphysical materialism. The visible (perception, experience, feltness, sensation, sensual surfaces) is rendered absolute in virtue of the principle that the material is real.

Under the auspices of this internalization fallacy, person, body, and body-movement must be regarded as unreal and hence invisible! This is an important part of the logic of the body-dead/brain-dead axiom.

For the purposes of this chapter it will be sufficent to focus exclusively on the procedure of desocialization. It is based on Warner's inversion of his fundamental idea in the discussion of the internalization fallacy. Warner works from a culturalist model of human being, and he has formulated a special conception of the social nature of being human. The concept is constructed from within the logical space of the experimental design in order to explode the myths of determinism and individualism endemic to a positivist reading of the design. It is not necessary for my discussion here to reconstruct the systematic details of Warner's conception; suffice it to say that, in my judgment, the task of constructing the conception of our social nature and the explosion of the two myths of positivism are both informative and cogent (Warner 1990:133–137). What I will do is discuss the conception itself as it directly fits my analysis thus far.

Warner has effected what I have elsewhere called the "Simmellian shift" (Varela 1992). He demonstrates Simmell's point, *fin de siècle,* that a Kantian model of social life demands a subject-to-subject format in which mutual social synthesizing among the actors defines the format. The Kantian concept of synthesis is the idea of constructional activity, and this became Harré's concept of the causal power of human agency. In honor of the revolutionary import of the concept, I will call this the Harré theorem. In sociology, the Harré theorem can be seen to provide the much needed philosophical foundation for the Thomas theorem that "if people define situations as real, they are real in their consequences." People are able to define situations as real precisely because the making of such definitions, and much else, is the power of real human agency. Warner uses this to build his conception of our constitutive sociality with the aid of social symbolic interaction theory from the Cooley and Mead tradition. The key idea that I want to examine is the social nature of freedom, the agentic act itself as self-mobilization (Warner 1990:134–138). This is certainly the heart of the darkness of modern individualism.

What is it about modern possessive individualism that makes it, in true Dostoyevskian fashion, fanatically, and, if need be, murderously possessive? My proposal is that the heart of its darkness—its secular religious fanaticism—is transcendental freedom: the absolute right and duty to be free from the *conditionality* of other(s). In the story of Dorian Grey, for example, the darkness of its heart, its murderousness, becomes exactly that. The sin of Dorian Grey is the willingness of "self" to murder "other" who may and does intervene in the exercise of that right to freedom as duty and who violates that freedom by conditioning it. Sartre was not quite on the mark in his frenzied exclamation that "hell is other people." That hell is complemented by the sin of Dorian Grey, who murdered his close friend because he was conditioning Dorian's freedom and thus compromising the fact of and the belief in being an absolute individual. Warner's insight into this situation is to recognize that the individualist thesis is wrong in its deep assumption that the nature of freedom and the very logic of agency are individualistic (Warner 1990:137–138).

The modern mechanistic-nominalist model of the individual is grounded in the root assumption of the original separation of the individual from others: the nature of the individual is individual. This idea of original separation means that agency itself is viewed as individualistic. This would seem to provide an interesting insight into the dogma of possessiveness that is constitutive of modern individualism. The assumption of separation is the principle defining the core of the doctrine of absolute freedom, which in turn constitutes the justification for the sin of Dorian Grey. And yet, the fundamental logic of individualism is fatally flawed, and so the moral objection to the "other" in the name of freedom is now no longer coherently justified.

If indeed people are social and thus in their personhood exemplify the Harréan theorem, then how could the mechanism of self-mobilization be individualistic? In other words, how could "self" be possible without the condition of the "other"? If one could seriously accept the incoherency of the kind of question mentioned earlier, namely, "Where is the explosion before the dynamite is detonated?" then surely one would have to believe that self-mobilization without the condition of "other" is a species of mysterious, spontaneous generation. After all, the principle in that kind of question is metaphysical, suggesting an occult ontology of natural kinds (the substance/quality model is presumed) such that there is a mysterious region, for instance, "within" the stick of dynamite wherein its explosions are located. If so, then self-mobilization *is* asocially and autonomously generated and in that case Freud was right all along: the "id" is the site of the primordial agency of personality! Warner, however, flatly denies that an individualist account could in principle be coherent. Self-mobilization *is* social—in principle the "other" is the primordial condition for the "self"—precisely because, in being social, one can direct oneself to respond only insofar as one considers how the other will respond in turn to one's own response. The social being of the individual is the primitive ground of its personal being. Warner concludes:

> Thus it's not because of what they are made of that the hidden generative processors . . . of the psychoanalytic tradition, cognitive psychology, and Chomskian linguistics can't possess the powers to produce speech-informed action. It's because they are conceived to operate individualistically. (Warner 1990:137–138)

Neither an asocial complex organism nor some part of it can thus conceivably be agentic in the human sense. Only when an organism is also a person, who, because of enculturation, is social in being and social in taking action as a person, can human agency be real—a productive force. And more deeply, the entities of the human, psychological, and social world are *joint* products, that is they involve the joint exercise of the cognitive powers of more than one. The logic of the agency of causal powers requires that the structural integrity of a natural kind not be violated. The positivist assumptions of materialism (material reductionism) and individualism (asocial organism), presupposed by experimental design and informing the behavioral scientists who are so committed, lead to the construction of theories of people that violate the sociocultural structural integrity of the human be-ing of people. It is because of this philosophical position that the person is improperly lost, and with it social action and its cultural content.

INTERNALIZATION FALLACY AND A PROPER CONCEPTION OF THE BODY

An individualistic conception of human being entails the tacit assumption of an asocial organism and thus in principle cannot account for the reality of the enactment of human agency—the social dynamics of self-mobilization. Now this principle liberates us to a fresh appreciation of the role of the human organism and body in human forms of life. We are liberated to comprehend that Freud's "id," Merleau-Ponty's "lived body," Sheets-Johnstone's "bodily logos," and Jackson's "knowledge of the body" (1989:119–136), can indeed be set aside as sensitizing but inadequate attempts seriously to implicate the body and movement in the intimate social affairs of persons. Certainly, as sensitizing concepts functioning somehow to ensure that Darwinian biology is never to be forgotten, and functioning to ensure that somehow the arts of movement might be remembered, they deserve to be appreciated. Body and movement, however, can never be seriously introduced into social living either from the psychoanalytic or from the existential phenomenological standpoints. Their individualistic position compels them to assume the concept of an asocial complex organism in their attempts to incorporate body and movement into cultural life.

The body, however, is the indexical site of the person, indeed, it is a body by virtue of the personhood of the individual. With a conception of body-instrument, movement can become an agentic option available to people in their person-centered social actions. But to say this is exactly not to say that such agentic display is enacted by the organism because persons are natural individuals. This locution betrays the conflation of the organism with the body. It is no longer a proper form for the preservation of human agency and its human value. Phenomenology and existentialism were for some time the defenders of the faith in human freedom against the threat to freedom from positivism. The conceptual form of the defense was a resort to "individualism," "livedness" (feeling, experience, sense), and some resort to a transcendentalist posture. This constituted the standpoint that entrapped phenomenology and existentialism within the human nature model and its unavoidable internalization fallacy. Merleau-Pointy's phenomenological existential resort to the lived body was no escape from this improper form of preserving human agency.

The transformation of natural into personal powers through the social mechanism of what Shotter calls "psychological symbiosis" (1973:143–147) enables us properly to order the relationships between the concepts of organism, person, action, and causal powers. *The grounding site of natural powers is the asocial and material individual organism.* This, however, is only the enabling condition for the exercise of agency. Its enactment requires the engagement in social acts through personhood and the resource of a concept of an entitative self. The difference between the conditions of enablement and engagement is radical: only the organism grounds our natural powers, and only the social act grounds our personal powers. *Hence, our everyday display of powers belongs to the person and not to the organism, and that is because their enactment can be accomplished only socially, not individually* (Warner 1990:138–141). The agency of the person is a social affordance, never an intentionality of the body. Bodily intentionality is a personal affordance, and that is because we are social. The concept of bodily intentionality within an individualist framework is a form of Rylean category mistake: it conflates the social grounding of our personal powers with the organismic grounding of our natural powers, in which case the consequence is that body and organism are improperly connected. And neither "experience," nor "livedness," nor "feeling" alone can convert the organism into the body.

The cultural variability in theories or myths of personhood and the self means of course that social life creates forms of persons and selves while the asocial and material organism is virtually constant. Yet, the last point is not quite right either. The principle of the personal affordance of the body because of the social affordance of personal agency allows a fresh understanding of the relevance of physical states to personal agency. Not only do social practices in various cultural forms of life create actions that human asocial organisms could never produce, but also those new actions represent the self-mobilization of both the person *and* the organism. Any resulting physical states are therefore certainly *mediated* by the organism, but they can be generated only by self-mobilized persons because of their culturally-informed social engagements (Warner 1990:140–141). Thus the organism may be relevant to an understanding of person, self, and action because of validly correlated physical states. It is nevertheless clear that that relevance can never be declared in the traditional form of a biologically original causal explanation (Gillett 1993:27–45). And any resultant gestural and other movement patterns found to be systematically correlated to personal self-mobilization can certainly be attributed to the organism of a body/person, but, again, that must be sociologically conceived as the condition of material mediation; that is, its generation is socially grounded and personally enacted (Gillett 1993:27–34, 39–41). The organism is an individual entity, but the body is a cultural entity—it is embodied in a substantial person with its pure agency. Thus the body is made visible by the invisible social act of being a person. Bodily intentionality, in the context of the cultural model of the ethogenic standpoint, is the social enactment of personal being.

THE JACKSONIAN MOVE: A DEAD END FOR A MERLEAU-PONTIAN ANTHROPOLOGY OF THE BODY

I will conclude this discussion with reference to Jackson's proposal to achieve a Merleau-Pontian anthropology of the body. The point I wish to make is that the Jacksonian move is another instructive example of the body-dead/brain-dead axiom in the social sciences. Most social scientists are endemically dead to the body, and more important, even when they are not they are still dead to the semiotics of bodily movement. There is an inability to see people "meaning" when they are moving, whether or not they are speaking, and especially when they are not speaking but engaged in using the body as an expressive action-sign system. Investigators may notice that people are moving and doing so significantly, but it ends there. The inability to apperceive such movement as *action* is due exactly to the failure to understand the theme of this chapter: the signifying act of body movement is a causal production and is so by virtue of the substance grounded powers of social persons in a local culture deploying a verbal but non-vocal gestural semiotic. As a consequence, today in the social sciences there is a systematic neglect of the fact and importance of *literacy* in the performance and study of human movement, a position seriously championed by Drid Williams in her semasiological theory of human movement for well over a decade (1975, 1979, 1982, 1991).

It is, then, not surprising that some may argue, even in principle, against any such position, but this is rather odd. It is quite clear that the sciences and some of the arts require their appropriate forms of literacy. Not to acknowledge this forces one into the incoherent position of insisting, for the sake of consistency, that, for instance, Western baroque, classical, romantic, and modern tonal and atonal music would have emerged and developed in the absence of musical literacy and its correlative notation systems. In the case of tonal music there is one notation system, whereas in that of atonal music there is a plethora of such systems. But Sheets-Johnstone tacitly suggests the dismissal of movement literacy and its correlative notation systems, and Jackson does so explicitly, in a neoromantic move perhaps.

The result is that this involves one not only in an incoherent position regarding Western music and literacy, but there is the professionally alarming consequence that renouncing movement literacy closes off future developments with regard to research, knowledge, and understanding concerning movement systems. The deeper point is the underlying issue of the suitable expansion of our conception of rationality beyond the restrictive version provided by the positivist tradition. This issue will itself be foreclosed by any such dogma against literacy. Intellectualism (deductivism, efficient rationality, formal rationality) may well entail literacy, but the reverse is not necessarily true. Both musical and movement notation systems strongly suggest exactly that. It is high time that the fight against the bogeyman of intellectualism, and therefore against literacy, in the name of freeing new forms of imagination, being, and feeling, be abandoned.

In the revolt against positivist science (as a powerful example), both the neo-Wittgensteinians and the new realists have won the battle to dethrone the hegemony of an intellectualist paradigm of rationality. Thus, for instance, Harré has recently made the strong point that scientific rational practices are predominantly material practices (i.e., using equipment and instruments for searching and finding) with some "thinking," and a severe stricture on deductivism (Harré, 1986a). The power of literacy is the provision of new and systematic methods, techniques, and procedures for the facilitation of new forms of imagination, being, and feeling.

In the twentieth century, the revolt against the rationalism of traditional tonal music emerged in the form of atonal music. The revolt was facilitated through the invention of new notation systems and not without—or in spite of—them. In reference to movement, the resort to the Merleau-Pontian body cannot realize that facilitation of our authorship. Movement literacy is that kind of new social act designed and enacted by persons for new paths of facilitation.

Four of the truly powerful sources of the revolt against the intellectualist paradigm of rationality are phenomenology (Husserl's final emphasis on rationalism's foundation in the *Lebenswelt,* [see Ferrara 1991:chap. 3]); hermeneutic phenomenology (Heidegger's *Dasein* as the poetry and depth of *Lebenswelt,* [see Ferrara 1991:chap. 3 & 4]); existentialism (Sartre's existence against essence finally combined with Marxist-inspired sociologism; and existential phenomenology (Merleau-Ponty's embodied being-in-the-world). The renunciation of movement literacy and its correlative notation systems has its origin, ultimately, in that philosophical and rational anti-intellectualist revolt.

Jackson articulates that influence unambiguously in his thesis that the anthropological emphasis on intellectualist rationality and language necessarily excludes the proper emphasis on the body, gesture, and movement in the everyday affairs of cultures (Jackson 1989:119–122). To understand his perspective on the issue, consider a select number of integrally connected statements found in the introductory essay to his collection of anthropological papers (1989):

> Anthropology . . . urges us not to subjugate lived experience to the tyranny of reason or the consolation of order . . . (p. 16)

> . . . [an] escape from lived experience is provided by the intellectualist notion that knowing is a kind of outside beholding rather than a matter of participation. (p. 15)

> . . . the separation of subject and object in traditional empiricism is in large measure a function of the sensory mode and metaphor it privileges: vision. (p. 6)

> The alienating effects of visualism can also be related to the impact of perspective and literacy. (p. 6)

> Literacy has the effect of isolating us and our ideas from the lived world of social experience. (p. 10)

> Now if it is true that linear perspective and literacy prevent coevalness, then there is a good case for trying to understand the world through bodily participation. (p. 11)

From the foregoing discussion of new realism and the ethogenic standpoint it is clear that Jackson's thesis must be rejected as is; it is simply theoretically wrongheaded and philosophically muddled. The Merleau-Pontian body may be conceptually sensitizing, but it is not conceptually adequate. The individual organism is a material entity, but the body is a cultural entity and it is embodied in a *substantial person.* Thus the body is made visible by the invisible social act of being a person. Heidegger's being-in-the-world or being-with-others does not save Merleau-Ponty's use of the term body from its conceptual inadequacy. From the ethogenic standpoint, that usage means that Merleau-Ponty picked up the wrong end of the stick. It is not the case that the "subject is his or her body," but rather that the "subject is an organism" and becomes his or her body when the individual becomes a person. The body is a personal affordance, and that is because the person is a social affordance. Thus, the personal enactment of a semiotic system of action-signs especially brings the *moving* body into view, so to speak.

In light of this, the test of the thesis that a Merleau-Pontian anthropology of the body is a dead end consists in the fact that neither Sheets-Johnstone nor Jackson ever present any empirical data or ethnographic descriptions of the body, gestures, or movement. It must be made very clear that they cannot do so in principle, and so they will never be able to do so in fact. This is an endemic feature of their conceptual commitment to existential phenomenology. Thus, they may not *talk about the body* and so avoid the intellectualist fallacy, but they can only *talk of the body* and so are trapped in the phenomenalist fallacy. Recalling the earlier discussion on the materialist, phenomenalist, and dynamical models of matter, we can clarify the meaning of this new idea of the phenomenalist fallacy in the present context. The intellectualist fallacy is rooted in the materialist substance/quality model, and the existential phenomenological perspective is rooted in the phenomenalist substanceless/quality model: thus the new idea of the phenomenalist fallacy. Talk of the body is first-person pronoun talk centered in the rhetoric of subjective experientialism. That this is absolutely the case is evident from the list of Jackson's statements and especially in view of his comment from the same introductory essay:

> But while I agree with both Foucault and Lévi-Strauss in eschewing any notion of the *individual subject* as the *primary source* and final arbiter of our understanding, I do not want to risk dissolving the lived experience of *the subject* into the anonymous field of discourse, allowing Episteme, or Language or Mind to take on the *epistemological privileges denied to consciousness and subjectivity* [emphasis supplied]. (Jackson 1989:1)

Neither Jackson, nor anyone else for that matter, can have it both ways. You cannot reject the "individual subject as a primary source" of understanding and at the same time affirm the "epistemological privileges" of the "consciousness and subjectivity" of the individual subject, and pretend to be able to do so with a magical resort to "lived experience" that mysteriously baptizes experience with the reality of, well, yes, substance! You are either in the materialist camp and you have substance or in the phenomenalist camp and you have qualities, but you cannot have both. And if the issue is the "primary source" problem—that is, that substance commits you to a substratum apart from its qualities—then neither "livedness" nor "experience" can be a substitute for substance conceived of in that materialist sense. And without the concept of substance, in this case an adequate one, there is no theoretical way to have a viable concept of an "individual subject."

What you *can* do, however, is to reject both the materialist model of substance and the phenomenalist model of quality, and accept in their stead a dynamical model of the immateriality of substance as the structure of powers and forces. Jackson reveals an incoherent preference for the astronomer's term "singularity" in reference to a suitable concept of the subject, but a dynamical model rather than a phenomenal model is the better choice. In other words, without a proper understanding of causal powers, the ethogenic view of person and its constitutive sociality, and without the distinction between organism and body articulated by the concept of the internalization fallacy, the incoherence and sterility of the Jacksonian move with its preference for a phenomenalist model of quality cannot be overcome.

As a result, that resort cannot be the means of realizing Merleau-Ponty's invitation to connect language and gesture. Jackson's commitment to Merleau-Ponty's existential phenomenology to the exclusion of his venture into philosophy of history and Saussure was one mistake; to then regress to James's radical empiricism was another, and it was fatal. Together they guarantee that the Jacksonian move is a degenerate form of Merleau-Ponty's vision and reach, because what is further guaranteed is that talking *of* the body can never graduate to talking *from* the body. To talk *from* the body is not only to experience the body as a lived organism but also to enact the movement of the body and thus to elect to articulate the experience of it (if that is your phenomenological interest). This enactment is in the first-person standpoint of an author's creating and using the semiotic of an action-sign system. The implication of this position is that movement scores are ethnographically superior to word glosses because they are recording talk from the enacted body. *Thus, because the movement itself is read and described literacy cannot be denied its centrality in an anthropology of the body.* Jackson's exclusive preference for phenomenological existentialism and radical empiricism will certainly give us an anthropology of embodiment, but such an anthropology will be philosophically self-deceptive, theoretically sterile, and ethnographically deficient.

It has been my contention throughout this chapter that the studies of human movement systems in this volume presuppose a conceptual framework best understood in terms of semasiology, elements of Harré's ethogenic standpoint and the new realist philosophy of science that generates it. It is this framework and this standpoint that permit us, I believe, to realize Merleau-Ponty's invitation to reach the semiotics of signifying lingual and action signs. And this volume stands as testimony.

REFERENCES

Baumer, F.L. (1977). *Modern European Thought: Continuity and Change in Ideas 1600–1950.* New York: Macmillan.

Berger, P. (1979). *The Heretical Imperative.* Garden City, New York: Anchor Press/ Doubleday.

Berman, M. (1970). *The Politics of Authenticity: Radical Individualism and the Emergence of Modern Society.* New York: Atheneum.

Bhaskar, R. (1978). *A Realist Theory of Science.* Brighton, Sussex, UK: Harvester Press.

———. (1979). *The Possibility of Naturalism.* Brighton, Sussex, UK: Harvester Press.

Bronowski, J. (1977). *A Sense of the Future: Essays in Natural Philosophy.* Cambridge, Mass.: Massachussetts Institute of Technology Press, pp. 163–195.

Bruner, J. (1990). *Acts of Meaning.* Cambridge, Mass.: Harvard University Press.

Cassirer, E. (1953). *Substance and Function.* New York: Dover.

Csordas, Thomas J. (1989) Embodiment as a paradigm for anthropology. *Ethos* pp. 5–47.

Davies, B. and R. Harré. (1990). Positioning: The discursive production of selves. *Journal for the Theory of Social Behavior* 20 (1) pp.43–63.

Delbruck, M. (1986). *Mind from Matter.* Oxford, UK: Blackwell Scientific.

Derfer, G. (1974). Science, poetry, and human specificity—an interview with J. Bronowski. *American Scholar* Summer, pp. 386–404.

Descombes, V. (1980). *Modern French Philosophy.* Cambridge, UK: Cambridge University Press.

Dewey, J. and A.F. Bentley. (1949). *Knowing and the Known.* New York: Beacon.

Dumont, L. (1986). *Essays on Individualism.* Chicago: University of Chicago Press.

Farnell, B. (1994). *Plains Indian Sign-talk and the Embodiment of Action.* Austin: University of Texas Press.

Ferrara, L. (1991). *Philosophy and the Analysis of Music.* New York: Greenwood.

Geertz, C. (1983). *Local Knowledge.* New York: Basic.

Gillett, G.R. (1993). Social causation and cognitive neuroscience. *Journal for the Theory of Social Behavior* 23(1):27–45.

Gould, S. J. (1977). *Ever Since Darwin.* New York: W. W. Norton.
———. (1985). Challenges to neo-Darwinism and their meaning for a revised view of human consciousness. In Sterling M. McMurrin (ed.) *The Tanner Lectures on Human Values.* Salt Lake City, Utah: University of Utah Press, vol.6 pp.55–73.

Grene, M. (1966). *Knower and the Known.* London: Faber & Faber.
———. (1985). Perception, interpretation, and the sciences: Toward a new philosophy of science. In David J. Depew (ed.) *Evolution at a Crossroads: The New Biology and the New Philosophy of Science.* Cambridge, Mass.: Massachussetts Institute of Technology Press, pp.1–20.6

Hall, H. (1983). Merleau-Ponty's philosophy of mind. In G. Floistad (ed.) *Contemporary Philosophy: A New Survey.* The Hague, Boston and London: Martinus Nijhoff, pp.343–361.

Hamlyn, D. (1989). *A History of Western Philosophy.* New York: Viking, Penguin.

Harré, R. (1983). Commentary from an ethogenic standpoint. *Journal for the Theory of Social Behaviour* 13(1):69–73.
———. (1984). *Personal Being.* Oxford, UK: Basil Blackwell.
———. (1986a). *Varieties of Realism.* Oxford, UK: Basil Blackwell.
———. (1986b). Persons and powers. In S.G. Shanker (ed.) *Philosophy in Britain Today.* London: Crowhelm, pp.135–153.
———. (1990). Explanation in psychology. *Annals of Theoretical Psychology* 6:105–124, 147–151.
———. (1991). *Physical Being.* Oxford, UK: Blackwell.

Harré, R. and E.H. Madden. (1975). *Causal Powers.* Oxford, UK: Basil Blackwell.

Hassan, I. (1985). The culture of post-modernism. *Theory, Culture and Society* Vol. 2(3):119–131.

Jackson, M. (1989). *Paths Toward a Clearing.* Bloomington, Ind.: Indiana University Press.

James, W. (1943). *Essays in Radical Empiricism and A Pluralistic Universe.* New York and London: Longmans Green & Co.

Keat, R. (1973). Positivism, naturalism, anti-naturalism in the social sciences. *Journal for the Theory of Social Behaviour* I:3–16.

Kumar, K. (1978). *Prophecy and Progress: The Sociology of*

Industrial and Post-Industrial Society. New York: Viking Penguin.

Langford, G. (1978). Persons are necessarily social. *Journal for the Theory of Social Behaviour* 8(3):263–283.

Lash, S. (1984). Geneology and the Body: Foucault, Deleuze, Nietzche. *Theory, Culture, & Society* vol.2(2):1–17.

———. (1989). *Sociology of Post-Modernism.* London and New York: Routledge, Chapman and Hall.

Lukes, S. (1973). *Individualism.* New York: Harper and Row.

Manicas, P. (1987). *A History & Philosophy of the Social Sciences.* Oxford, UK: Basil Blackwell.

Margolis, J. (1984). *Culture and Cultural Entities: Toward a New Unity of Science.* Dordrecht, Boston and Lancaster: D. Reidel.

Mayr, E. (1988). *Toward a New Philosophy of Biology.* Cambridge, Mass.: Belknap and Harvard University Press.

Merleau-Ponty, M. (1964a). *Sense and Nonsense.* Evanston, Ill.: Northwestern University Press.

———. (1964b). *Signs.* Evanston, Ill.: Northwestern University Press.

———. (1967). *The Structure of Behaviour.* Boston: Beacon Press.

———. (1968). *The Visible and the Invisible.* Evanston, Ill.: Northwestern University Press.

———. (1962). *The Phenomenology of Perception.* (translated by C.Smith). London: Routledge and Kegan Paul.

Morris, C. (1972). *The Discovery of the Individual.* New York: Harper & Row.

Mühlhäusler, P. and R. Harré. (1990). *Pronouns and People: The Linguistic Construction of Social and Personal Identity.* Oxford, UK: Basil Blackwell.

Puri, R. and D. Hart-Johnson. (1982). Thinking with movement: improvising or composing? *Journal for the Anthropological Study of Human Movement* 2(2):71–88.

Rossi, I. (1974). Intellectual antecedents of Lévi-Strauss's notion of the unconscious. In I. Rossi (ed.) *The Unconscious in Culture.* New York: Dutton, pp. 7–30.

Russow, L.M. (1988). Merleau-Ponty and the myth of bodily intentionality. *Nous* 22:35–47.

Sartre, J.P. (1968). *In Search of Method.* New York: Vintage.

Sheets, M. (1966). *Phenomenology of the Dance.* Madison and Milwaukee, Wis.: University of Wisconsin Press.

Sheets-Johnstone. M. (1981). Thinking in movement. *Journal of Aesthetics and Art Criticism* 39(4):339–407.

———. (1983). Interdisciplinary travel: From dance to philosophical anthropology. *Journal for the Anthropological Study of Human Movement* 2(3):129–142.

———. (1990). *The Roots of Thinking.* Philadelphia: Temple University Press.

Shotter, J. (1973). Acquired powers: The transformation of natural into personal powers. *Journal for the Theory of Social Behaviour,* 3(2):141–155.

Spurling, L. (1977). *Phenomenology and the Social World.* London: Routledge & Kegan Paul.

Stark, W. (1963). *The Fundamental Forms of Social Thought.* New York: Fordham.

Strawson, P. (1959). *Individuals.* London: Methuen.

———. (1992). *Analysis and Metaphysics: An Introduction to Philosophy.* Oxford, UK: Oxford University Press.

Toulmin, S. 1979. The inwardness of mental life. *Critical Inquiry* Autumn:1–16.

Turner, B. (1984). *The Body and Society.* Oxford, UK: Basil Blackwell.

Varela, C. (1973). *The Crisis of Western Sociology: The Problem of Social Interaction, the Self, and Unawareness for Social Theory.* Unpublished Ph.D. dissertation, New York University, New York, N. Y.

———. (1984). Pocock, Williams, Gouldner: Initial reactions of three social scientists to the problem of objectivity. *Journal for the Anthropological Study of Human Movement* 3:53–73.

———. (forthcoming). *Freud to Mead: The Third Psychologist's Fallacy and the Social Nature of Unawareness.*

———. (1993). Semasiology and the ethogenic standpoint: the proper alignment of causal powers and the action sign. *Journal for the Anthropological Study of Human Movement* 7(4):219–249.

———. (1992). The social construction of psychological reality: The unconscious. Ms.

Warner, C.T. (1990). Locating agency. *Annals of Theoretical Psychology* 6:133–145.

Williams, D. (1975). *The Role of Movement in Selected Symbol Systems.* Unpublished D.Phil. Dissertation, Oxford University, Oxford, UK.

———. (1979). The human action sign and semasiology. *CORD Research Annual X.* New York: New York University.

————. (1982). Semasiology: A semantic anthropologist's view of human movement and actions. In D. Parkin (ed.) *Semantic Anthropology* ASA Vol 22. London:Academic.

————. (1991). *Ten Lectures on Theories of the Dance.* Metuchen, N.J.: Scarecrow Press.

Zijderfeld, A. (1970). *The Abstract Society.* Garden City, N. Y.: Anchor, Doubleday.

CONTRIBUTORS

BRENDA FARNELL is a visiting professor in the anthropology department at the University of Iowa. She earned her Ph.D. in sociocultural anthropology at Indiana University (Bloomington). Born in England, she also holds a teaching diploma from I.M. Marsh College of Physical Education of Liverpool University, a Diploma in Dance and Dance Education from the Laban Centre for Movement and Dance of London University and an M.A. in the Anthropology of Human Movement from New York University. Her research interests include ethnopoetics and performance in Plains Indian Sign Language, Assiniboine oral narrative, deixis, and dances of the Northern Plains. She is the author of *Do You See What I Mean: Plains Indian Sign-Talk and the Embodiment of Action* and an interactive multi-media CD Rom, *Wiyuta: Assiniboine Storytelling with Signs* (University of Texas Press, 1994).

LEE-ELLEN FRIEDLAND is a folklorist who studies European- and African-derived dance traditions in the United States. Her research and publications have addressed such subjects as movement ethnography, expressive culture and national identity, revitalization movements, and the history of vernacular dance scholarship. She is director of Ethnologica, a Washington D.C. consulting firm that specializes in ethnographic research and cultural resource planning.

DIANA HART-JOHNSON holds an M.A. in the anthropology of human movement from New York University and a B.F.A. in dance from Juilliard. She was a soloist in the Martha Graham Dance Company prior to 1983, performing both solo and principal roles. She has taught dance and choreographed works at several U.S. universities, including the University of Massachusetts, the University of Wisconsin-Madison, Ithaca College and the University of Iowa, as well as at the Martha Graham School and Interlochen Arts Academy. Since 1983 she has co-directed a school-age child care program and community school project in Sunset Park, New York under the auspices of the Center for Family Life. There she created and now directs the performing arts component while performing several other administrative duties as well. She has directed twenty-seven major productions there and has also completed commissioned works for Kanopy Dance Theatre and the Dave Bromberg Band. She has published several articles in the *Journal for the Anthropological Study of Human Movement.*

ADRIENNE L. KAEPPLER is curator of oceanic ethnology at the National Museum of Natural History at the Smithsonian Institution in Washington, D.C. She attended the University of Wisconsin-Milwaukee and received her B.A., M.A., and Ph.D. degrees from the University of Hawaii. From 1967 to 1980 she was an anthropologist on the staff of the Bishop Museum in Honolulu, Hawaii. She has taught anthropology, ethnomusicology, and anthropology of dance at the Universities of Hawaii and Maryland and at Queen's University in Belfast, Northern Ireland. She carried out field research in Tonga, Hawaii, Tahiti, Easter Island, the Solomon Islands, New Guinea, and Japan. Her research focuses on the interrelationships between social structure and the arts, especially dance, music, and the visual arts. She has published widely on these subjects and is currently finishing two books on cross-cultural aesthetics and Hawaiian dance and ritual.

ADAM KENDON studied biology and experimental psychology at Cambridge, England and was awarded a D.Phil. from Oxford University in 1963 after a dissertation on the temporal structure of conversation. He has undertaken research on face-to-face interaction and gestural communication at Oxford University, the University of Pittsburgh, Bronx State Hospital (New York), Australian National University and Indiana University. He has taught at Cornell University, Connecticut College, and the University of Pennsylvania. The author of numerous publications on the microstructure of face-to-face interaction and the nature of gesture and its relationship with spoken language, he published a book entitled *Sign Languages of Aboriginal Australia* (Cambridge University Press, 1988), which includes the results of original fieldwork with Australian Aborigines undertaken between 1978 and 1986.

GAYNOR MACDONALD recently completed a two-year secondment, teaching anthropology at the International Christian University in Tokyo, Japan, during a leave of absence from the University of Western Sydney, Australia, where she has been lecturing in anthropology and Aboriginal studies since 1986. She conducted fieldwork with the Wiradjuri people of Australia for ten years, during which time she completed her Ph.D. at the University of Sydney. She has also done fieldwork in the Torres Strait Islands. Her major research interests include Aboriginal conflict management and expression, self-determination, and Aboriginal-government relations, as well as contemporary lifeways and culture of Aboriginal people.

RAJIKA PURI is an internationally known performer of three idioms of Indian Classical dance: Bharata Natyam, Odissi and Kuchipudi. She holds a B.A. (Hons.) in English Literature, Delhi University and an M. A. in the anthropology of human movement, New York University. She has published articles on Indian Classical dance in the *Journal for the Anthropological Study of Human Movement* and *Semiotica*. After many years in the United States, she has returned to India and now lives in Bombay, from where she travels widely in order to teach and perform.

BONNIE URCIUOLI is director of the Linguistics Program at Hamilton College in Clinton, New York, and has also taught linguistic anthropology at Indiana University in Bloomington, Indiana. She received a Ph.D. in the Anthropology and Linguistics joint program at the University of Chicago in 1984. She has done extended research in the ethnography of language contact and ethnic/racial/class identity among Puerto Rican families on the Lower East Side and in the Bronx in New York City.

CHARLES R. VARELA is a professor of sociology and psychology at Union County College, New Jersey. He completed a B.A. at Brockport College, New York; an M.A. in Human Relations Studies and a Ph.D. in sociology at New York University. His major interest is in the sociology of knowledge; especially religion, philosophy, the natural and social sciences, literature and music. He is the author of *Freud to Mead: The Third Psychologist's Fallacy and the Social Nature of Unawareness* (forthcoming) and has recently completed a second book, *The Social Construction of Psychological Reality: The Unconscious.*

DRID WILLIAMS was a member of the anthropology department at the United States International University in Nairobi, Kenya, having previously served on the faculty of Moi University, Kenya. She completed three graduate degrees in social anthropology (Dip., B. Litt. and D. Phil) from Oxford University between 1970 and 1976 and is the architect of a theory of human actions and movement called "semasiology." She has directed an M.A. program in the anthropology of human movement and Aboriginal performing arts at the University of Sydney, Australia and, prior to this, an M.A. program at New York University. The author of numerous articles on the dance, liturgies and martial arts and *Ten Lectures on Theories of the Dance* (Scarecrow Press, N.J., 1991). She also holds an M.A. degree in library science and current research interests involve the bibliographic organization of materials on the dance world-wide. She has done fieldwork among Carmelite nuns and Dominican friars in England; the Guardian Angels in New York City; and most recently amongst Cape York Aboriginal communities in Northern Queensland. Dr. Williams is also founder and senior editor of the *Journal for the Anthropological Study of Human Movement.*

NAME INDEX

SUBJECT INDEX